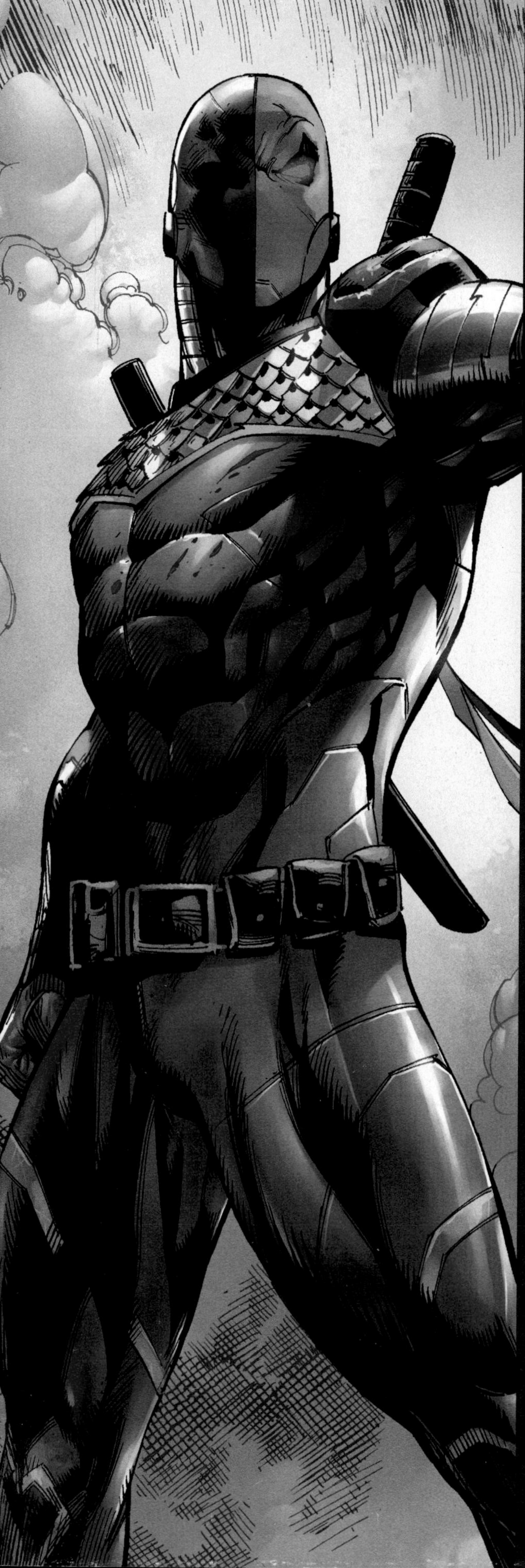

VOLUME 1

GODS OF WAR

DEATHSTROKE

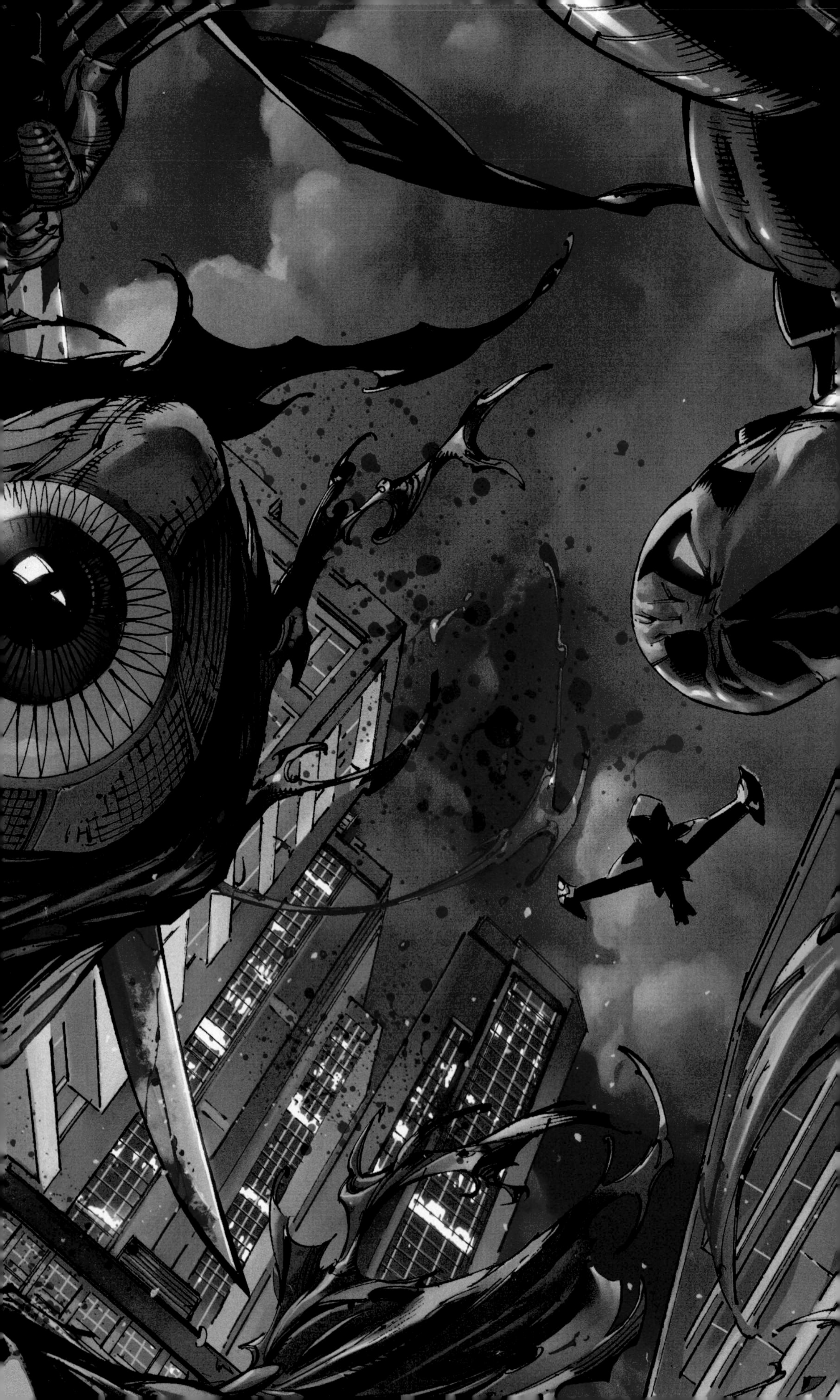

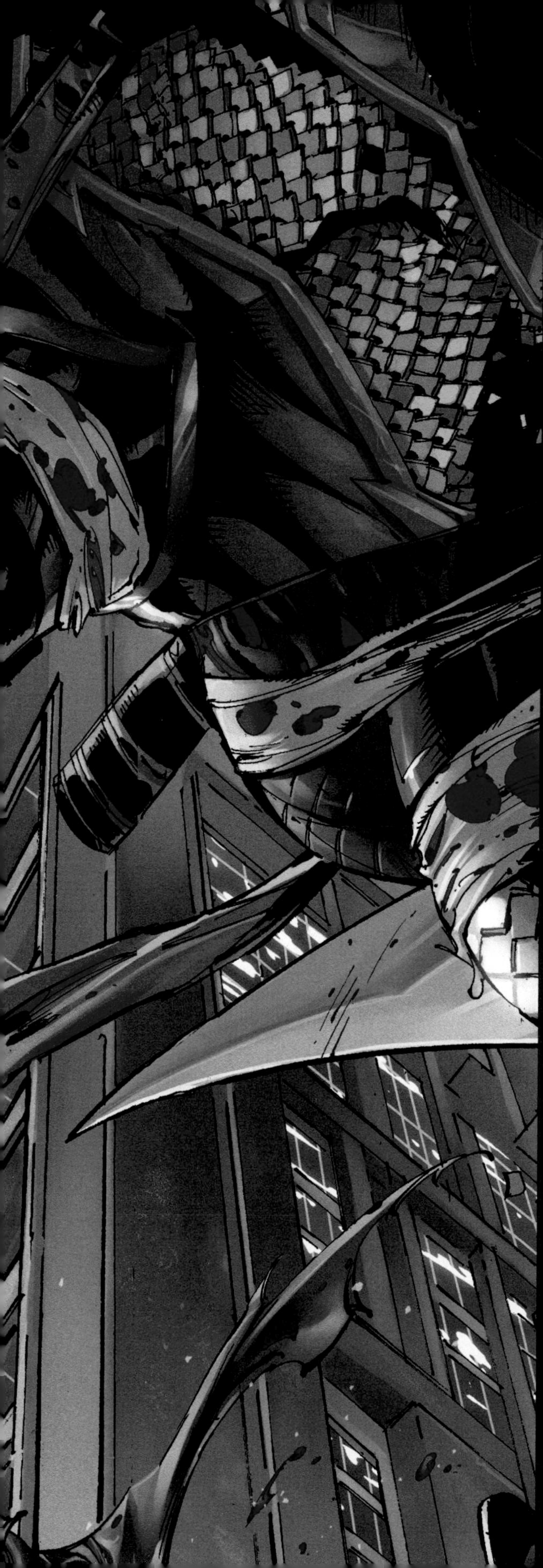

VOLUME 1

GODS OF WAR

DEATHSTROKE

WRITTEN BY
TONY S. DANIEL

PENCILS BY
TONY S. DANIEL

INKS BY
SANDU FLOREA

COLOR BY
TOMEU MOREY

LETTERS BY
ROB LEIGH

COVER ART AND
ORIGINAL SERIES COVERS BY
TONY S. DANIEL
SANDU FLOREA
TOMEU MOREY

DEATHSTROKE CREATED BY
MARV WOLFMAN
AND **GEORGE PÉREZ**

EDDIE BERGANZA Editor – Original Series
JEREMY BENT Assistant Editor – Original Series
LIZ ERICKSON Editor
ROBBIN BROSTERMAN Design Director – Books
DAMIAN RYLAND Publication Design

BOB HARRAS Senior VP – Editor-in-Chief, DC Comics

DIANE NELSON President
DAN DIDIO and JIM LEE Co-Publishers
GEOFF JOHNS Chief Creative Officer
AMIT DESAI Senior VP – Marketing & Franchise Management
AMY GENKINS Senior VP – Business & Legal Affairs
NAIRI GARDINER Senior VP – Finance
JEFF BOISON VP – Publishing Planning
MARK CHIARELLO VP – Art Direction & Design
JOHN CUNNINGHAM VP – Marketing
TERRI CUNNINGHAM VP – Editorial Administration
LARRY GANEM VP – Talent Relations & Services
ALISON GILL Senior VP – Manufacturing & Operations
HANK KANALZ Senior VP – Vertigo & Integrated Publishing
JAY KOGAN VP – Business & Legal Affairs, Publishing
JACK MAHAN VP – Business Affairs, Talent
NICK NAPOLITANO VP – Manufacturing Administration
SUE POHJA VP – Book Sales
FRED RUIZ VP – Manufacturing Operations
COURTNEY SIMMONS Senior VP – Publicity
BOB WAYNE Senior VP – Sales

DEATHSTROKE VOLUME 1: GODS OF WAR

DC Comics, 4000 Warner Blvd., Burbank, CA 91522
A Warner Bros. Entertainment Company.
Printed by RR Donnelley, Owensville, MO, USA. 5/15/15. First Printing.
ISBN 978-1-4012-5471-1

Library of Congress Cataloging-in-Publication Data

Daniel, Tony S. (Antonio Salvador), author, illustrator.
Deathstroke / Tony Daniel.
pages cm. — (The New 52!)
ISBN 978-1-4012-5471-1 (v. 1 : paperback) 1. Assassins—Comic books, strips, etc. 2. Graphic novels. I. Title.
PN6728.D363D36 2015
741.5'973—dc23
2014049024

SUSTAINABLE FORESTRY INITIATIVE

Certified Chain of Custody
20% Certified Forest Content,
80% Certified Sourcing
www.sfiprogram.org
SFI-01042
APPLIES TO TEXT STOCK ONLY

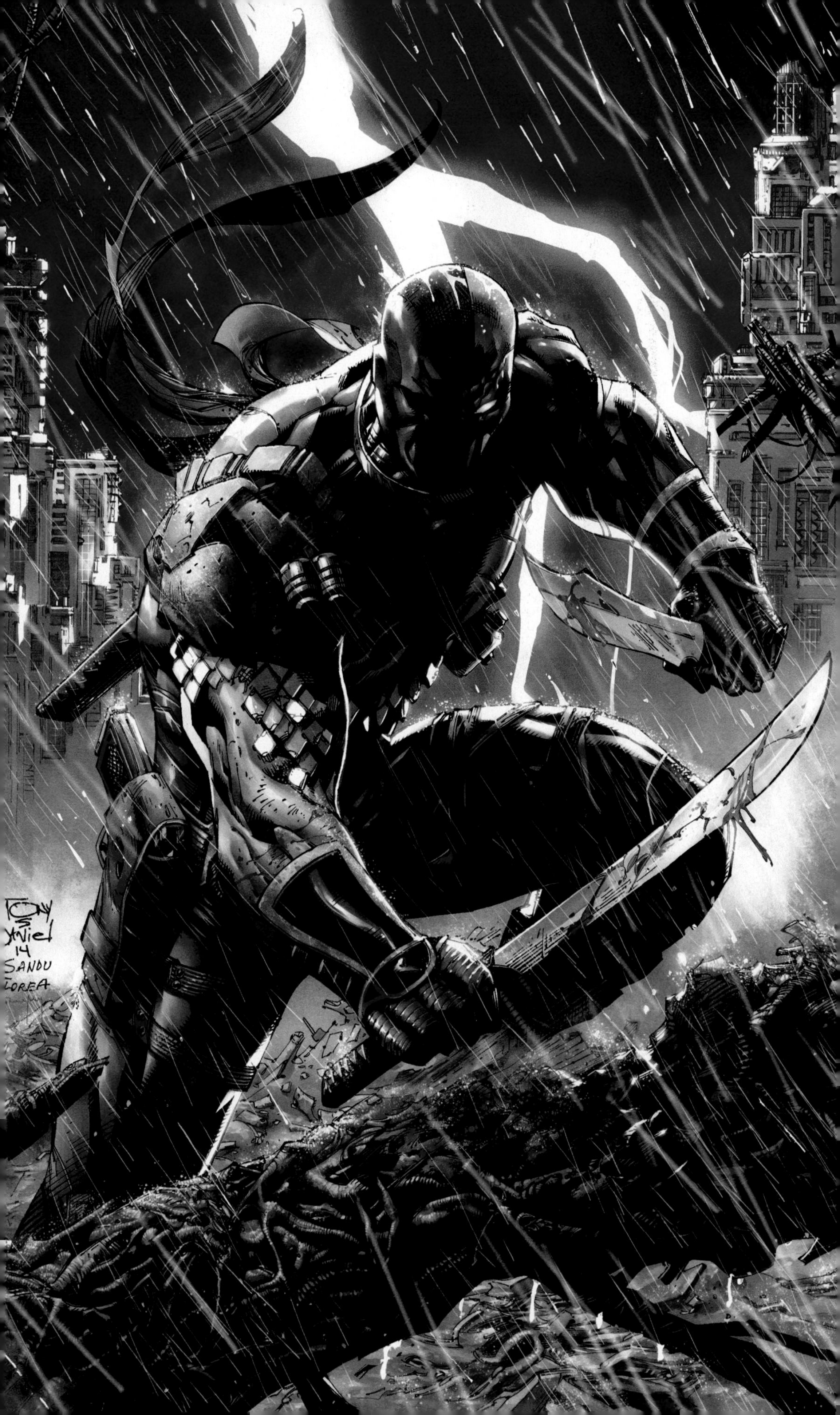
TONY S DANIEL 14
SANDU FLOREA

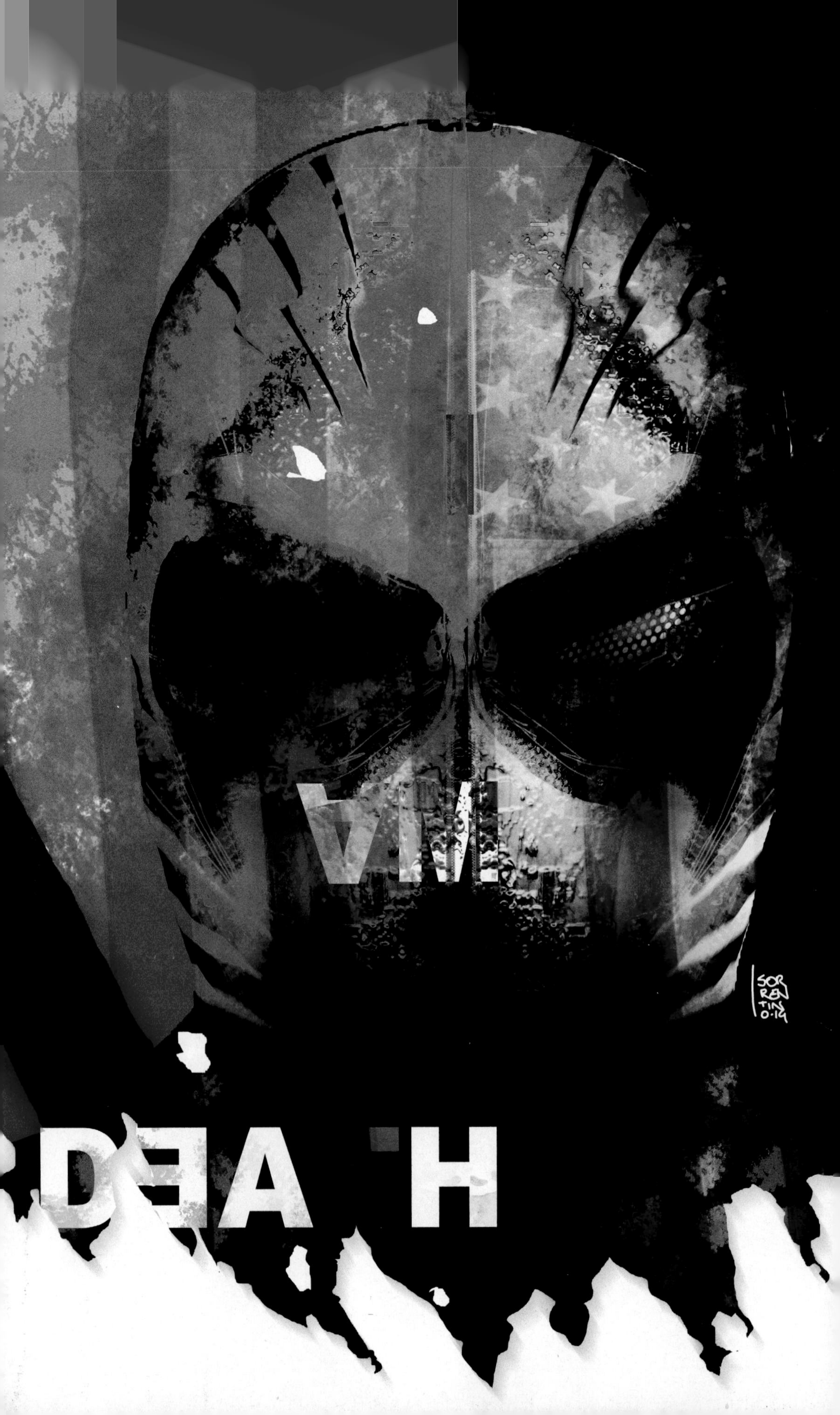

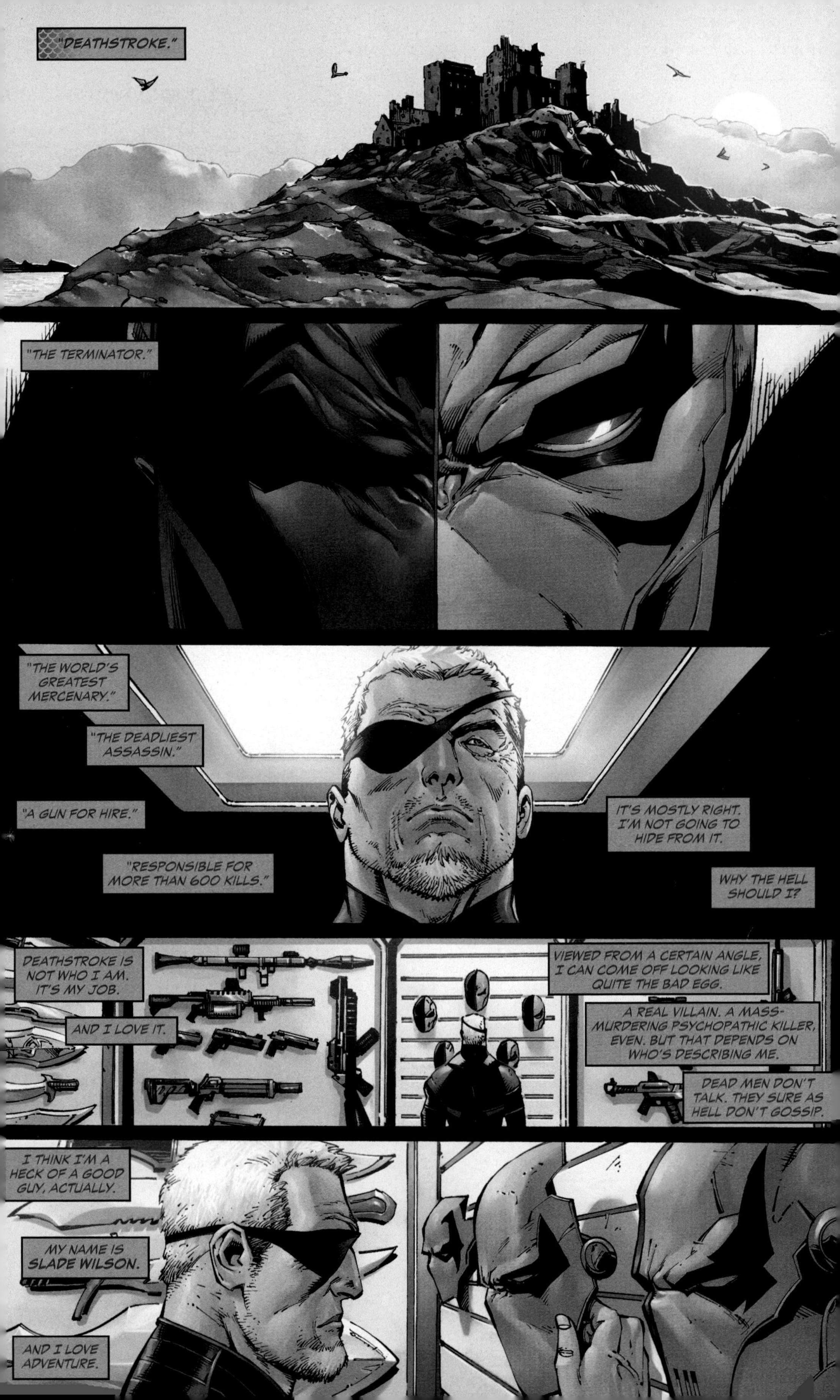
"DEATHSTROKE."
"THE TERMINATOR."
"THE WORLD'S GREATEST MERCENARY."
"THE DEADLIEST ASSASSIN."
"A GUN FOR HIRE."
"RESPONSIBLE FOR MORE THAN 600 KILLS."
IT'S MOSTLY RIGHT. I'M NOT GOING TO HIDE FROM IT.
WHY THE HELL SHOULD I?
DEATHSTROKE IS NOT WHO I AM. IT'S MY JOB.
AND I LOVE IT.
VIEWED FROM A CERTAIN ANGLE, I CAN COME OFF LOOKING LIKE QUITE THE BAD EGG.
A REAL VILLAIN. A MASS-MURDERING PSYCHOPATHIC KILLER, EVEN. BUT THAT DEPENDS ON WHO'S DESCRIBING ME.
DEAD MEN DON'T TALK. THEY SURE AS HELL DON'T GOSSIP.
I THINK I'M A HECK OF A GOOD GUY, ACTUALLY.
MY NAME IS SLADE WILSON.
AND I LOVE ADVENTURE.

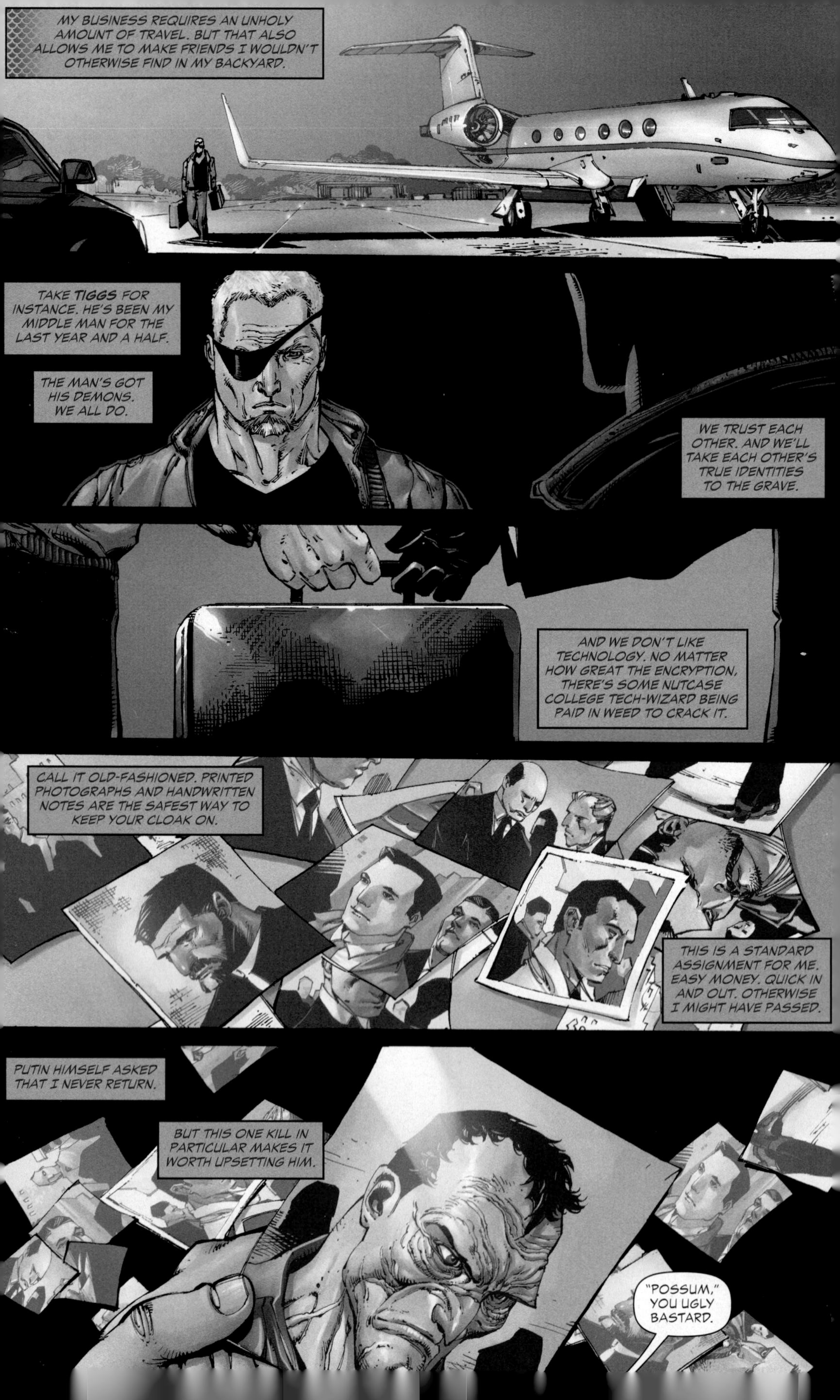
MY BUSINESS REQUIRES AN UNHOLY AMOUNT OF TRAVEL. BUT THAT ALSO ALLOWS ME TO MAKE FRIENDS I WOULDN'T OTHERWISE FIND IN MY BACKYARD.
TAKE TIGGS FOR INSTANCE. HE'S BEEN MY MIDDLE MAN FOR THE LAST YEAR AND A HALF.
THE MAN'S GOT HIS DEMONS. WE ALL DO.
WE TRUST EACH OTHER. AND WE'LL TAKE EACH OTHER'S TRUE IDENTITIES TO THE GRAVE.
AND WE DON'T LIKE TECHNOLOGY. NO MATTER HOW GREAT THE ENCRYPTION, THERE'S SOME NUTCASE COLLEGE TECH-WIZARD BEING PAID IN WEED TO CRACK IT.
CALL IT OLD-FASHIONED. PRINTED PHOTOGRAPHS AND HANDWRITTEN NOTES ARE THE SAFEST WAY TO KEEP YOUR CLOAK ON.
THIS IS A STANDARD ASSIGNMENT FOR ME. EASY MONEY. QUICK IN AND OUT. OTHERWISE I MIGHT HAVE PASSED.
PUTIN HIMSELF ASKED THAT I NEVER RETURN.
BUT THIS ONE KILL IN PARTICULAR MAKES IT WORTH UPSETTING HIM.
"POSSUM," YOU UGLY BASTARD.

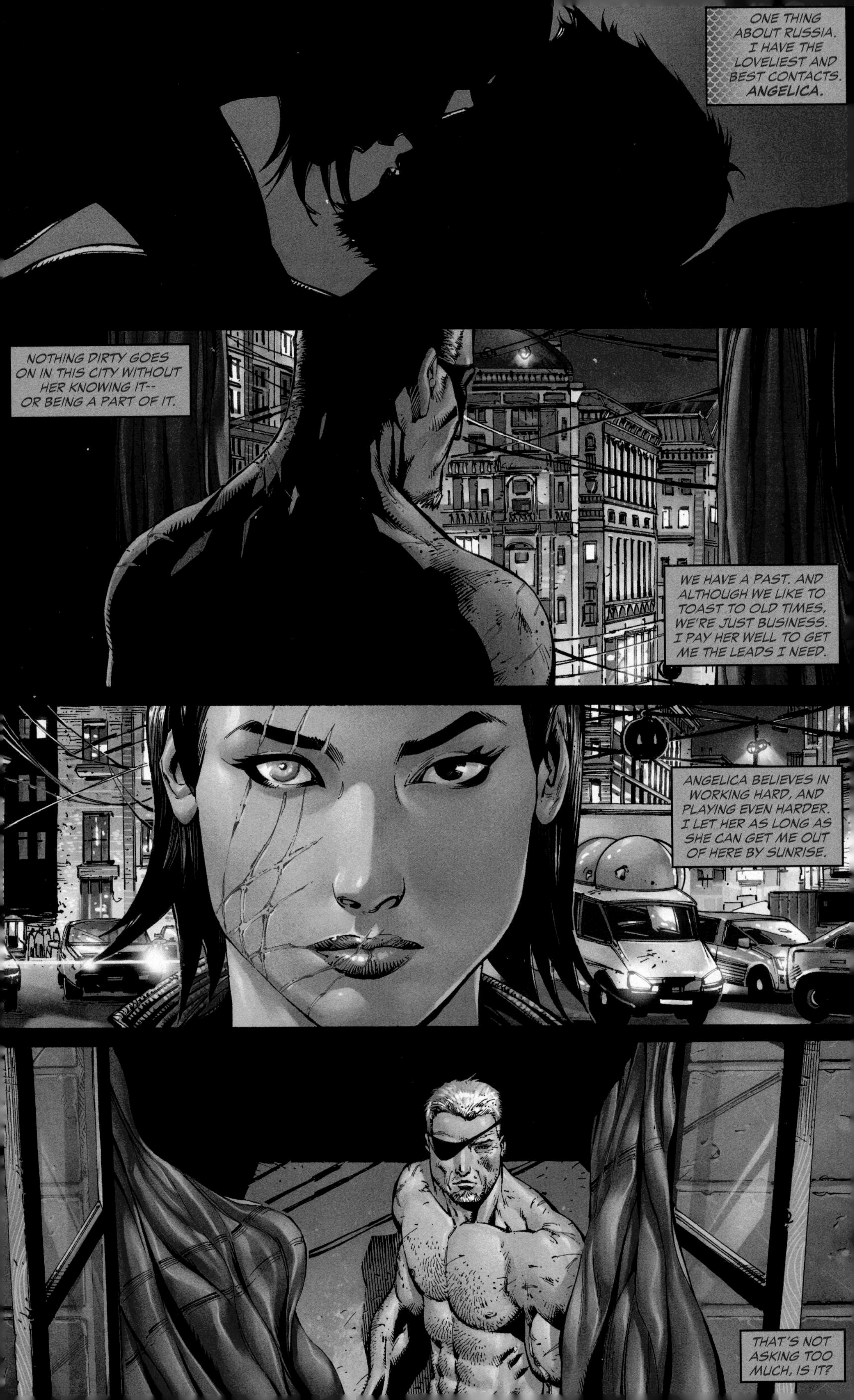
ONE THING ABOUT RUSSIA. I HAVE THE LOVELIEST AND BEST CONTACTS. ANGELICA.
NOTHING DIRTY GOES ON IN THIS CITY WITHOUT HER KNOWING IT-- OR BEING A PART OF IT.
WE HAVE A PAST. AND ALTHOUGH WE LIKE TO TOAST TO OLD TIMES, WE'RE JUST BUSINESS. I PAY HER WELL TO GET ME THE LEADS I NEED.
ANGELICA BELIEVES IN WORKING HARD, AND PLAYING EVEN HARDER. I LET HER AS LONG AS SHE CAN GET ME OUT OF HERE BY SUNRISE.
THAT'S NOT ASKING TOO MUCH, IS IT?

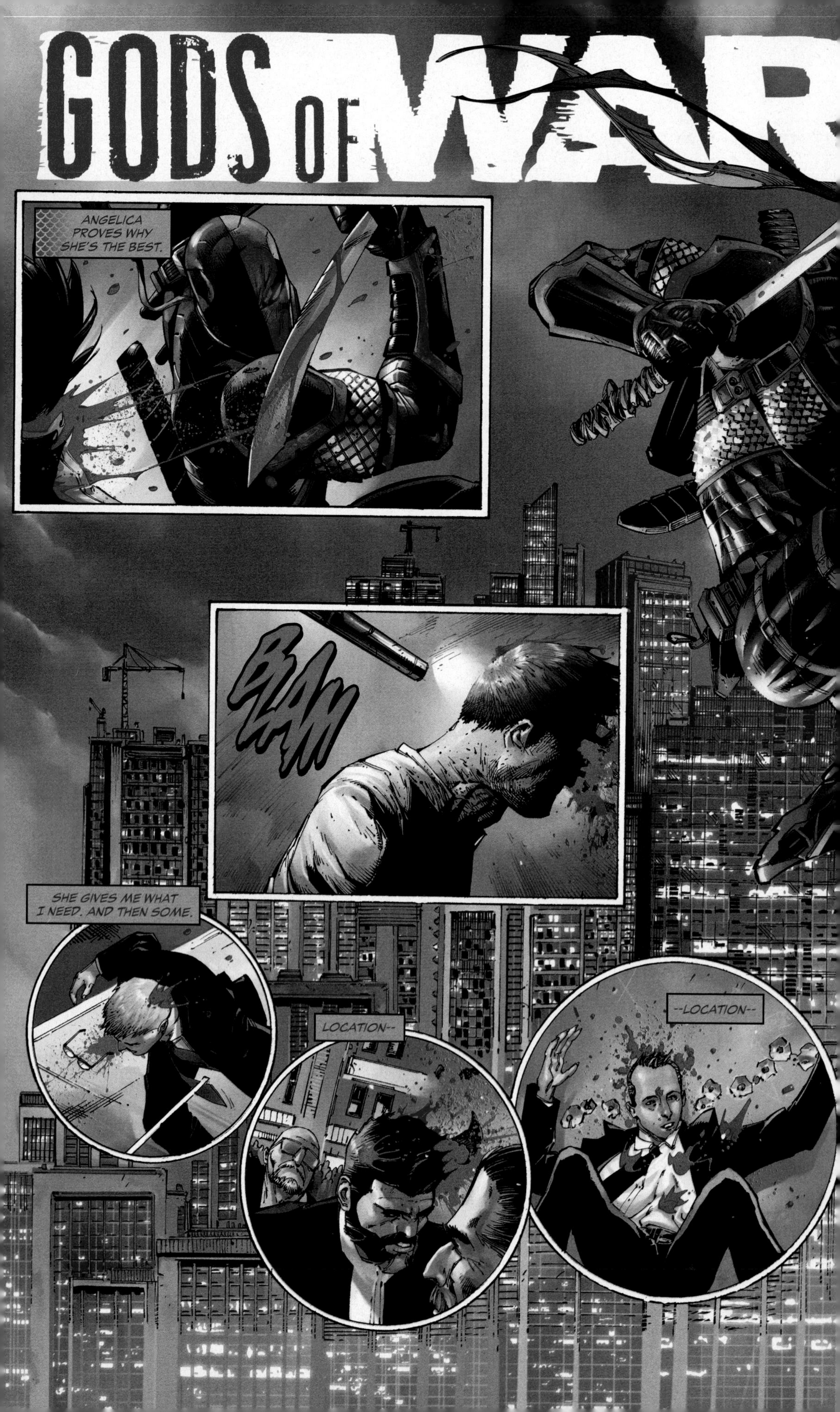
GODS OF WAR
ANGELICA PROVES WHY SHE'S THE BEST.
BLAM
SHE GIVES ME WHAT I NEED. AND THEN SOME.
LOCATION--
--LOCATION--

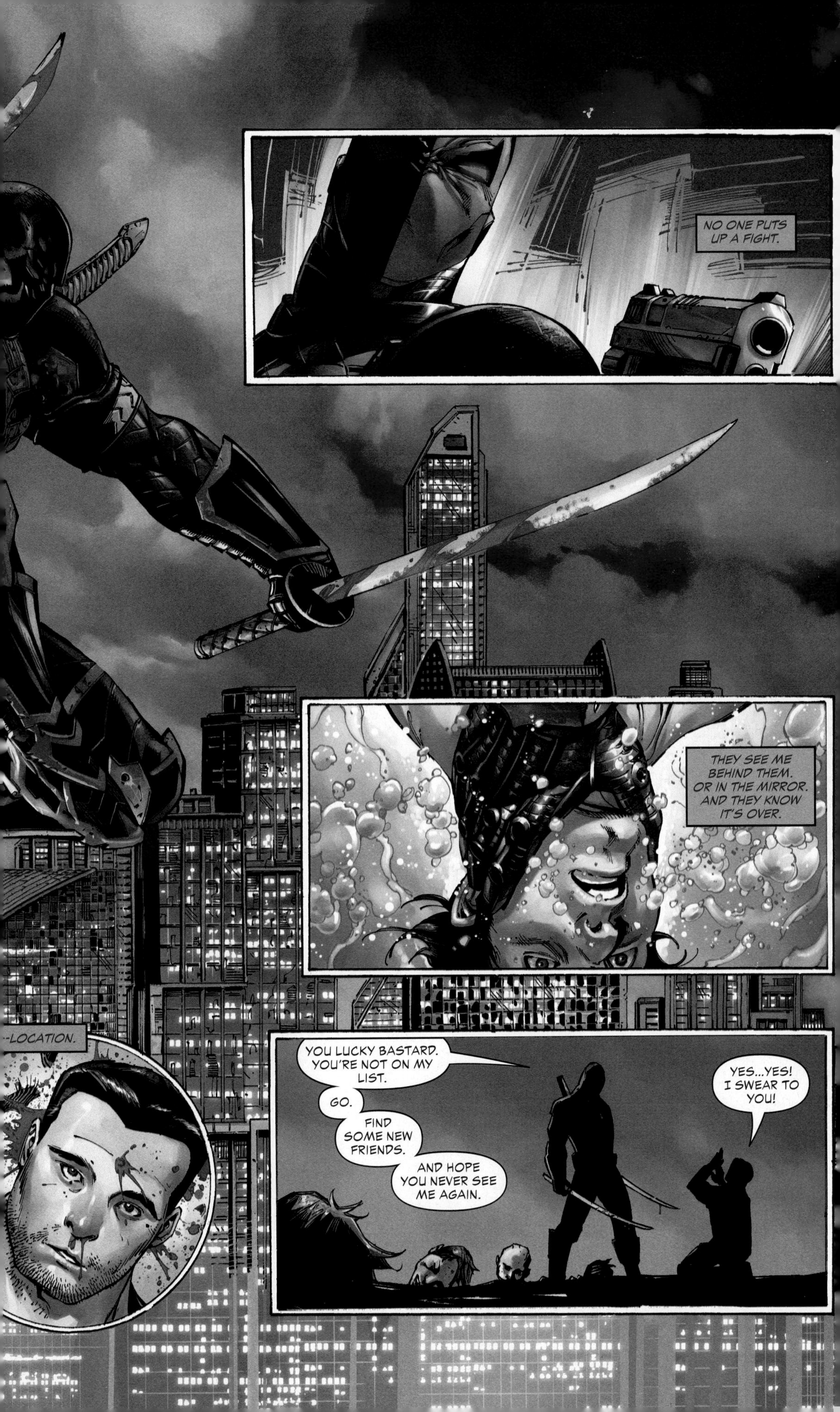
NO ONE PUTS UP A FIGHT.
THEY SEE ME BEHIND THEM. OR IN THE MIRROR. AND THEY KNOW IT'S OVER.
--LOCATION.
YOU LUCKY BASTARD. YOU'RE NOT ON MY LIST.
GO.
FIND SOME NEW FRIENDS.
AND HOPE YOU NEVER SEE ME AGAIN.
YES...YES! I SWEAR TO YOU!

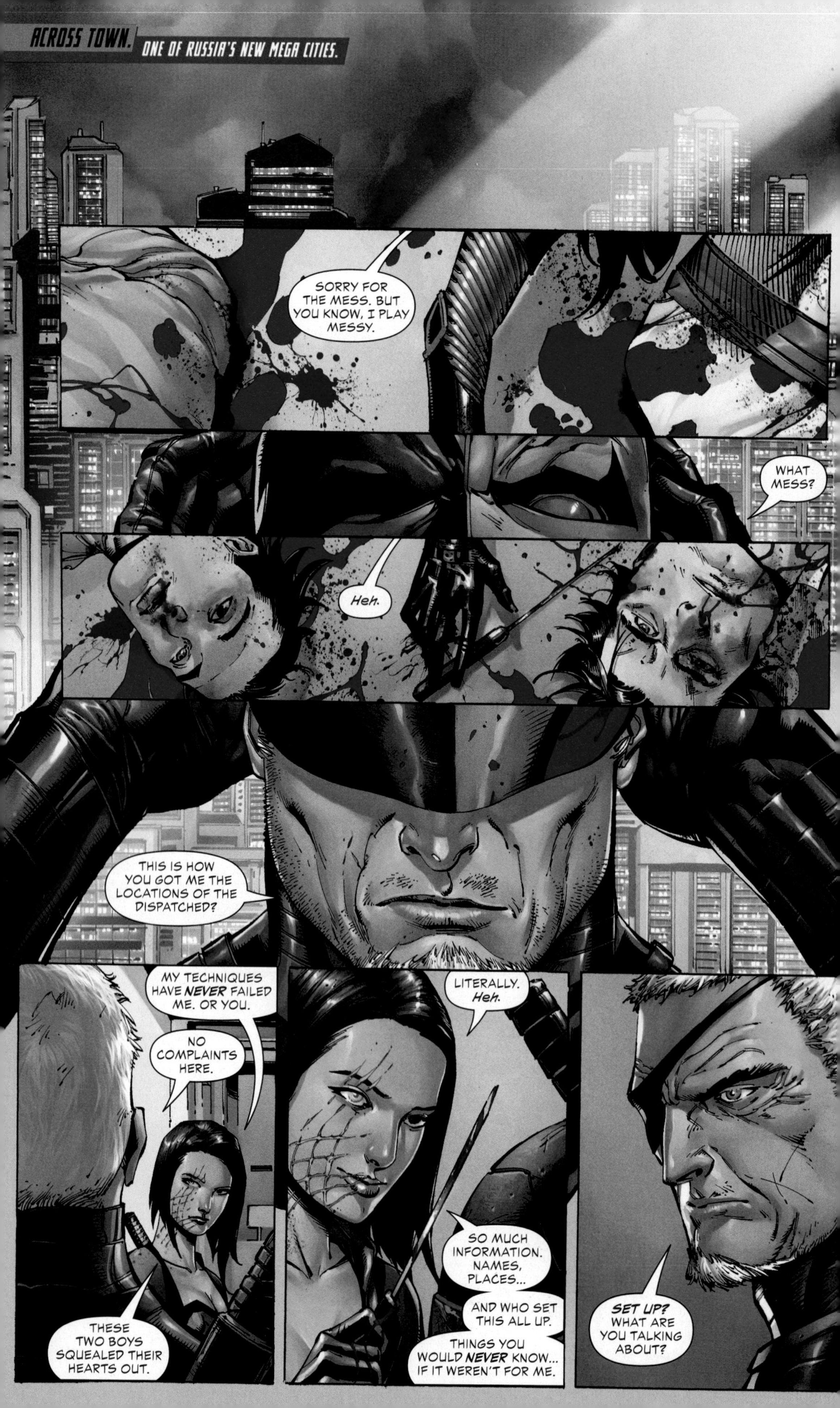
ACROSS TOWN.
ONE OF RUSSIA'S NEW MEGA CITIES.
SORRY FOR THE MESS. BUT YOU KNOW, I PLAY MESSY.
WHAT MESS?
Heh.
THIS IS HOW YOU GOT ME THE LOCATIONS OF THE DISPATCHED?
MY TECHNIQUES HAVE NEVER FAILED ME. OR YOU.
NO COMPLAINTS HERE.
THESE TWO BOYS SQUEALED THEIR HEARTS OUT.
LITERALLY. Heh.
SO MUCH INFORMATION. NAMES, PLACES...
AND WHO SET THIS ALL UP.
THINGS YOU WOULD NEVER KNOW... IF IT WEREN'T FOR ME.
SET UP? WHAT ARE YOU TALKING ABOUT?

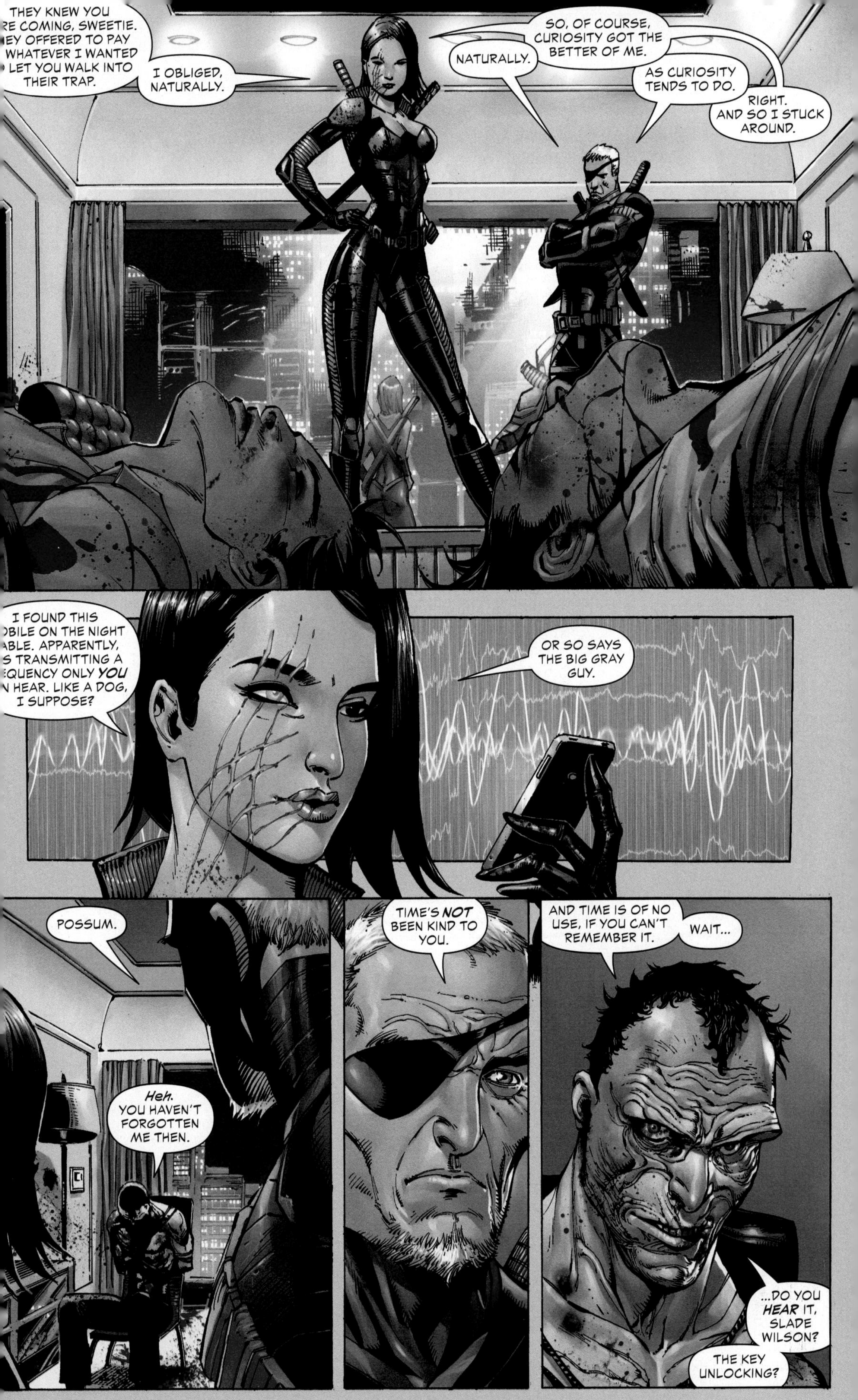
THEY KNEW YOU
RE COMING, SWEETIE.
EY OFFERED TO PAY
WHATEVER I WANTED
LET YOU WALK INTO
THEIR TRAP.
I OBLIGED, NATURALLY.
NATURALLY.
SO, OF COURSE, CURIOSITY GOT THE BETTER OF ME.
AS CURIOSITY TENDS TO DO.
RIGHT. AND SO I STUCK AROUND.
I FOUND THIS
OBILE ON THE NIGHT
ABLE. APPARENTLY,
S TRANSMITTING A
EQUENCY ONLY *YOU*
N HEAR. LIKE A DOG,
I SUPPOSE?
OR SO SAYS THE BIG GRAY GUY.
POSSUM.
Heh. YOU HAVEN'T FORGOTTEN ME THEN.
TIME'S ***NOT*** BEEN KIND TO YOU.
AND TIME IS OF NO USE, IF YOU CAN'T REMEMBER IT.
WAIT...
...DO YOU ***HEAR*** IT, SLADE WILSON?
THE KEY UNLOCKING?

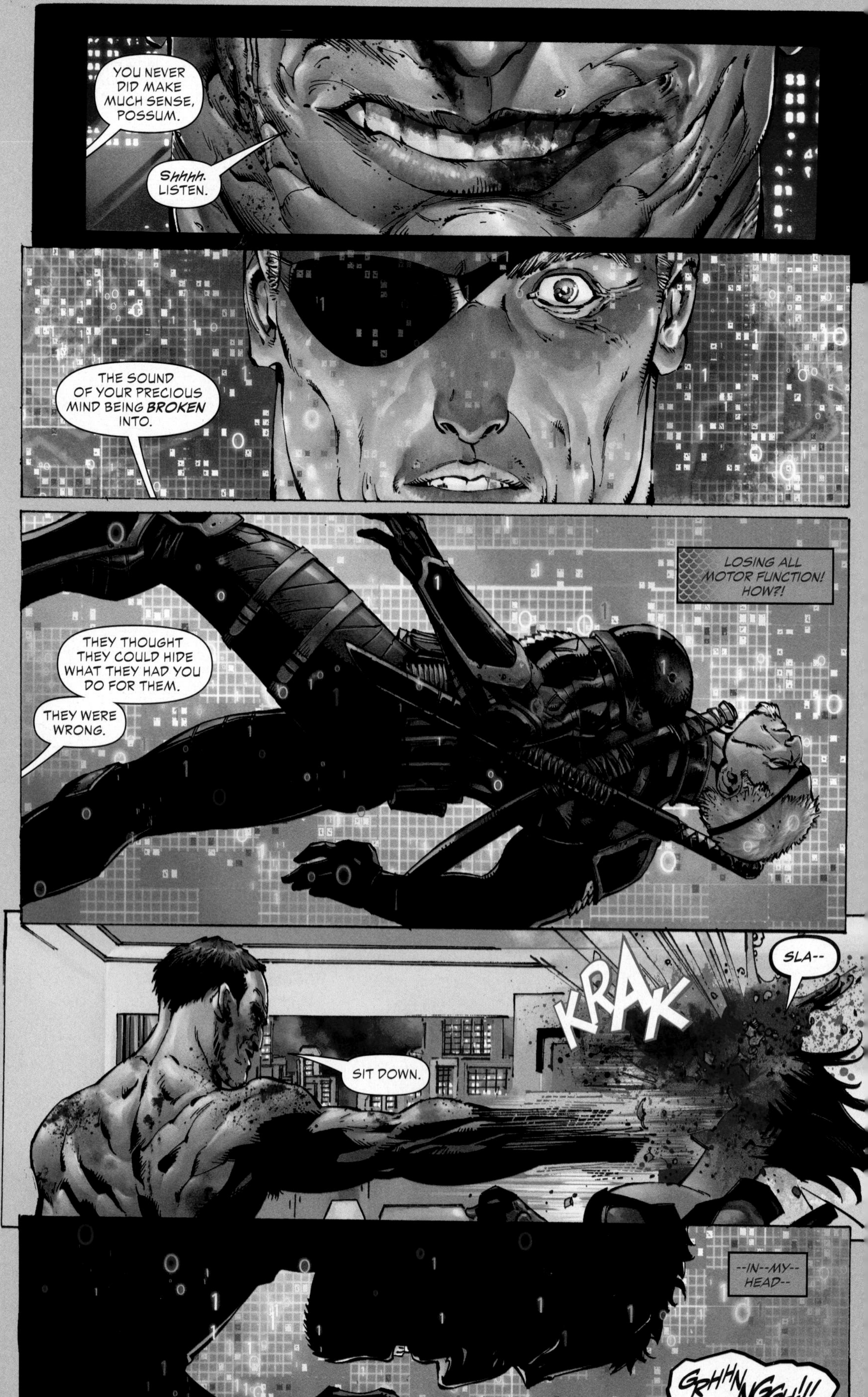
YOU NEVER DID MAKE MUCH SENSE, POSSUM.
Shhhh. LISTEN.
THE SOUND OF YOUR PRECIOUS MIND BEING BROKEN INTO.
LOSING ALL MOTOR FUNCTION! HOW?!
THEY THOUGHT THEY COULD HIDE WHAT THEY HAD YOU DO FOR THEM.
THEY WERE WRONG.
SLA--
KRAK
SIT DOWN.
--IN--MY--HEAD--
GRHHNNGGH!!!

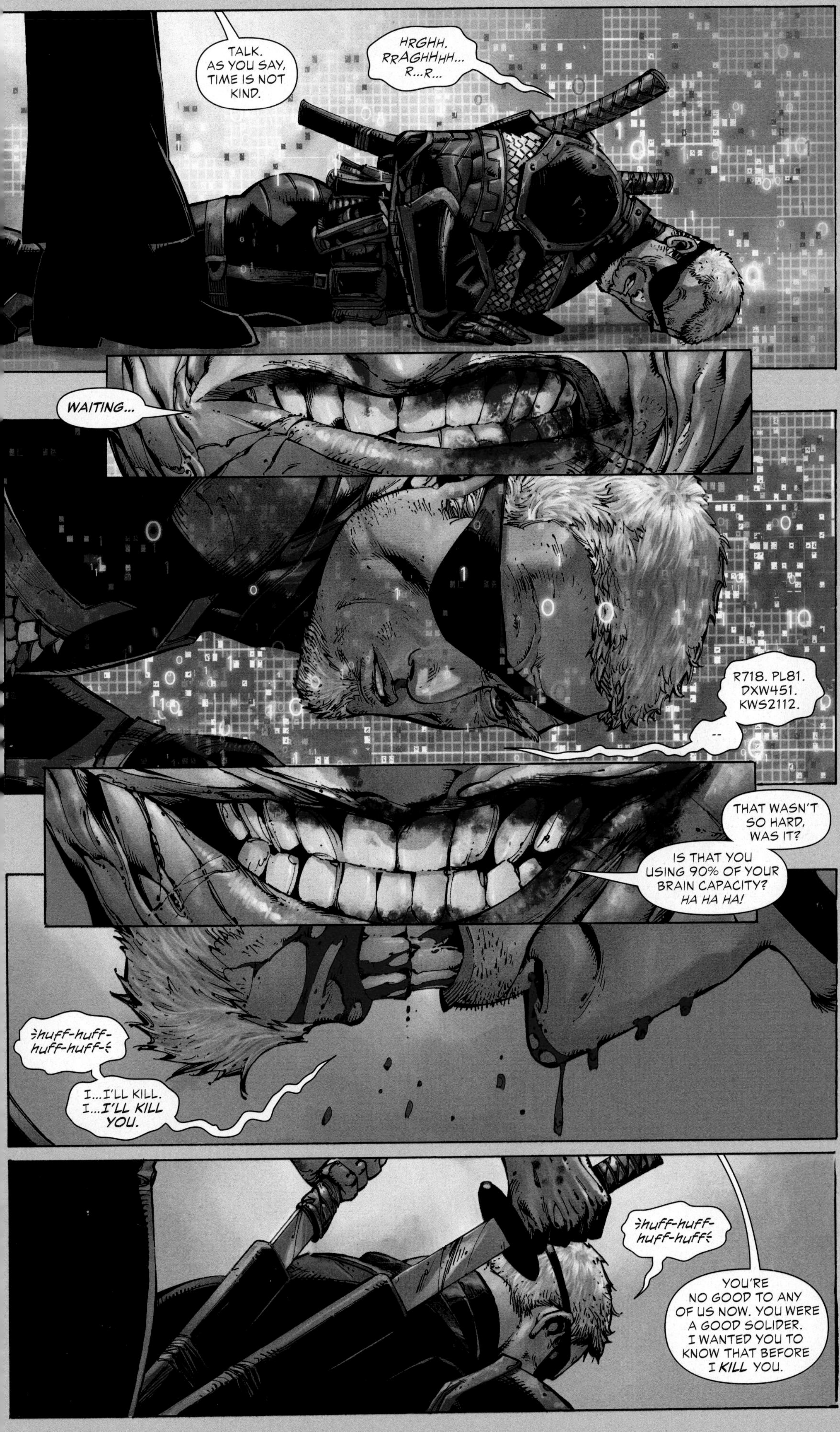
TALK. AS YOU SAY, TIME IS NOT KIND.
HRGHH. RRAGHHHH... R...R...
WAITING...
R718. PL81. DXW451. KWS2112. --
THAT WASN'T SO HARD, WAS IT?
IS THAT YOU USING 90% OF YOUR BRAIN CAPACITY? *HA HA HA!*
huff-huff-huff-huff-
I...I'LL KILL. I...***I'LL KILL*** YOU.
huff-huff-huff-huff
YOU'RE NO GOOD TO ANY OF US NOW. YOU WERE A GOOD SOLIDER. I WANTED YOU TO KNOW THAT BEFORE I ***KILL*** YOU.

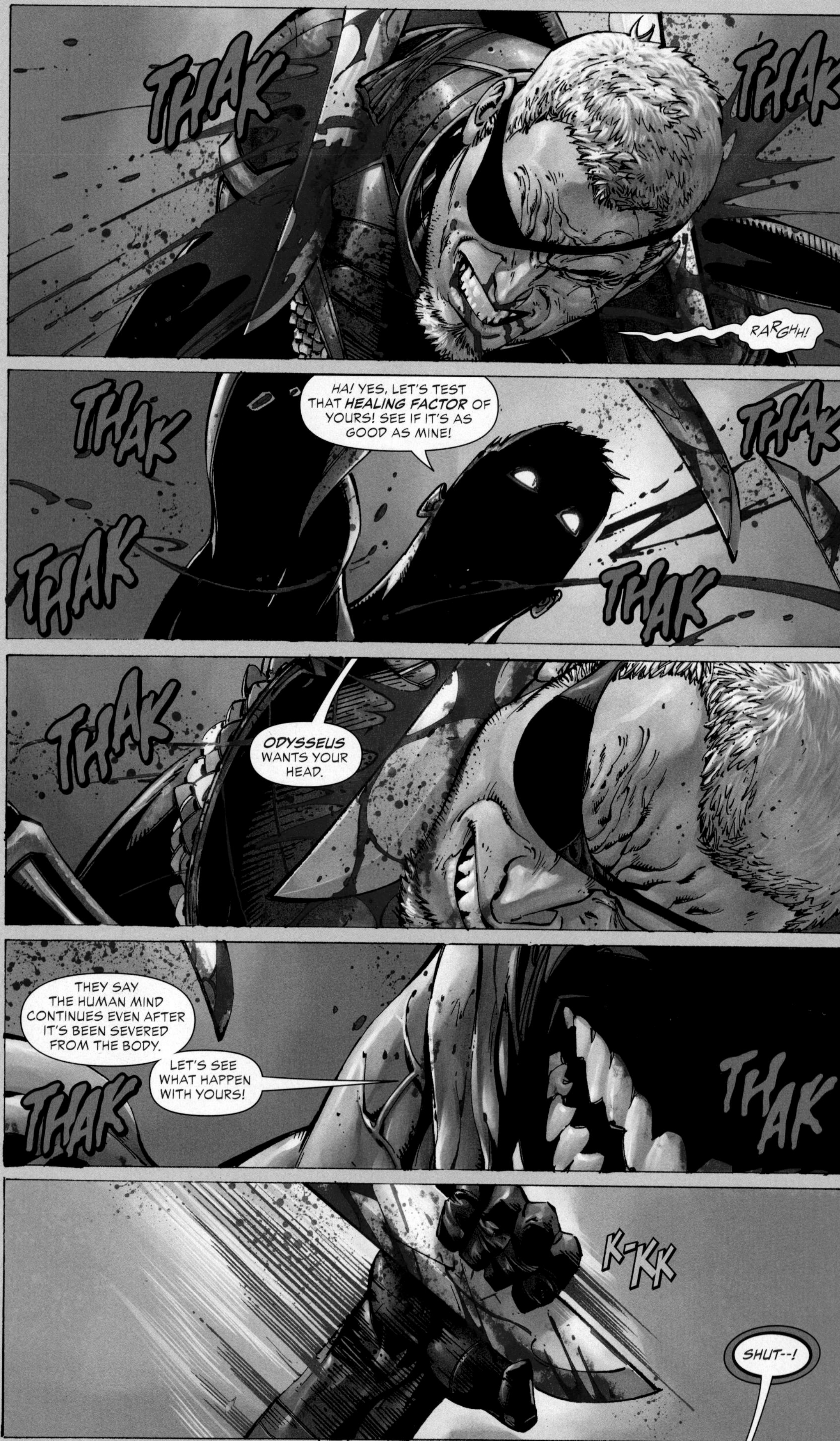
THAK
THAK
RARGHH!
THAK
HA! YES, LET'S TEST THAT HEALING FACTOR OF YOURS! SEE IF IT'S AS GOOD AS MINE!
THAK
THAK
THAK
THAK
ODYSSEUS WANTS YOUR HEAD.
THEY SAY THE HUMAN MIND CONTINUES EVEN AFTER IT'S BEEN SEVERED FROM THE BODY.
LET'S SEE WHAT HAPPEN WITH YOURS!
THAK
THAK
K-KK
SHUT--!

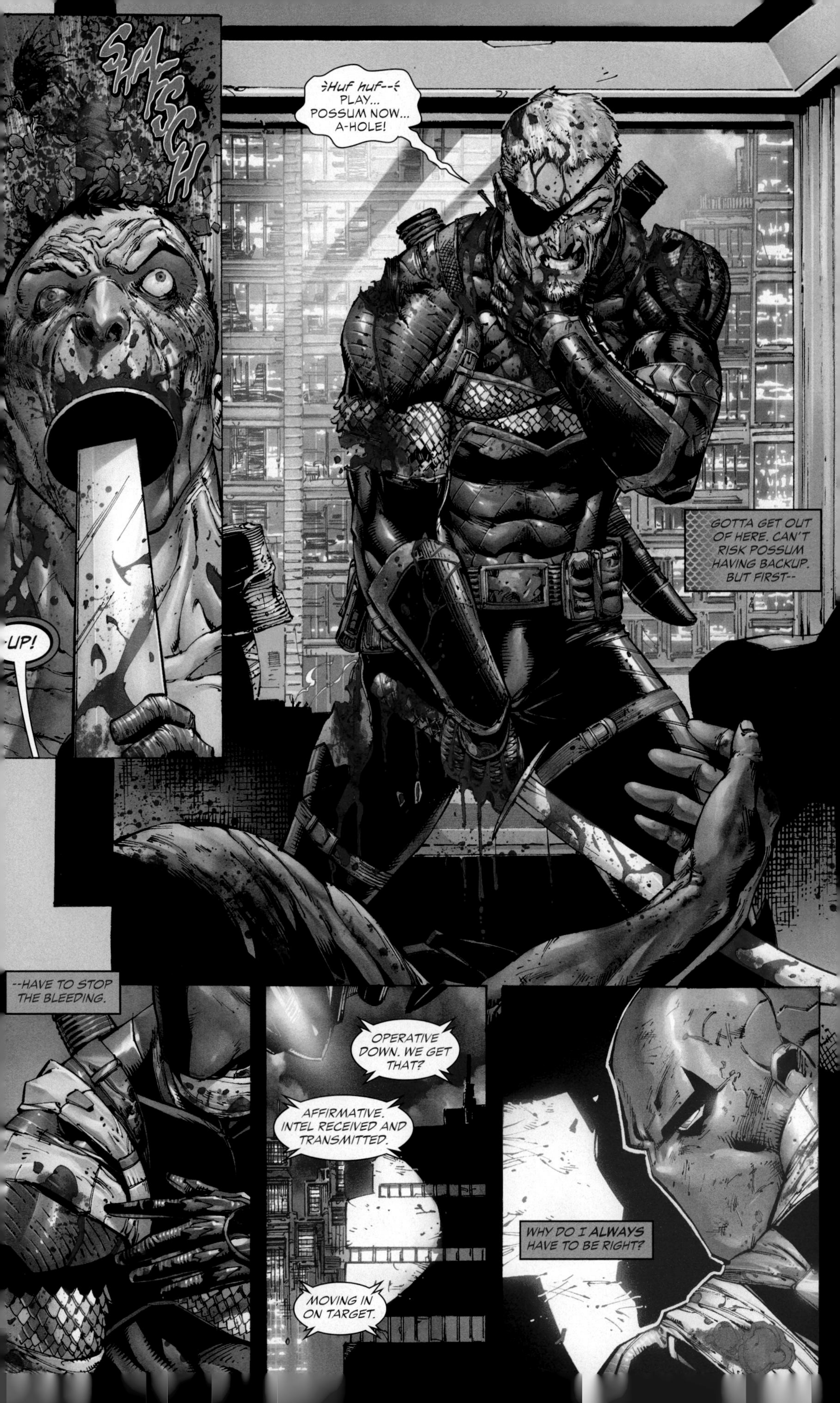
SHASCH
-UP!
Huf huf--
PLAY...
POSSUM NOW...
A-HOLE!
GOTTA GET OUT OF HERE. CAN'T RISK POSSUM HAVING BACKUP. BUT FIRST--
--HAVE TO STOP THE BLEEDING.
OPERATIVE DOWN. WE GET THAT?
AFFIRMATIVE. INTEL RECEIVED AND TRANSMITTED.
MOVING IN ON TARGET.
WHY DO I ALWAYS HAVE TO BE RIGHT?

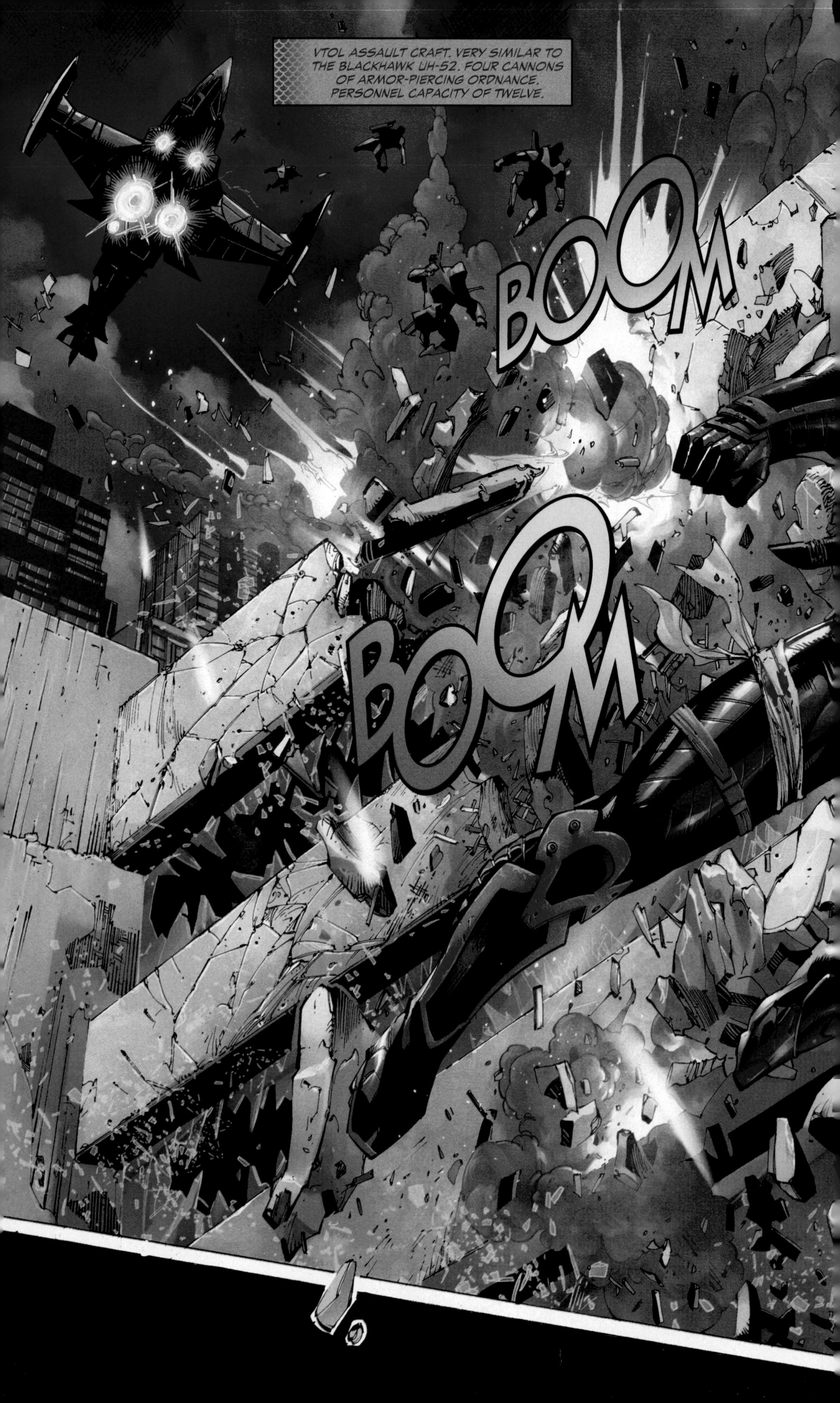
VTOL ASSAULT CRAFT. VERY SIMILAR TO THE BLACKHAWK UH-52. FOUR CANNONS OF ARMOR-PIERCING ORDNANCE. PERSONNEL CAPACITY OF TWELVE.
BOOM
BOOM

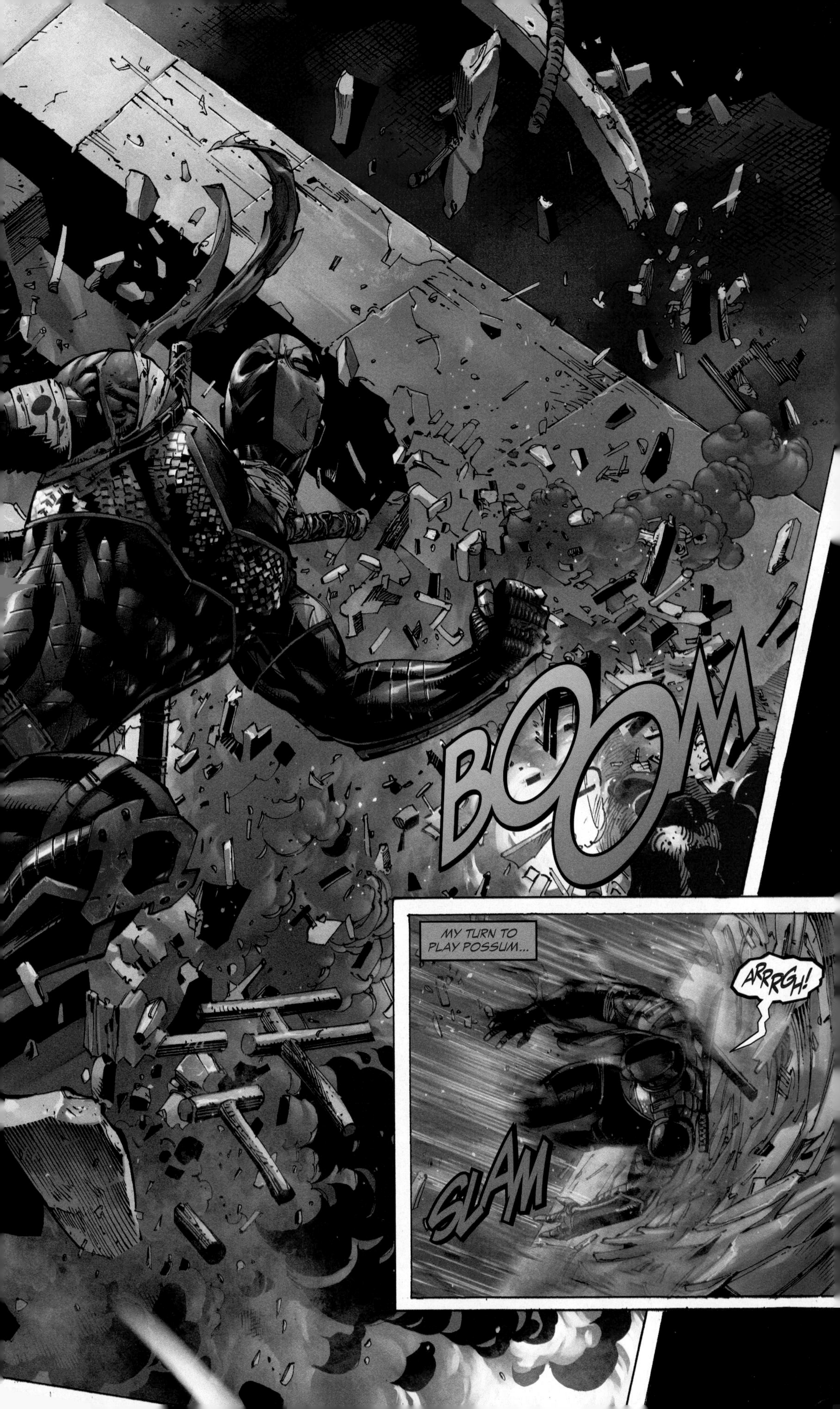

BOOM
MY TURN TO PLAY POSSUM...
ARRRGH!
SLAM

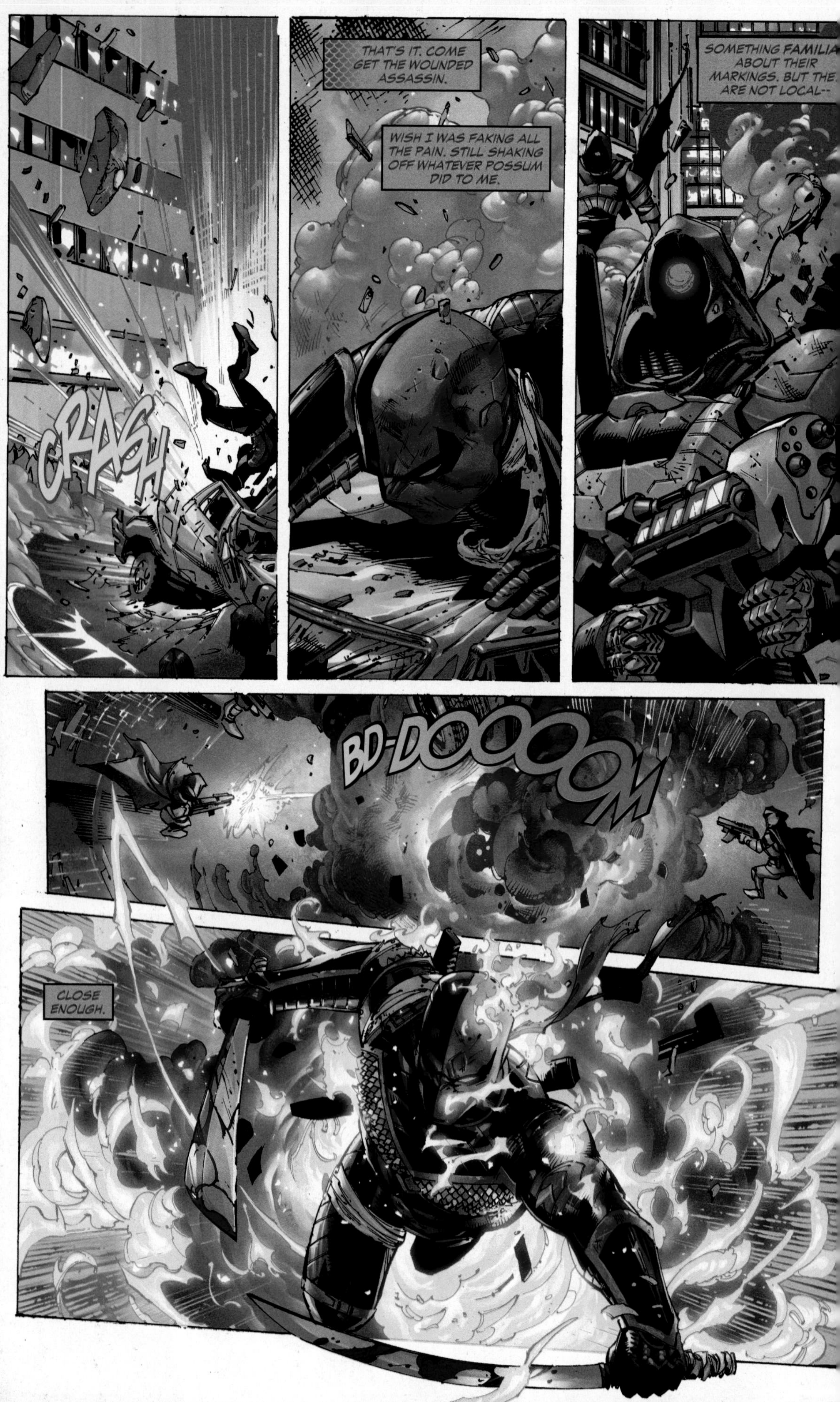
CRASH
THAT'S IT. COME GET THE WOUNDED ASSASSIN.
WISH I WAS FAKING ALL THE PAIN. STILL SHAKING OFF WHATEVER POSSUM DID TO ME.
SOMETHING FAMILIA ABOUT THEIR MARKINGS. BUT THE ARE NOT LOCAL--
BD-DOOOOOM
CLOSE ENOUGH.

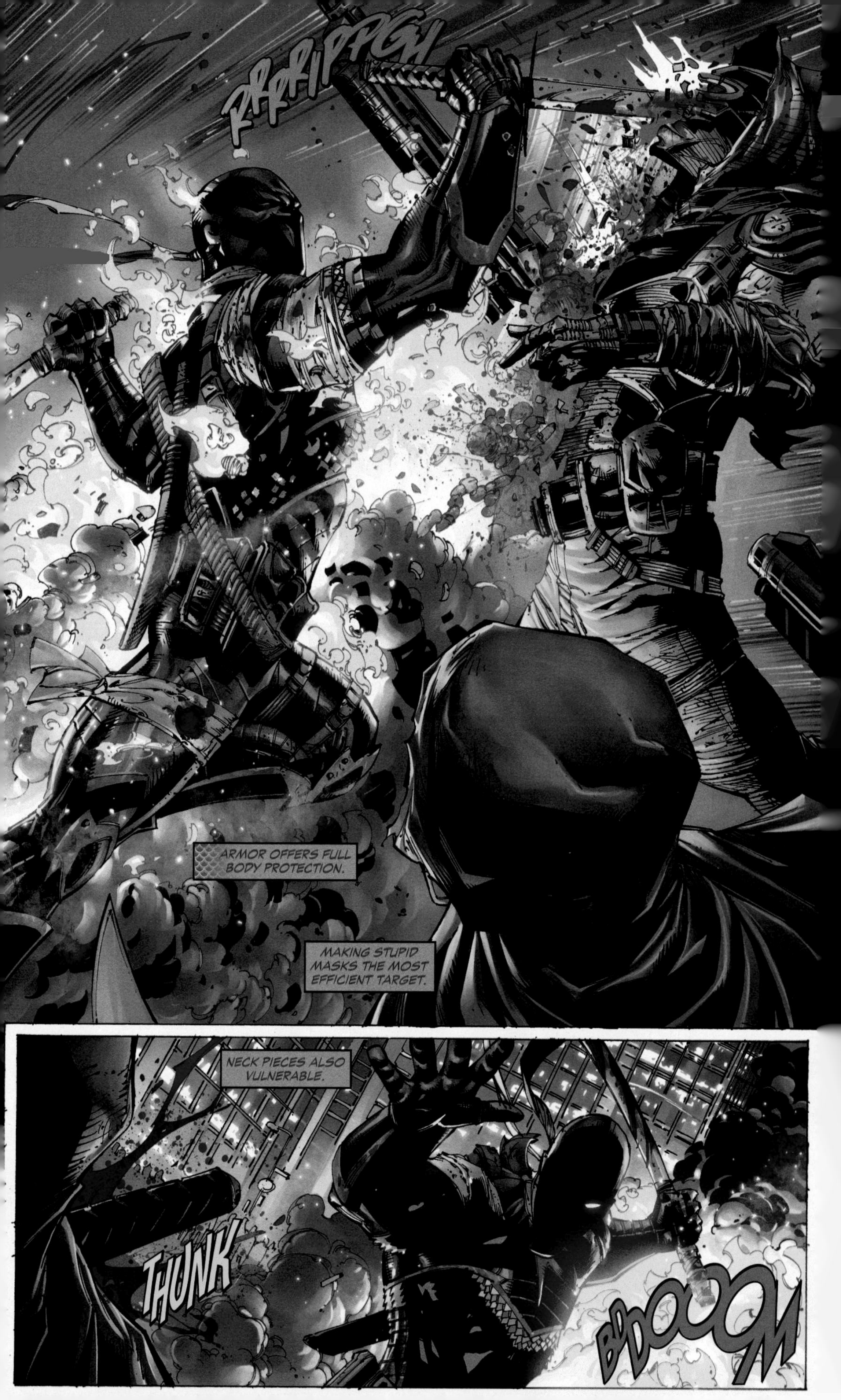

RRRIPPPGH
ARMOR OFFERS FULL BODY PROTECTION.
MAKING STUPID MASKS THE MOST EFFICIENT TARGET.
NECK PIECES ALSO VULNERABLE.
THUNK
BDOOOM

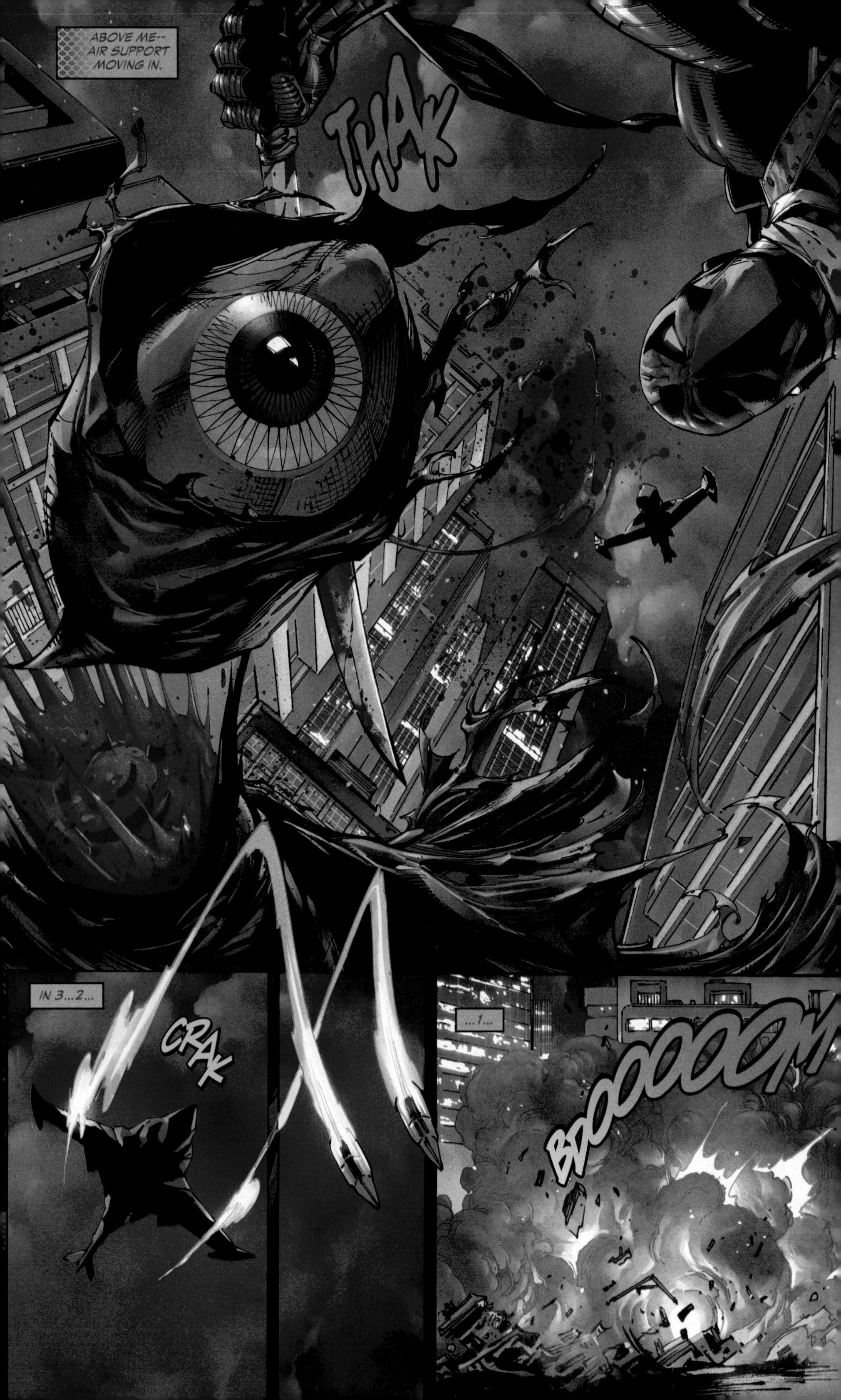

ABOVE ME--
AIR SUPPORT
MOVING IN.
THAK
IN 3...2...
CRAK
...1...
BDOOOOOOM

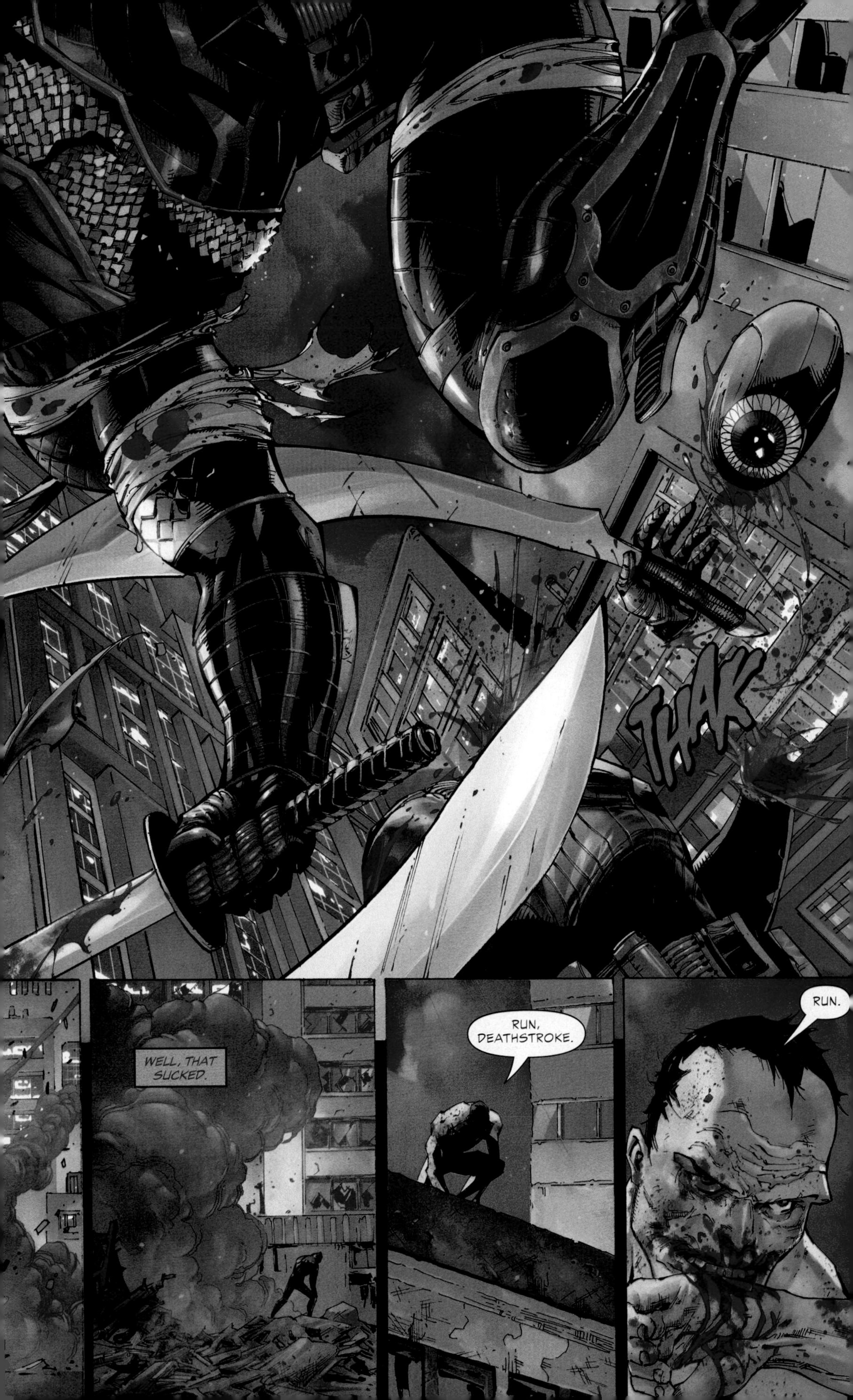
THAK
WELL, THAT SUCKED.
RUN, DEATHSTROKE.
RUN.

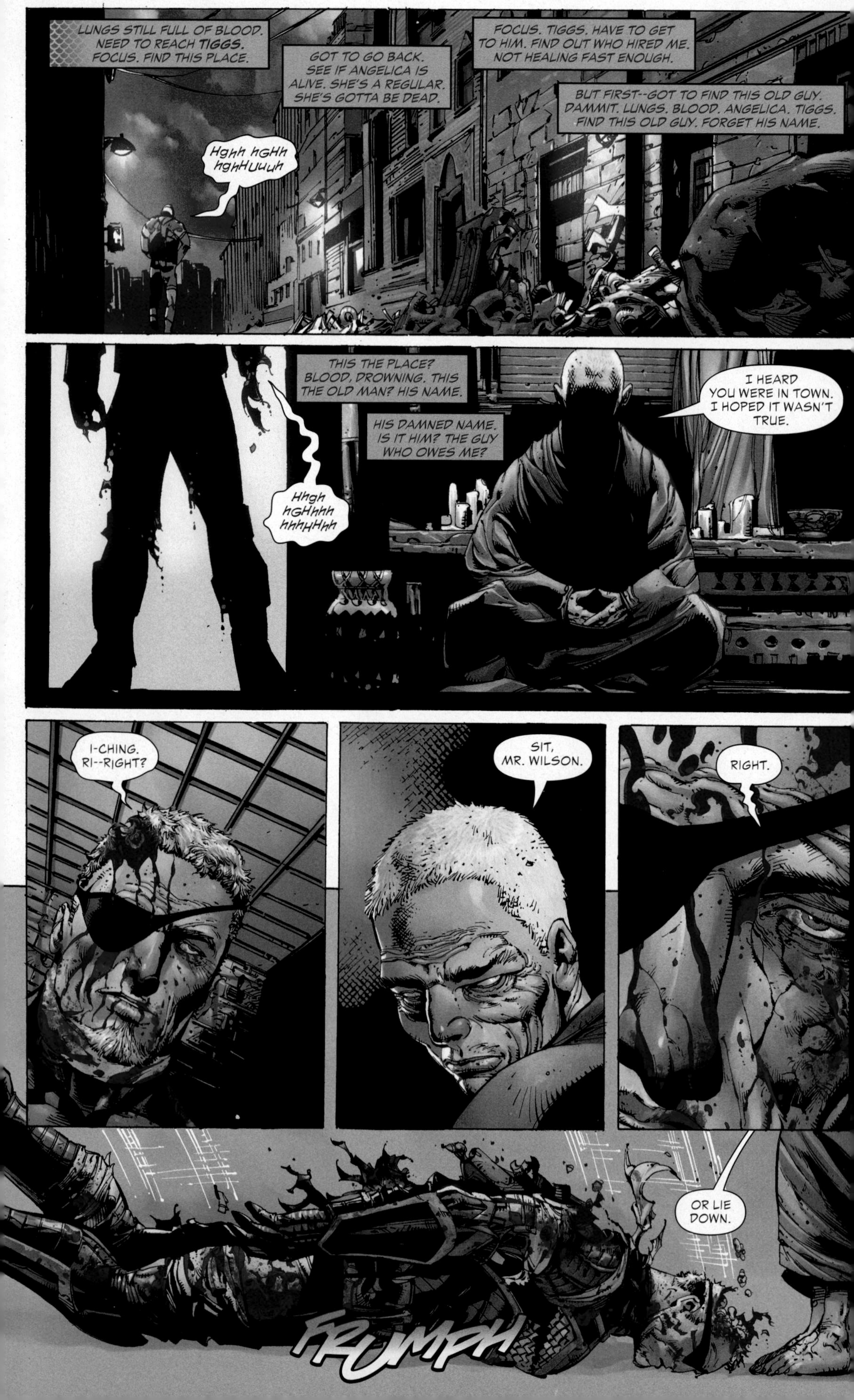
LUNGS STILL FULL OF BLOOD. NEED TO REACH TIGGS. FOCUS. FIND THIS PLACE.
GOT TO GO BACK. SEE IF ANGELICA IS ALIVE. SHE'S A REGULAR. SHE'S GOTTA BE DEAD.
FOCUS. TIGGS. HAVE TO GET TO HIM. FIND OUT WHO HIRED ME. NOT HEALING FAST ENOUGH.
BUT FIRST--GOT TO FIND THIS OLD GUY. DAMMIT. LUNGS. BLOOD. ANGELICA. TIGGS. FIND THIS OLD GUY. FORGET HIS NAME.
Hghh hGHh hghHuuuh
THIS THE PLACE? BLOOD, DROWNING. THIS THE OLD MAN? HIS NAME.
HIS DAMNED NAME. IS IT HIM? THE GUY WHO OWES ME?
Hhgh hGHhhh hhhHHhh
I HEARD YOU WERE IN TOWN. I HOPED IT WASN'T TRUE.
I-CHING. RI--RIGHT?
SIT, MR. WILSON.
RIGHT.
OR LIE DOWN.
FRUMPH

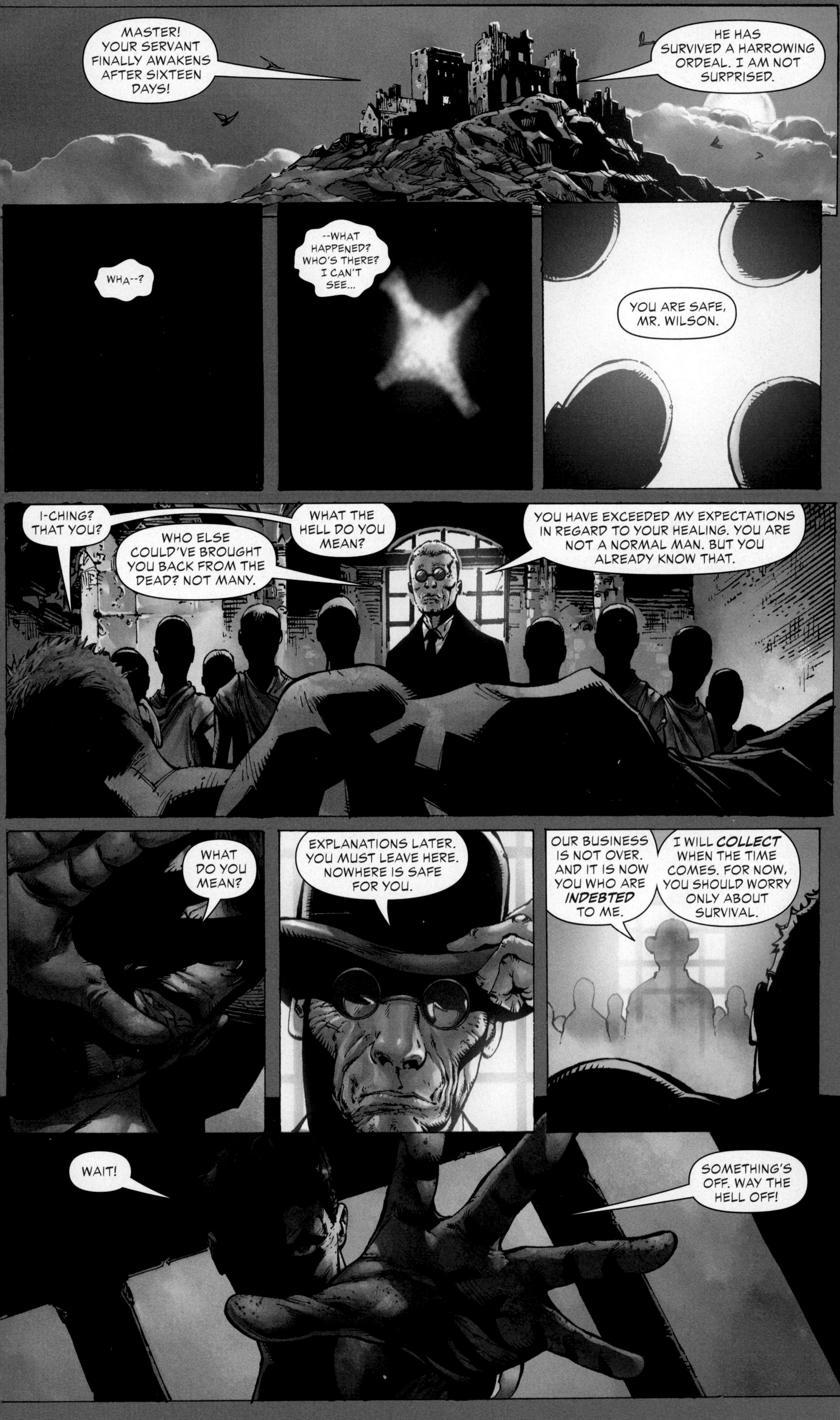
MASTER! YOUR SERVANT FINALLY AWAKENS AFTER SIXTEEN DAYS!
HE HAS SURVIVED A HARROWING ORDEAL. I AM NOT SURPRISED.
WHA--?
--WHAT HAPPENED? WHO'S THERE? I CAN'T SEE...
YOU ARE SAFE, MR. WILSON.
I-CHING? THAT YOU?
WHO ELSE COULD'VE BROUGHT YOU BACK FROM THE DEAD? NOT MANY.
WHAT THE HELL DO YOU MEAN?
YOU HAVE EXCEEDED MY EXPECTATIONS IN REGARD TO YOUR HEALING. YOU ARE NOT A NORMAL MAN. BUT YOU ALREADY KNOW THAT.
WHAT DO YOU MEAN?
EXPLANATIONS LATER. YOU MUST LEAVE HERE. NOWHERE IS SAFE FOR YOU.
OUR BUSINESS IS NOT OVER. AND IT IS NOW YOU WHO ARE INDEBTED TO ME.
I WILL COLLECT WHEN THE TIME COMES. FOR NOW, YOU SHOULD WORRY ONLY ABOUT SURVIVAL.
WAIT!
SOMETHING'S OFF. WAY THE HELL OFF!

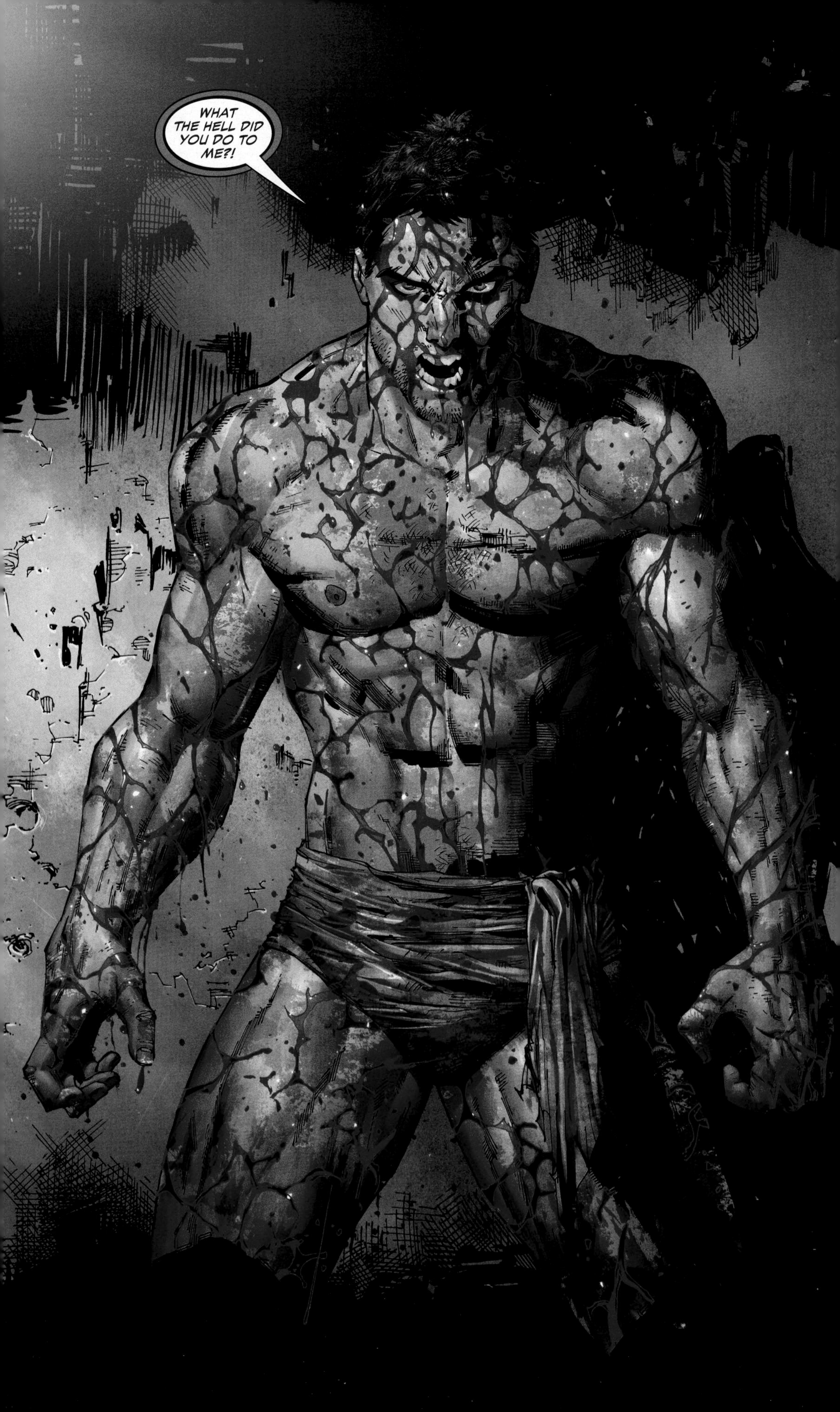
WHAT THE HELL DID YOU DO TO ME?!

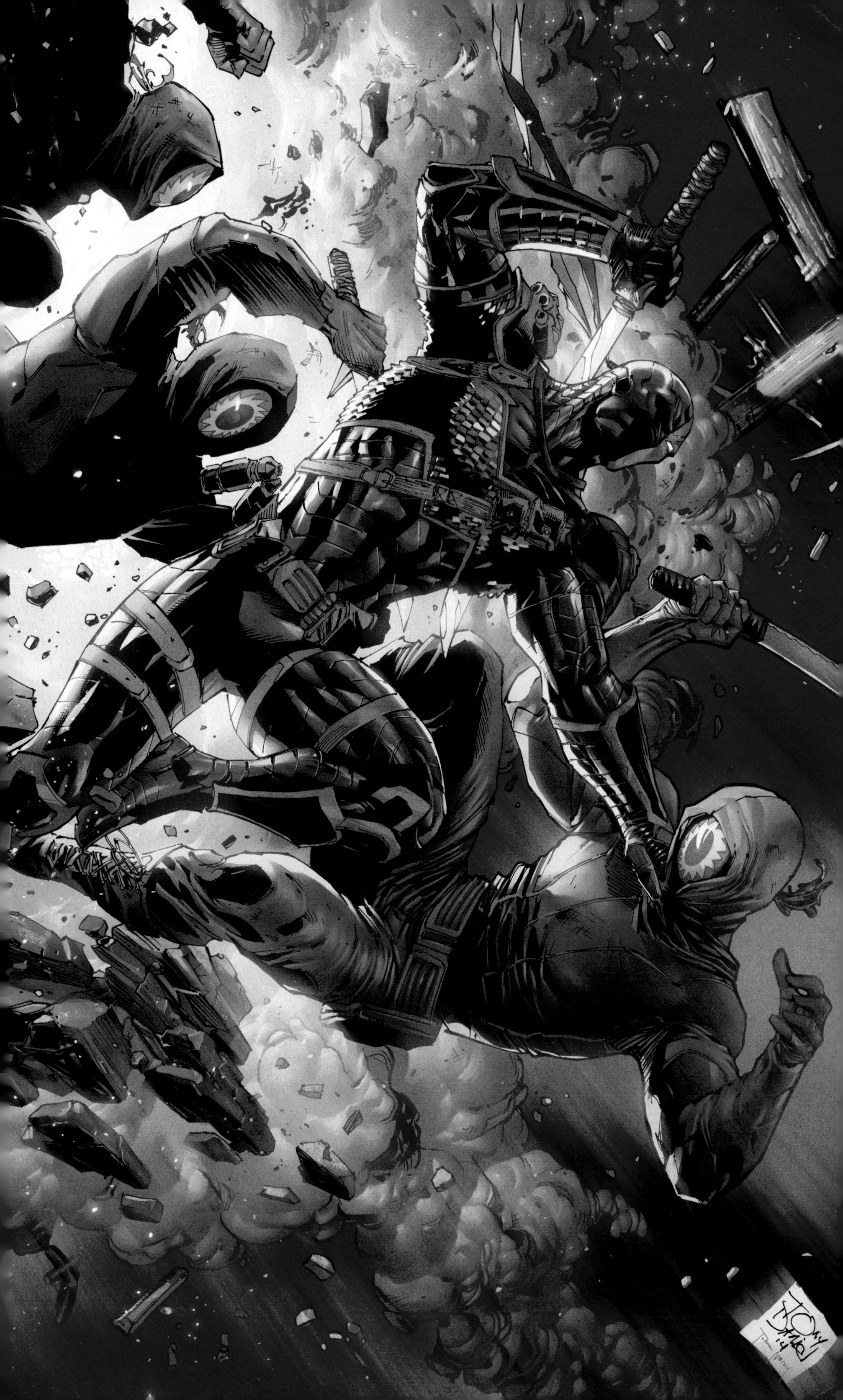

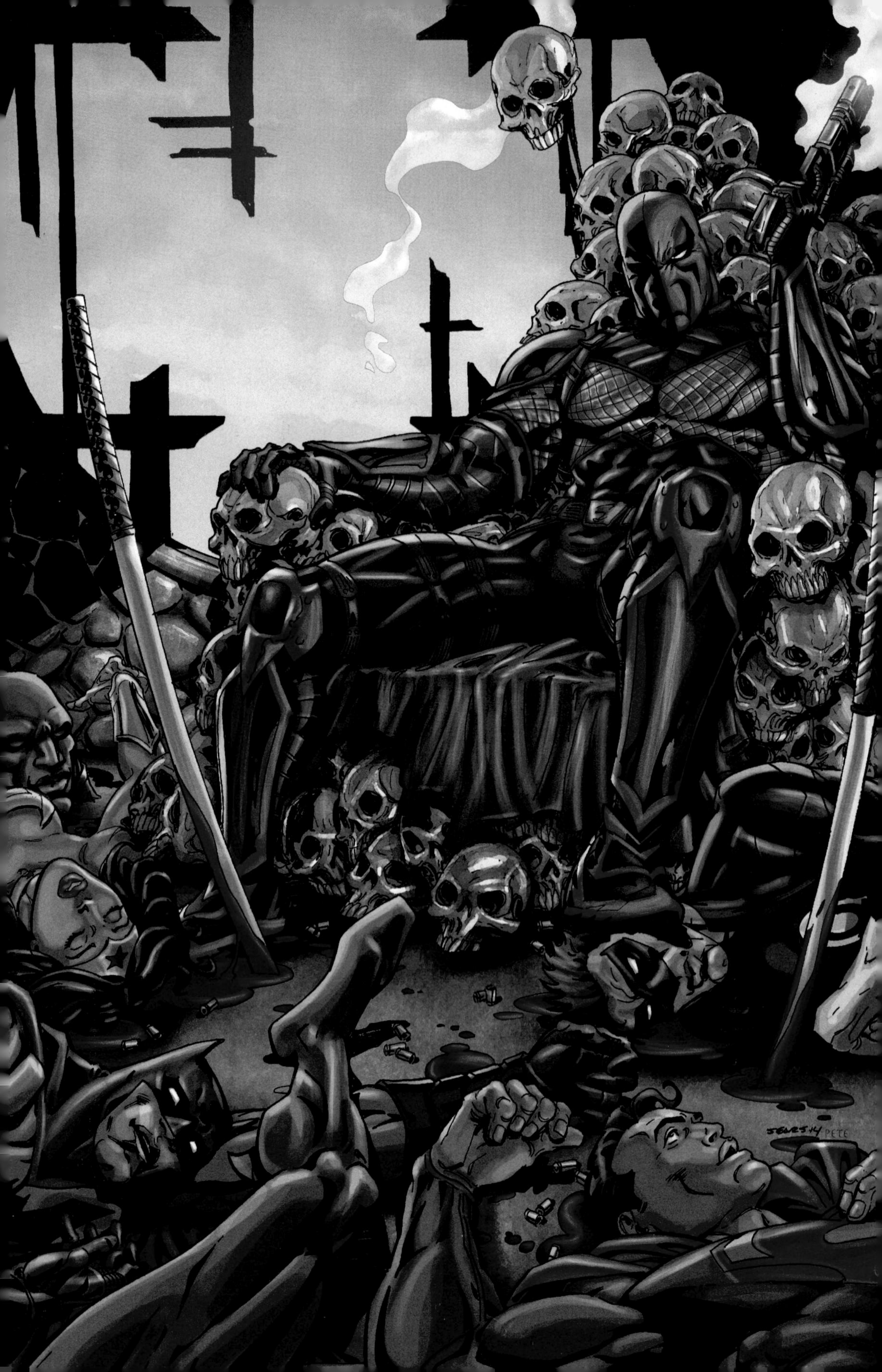

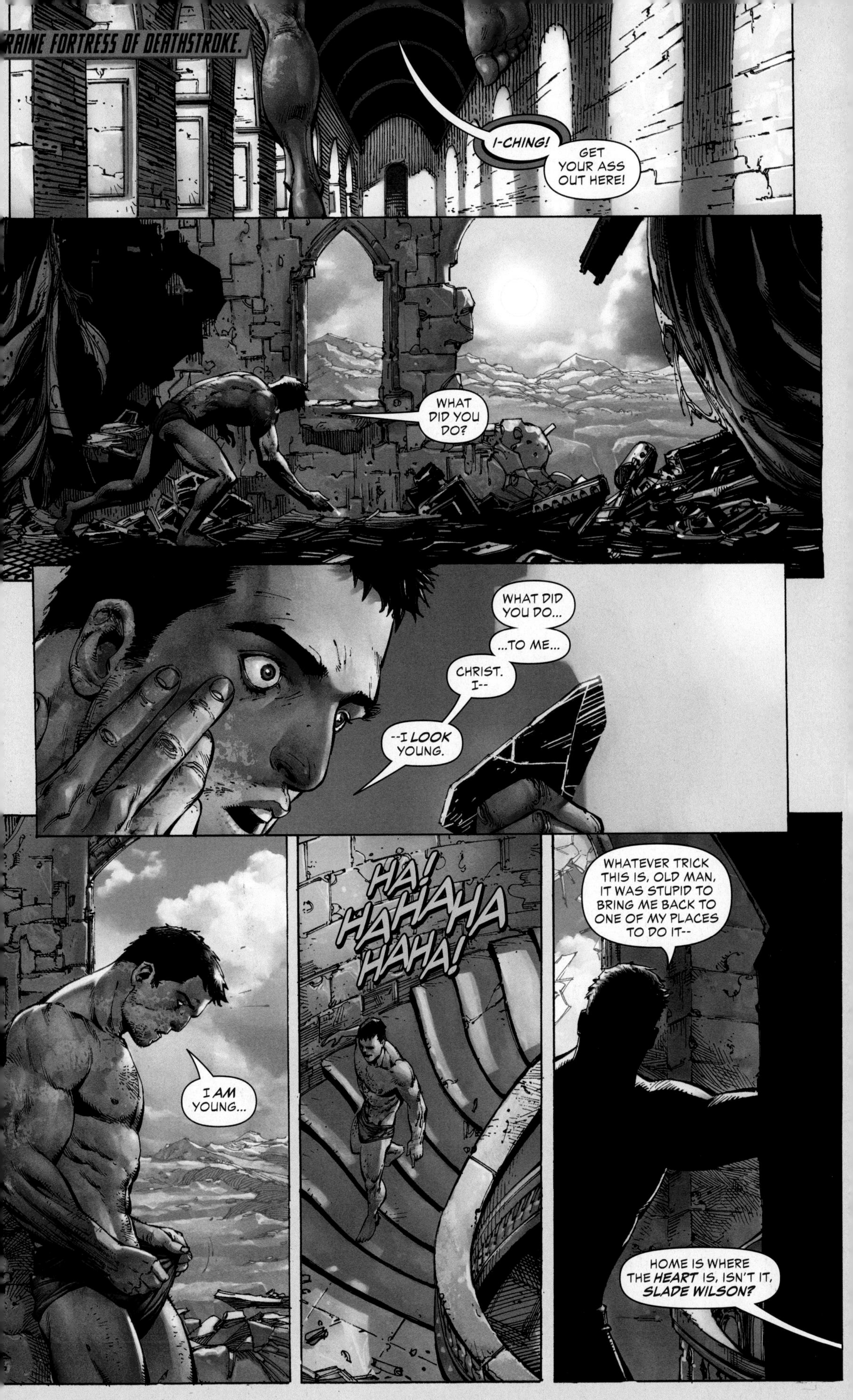

RAINE FORTRESS OF DEATHSTROKE.
I-CHING!
GET YOUR ASS OUT HERE!
WHAT DID YOU DO?
WHAT DID YOU DO...
...TO ME...
CHRIST. I--
--I LOOK YOUNG.
I AM YOUNG...
HA! HAHAHA HAHA!
WHATEVER TRICK THIS IS, OLD MAN, IT WAS STUPID TO BRING ME BACK TO ONE OF MY PLACES TO DO IT--
HOME IS WHERE THE HEART IS, ISN'T IT, SLADE WILSON?

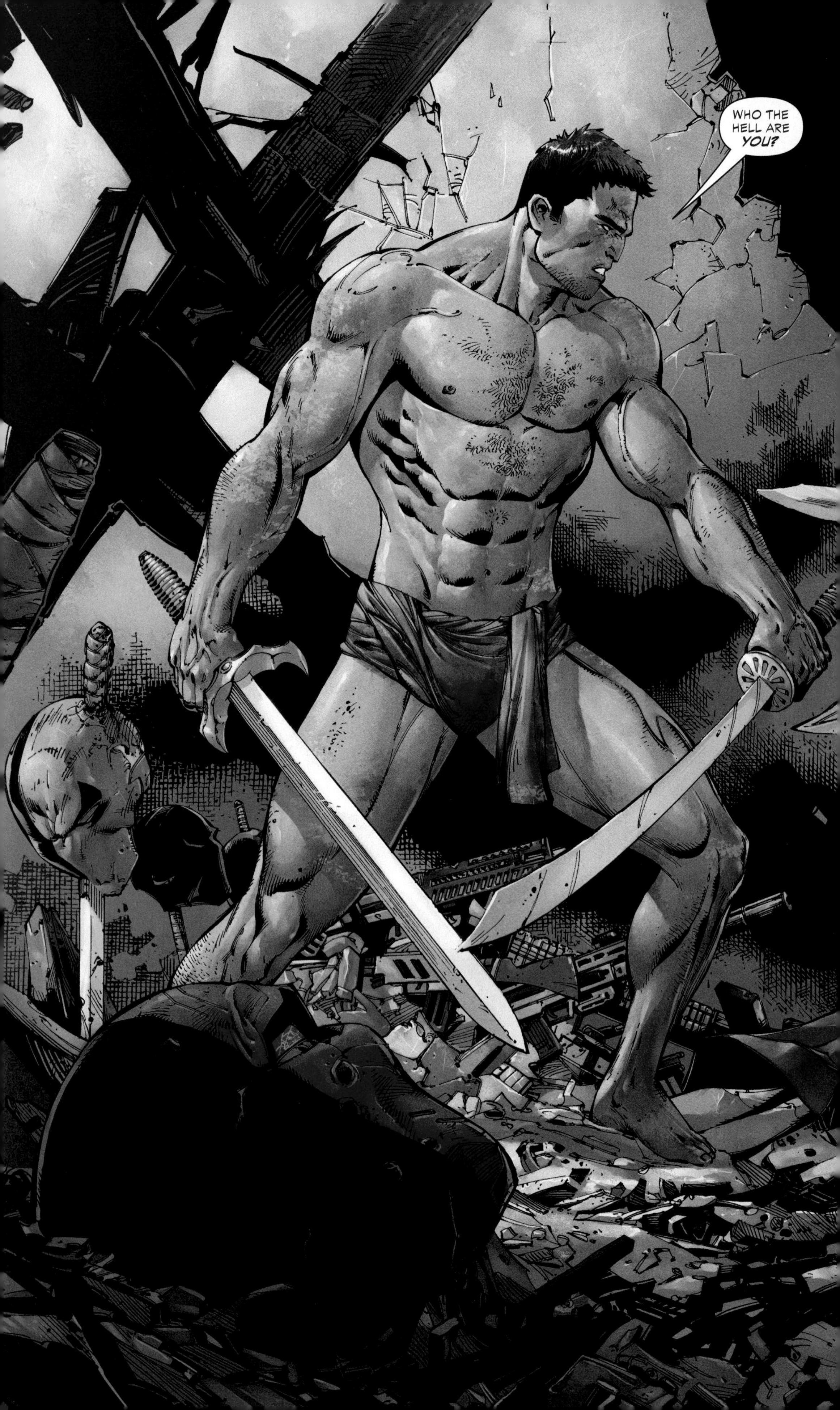
WHO THE HELL ARE YOU?

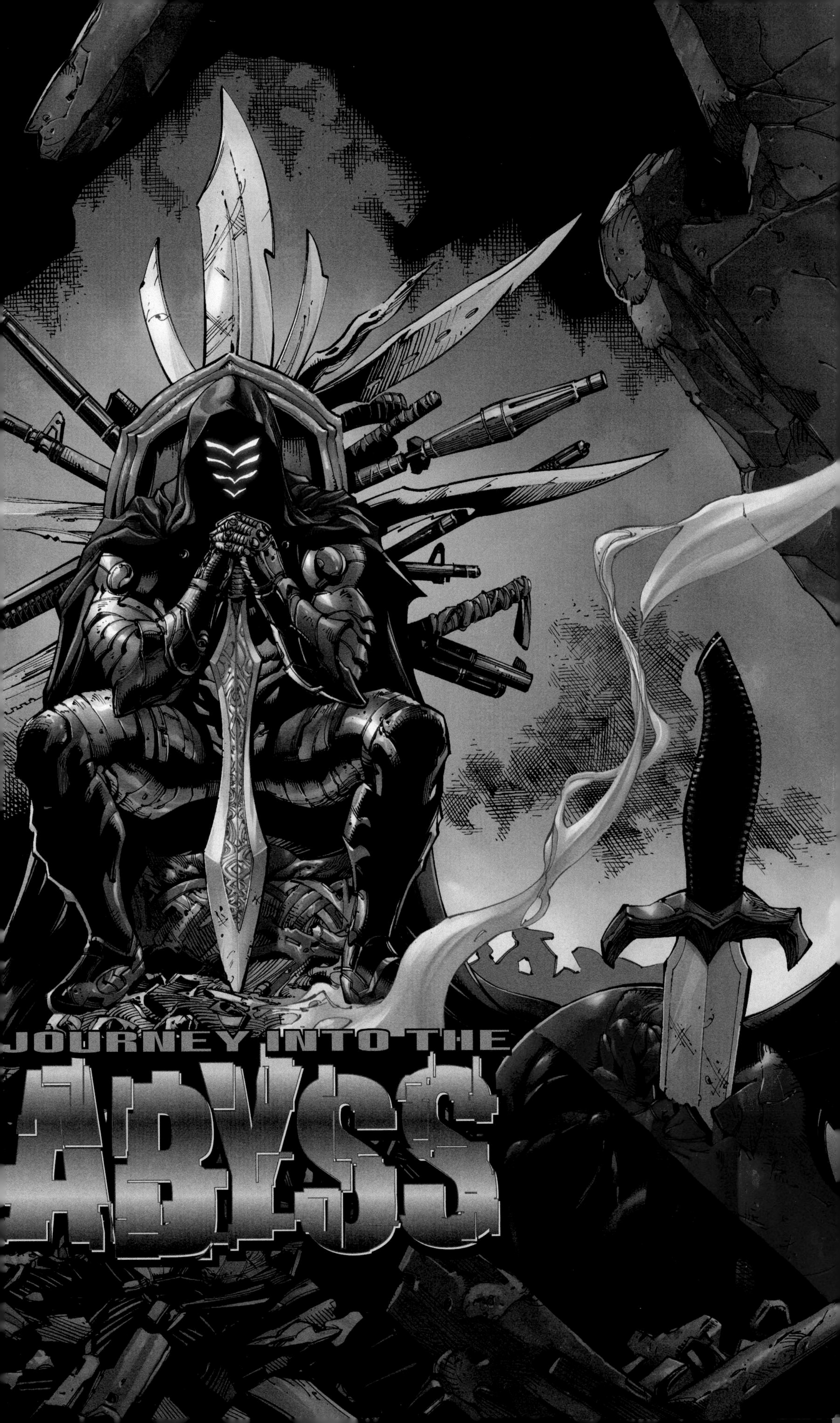
JOURNEY INTO THE
ABYSS

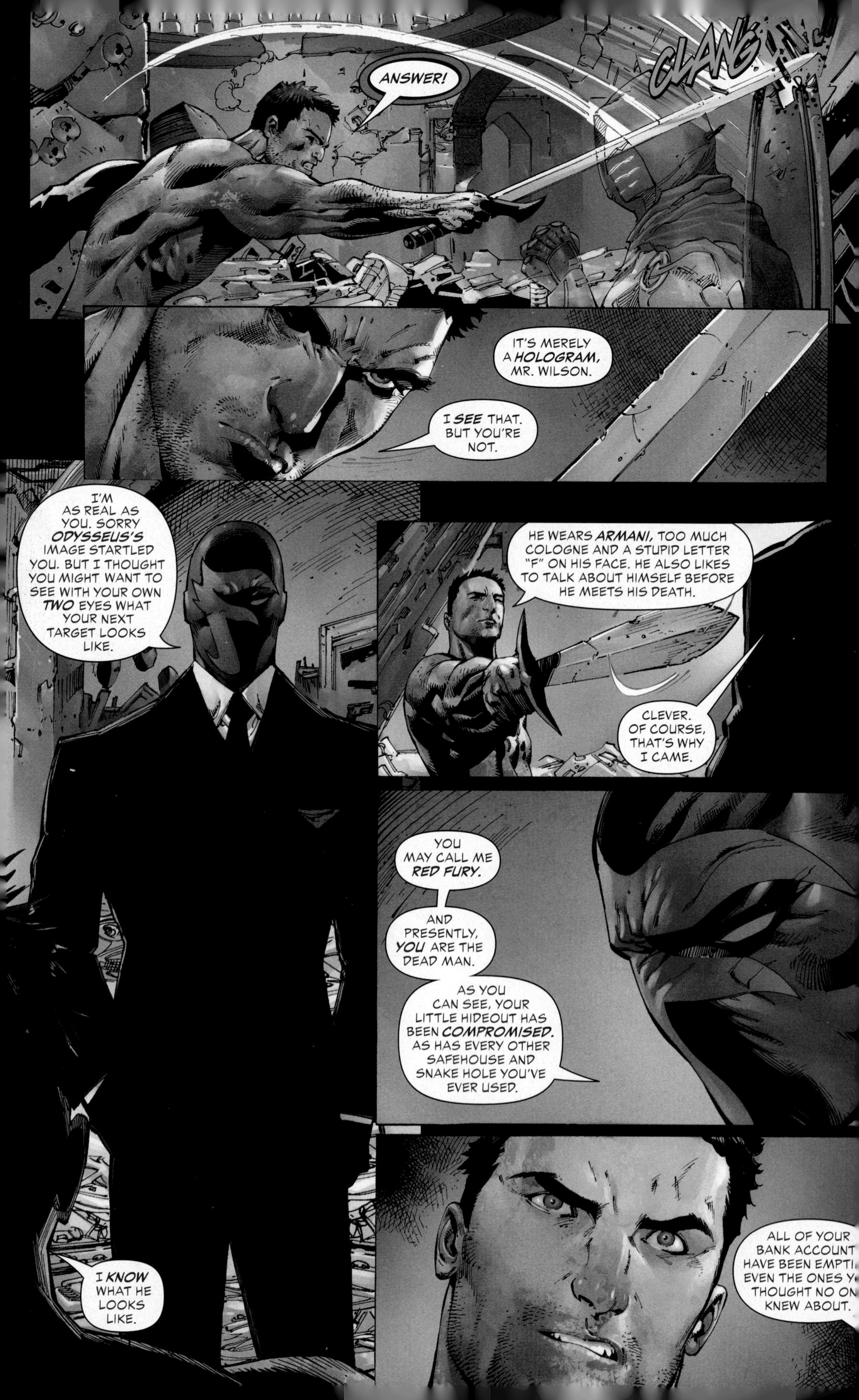
CLANG
ANSWER!
IT'S MERELY A HOLOGRAM, MR. WILSON.
I SEE THAT. BUT YOU'RE NOT.
I'M AS REAL AS YOU. SORRY ODYSSEUS'S IMAGE STARTLED YOU. BUT I THOUGHT YOU MIGHT WANT TO SEE WITH YOUR OWN TWO EYES WHAT YOUR NEXT TARGET LOOKS LIKE.
HE WEARS ARMANI, TOO MUCH COLOGNE AND A STUPID LETTER "F" ON HIS FACE. HE ALSO LIKES TO TALK ABOUT HIMSELF BEFORE HE MEETS HIS DEATH.
CLEVER. OF COURSE, THAT'S WHY I CAME.
YOU MAY CALL ME RED FURY.
AND PRESENTLY, YOU ARE THE DEAD MAN.
AS YOU CAN SEE, YOUR LITTLE HIDEOUT HAS BEEN COMPROMISED. AS HAS EVERY OTHER SAFEHOUSE AND SNAKE HOLE YOU'VE EVER USED.
I KNOW WHAT HE LOOKS LIKE.
ALL OF YOUR BANK ACCOUNT HAVE BEEN EMPTI EVEN THE ONES Y THOUGHT NO ON KNEW ABOUT.

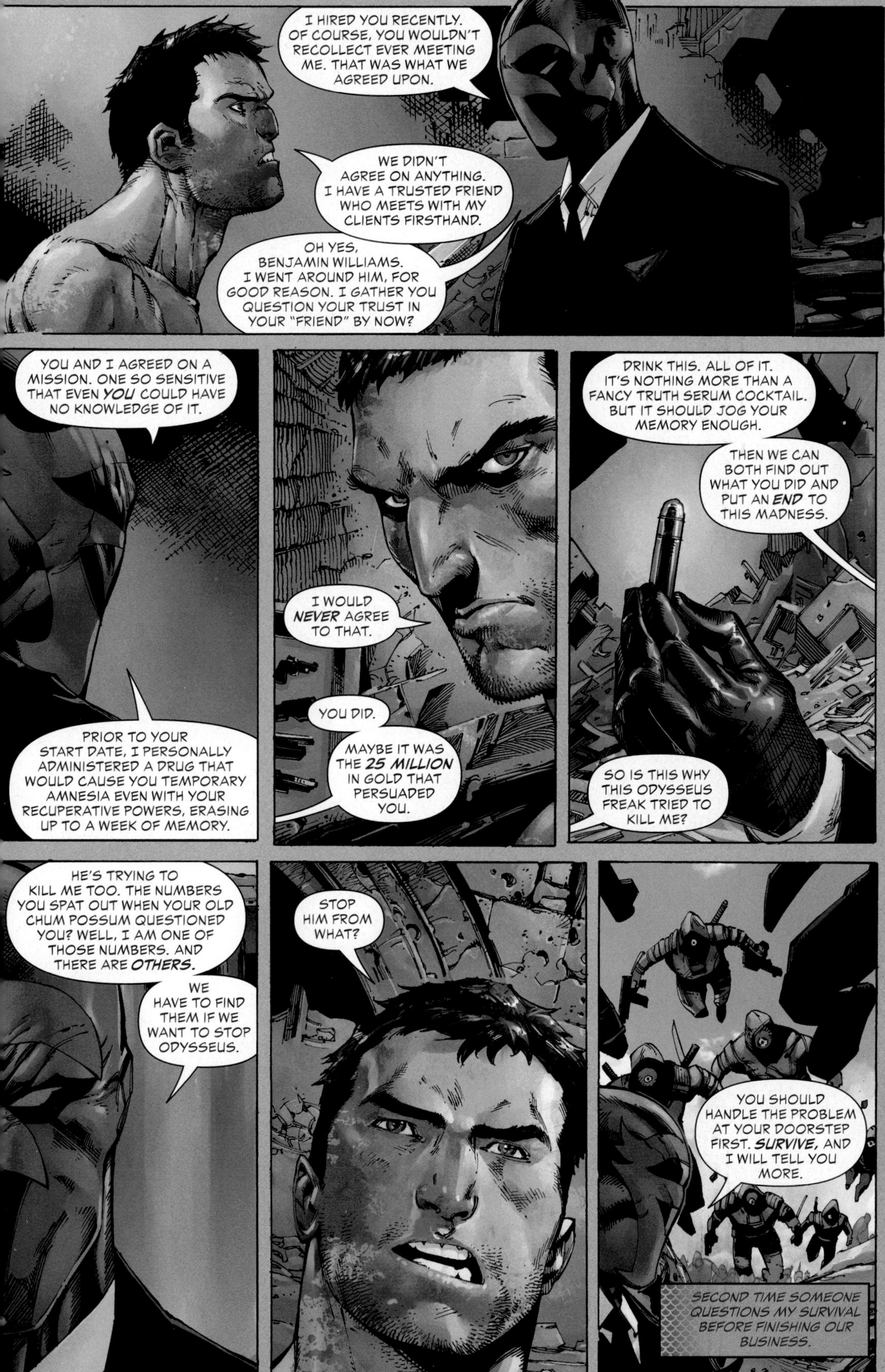
I HIRED YOU RECENTLY. OF COURSE, YOU WOULDN'T RECOLLECT EVER MEETING ME. THAT WAS WHAT WE AGREED UPON.
WE DIDN'T AGREE ON ANYTHING. I HAVE A TRUSTED FRIEND WHO MEETS WITH MY CLIENTS FIRSTHAND.
OH YES, BENJAMIN WILLIAMS. I WENT AROUND HIM, FOR GOOD REASON. I GATHER YOU QUESTION YOUR TRUST IN YOUR "FRIEND" BY NOW?
YOU AND I AGREED ON A MISSION. ONE SO SENSITIVE THAT EVEN YOU COULD HAVE NO KNOWLEDGE OF IT.
I WOULD NEVER AGREE TO THAT.
PRIOR TO YOUR START DATE, I PERSONALLY ADMINISTERED A DRUG THAT WOULD CAUSE YOU TEMPORARY AMNESIA EVEN WITH YOUR RECUPERATIVE POWERS, ERASING UP TO A WEEK OF MEMORY.
YOU DID.
MAYBE IT WAS THE 25 MILLION IN GOLD THAT PERSUADED YOU.
DRINK THIS. ALL OF IT. IT'S NOTHING MORE THAN A FANCY TRUTH SERUM COCKTAIL. BUT IT SHOULD JOG YOUR MEMORY ENOUGH.
THEN WE CAN BOTH FIND OUT WHAT YOU DID AND PUT AN END TO THIS MADNESS.
SO IS THIS WHY THIS ODYSSEUS FREAK TRIED TO KILL ME?
HE'S TRYING TO KILL ME TOO. THE NUMBERS YOU SPAT OUT WHEN YOUR OLD CHUM POSSUM QUESTIONED YOU? WELL, I AM ONE OF THOSE NUMBERS. AND THERE ARE OTHERS.
WE HAVE TO FIND THEM IF WE WANT TO STOP ODYSSEUS.
STOP HIM FROM WHAT?
YOU SHOULD HANDLE THE PROBLEM AT YOUR DOORSTEP FIRST. SURVIVE, AND I WILL TELL YOU MORE.
SECOND TIME SOMEONE QUESTIONS MY SURVIVAL BEFORE FINISHING OUR BUSINESS.
I DON'T LIKE IT.

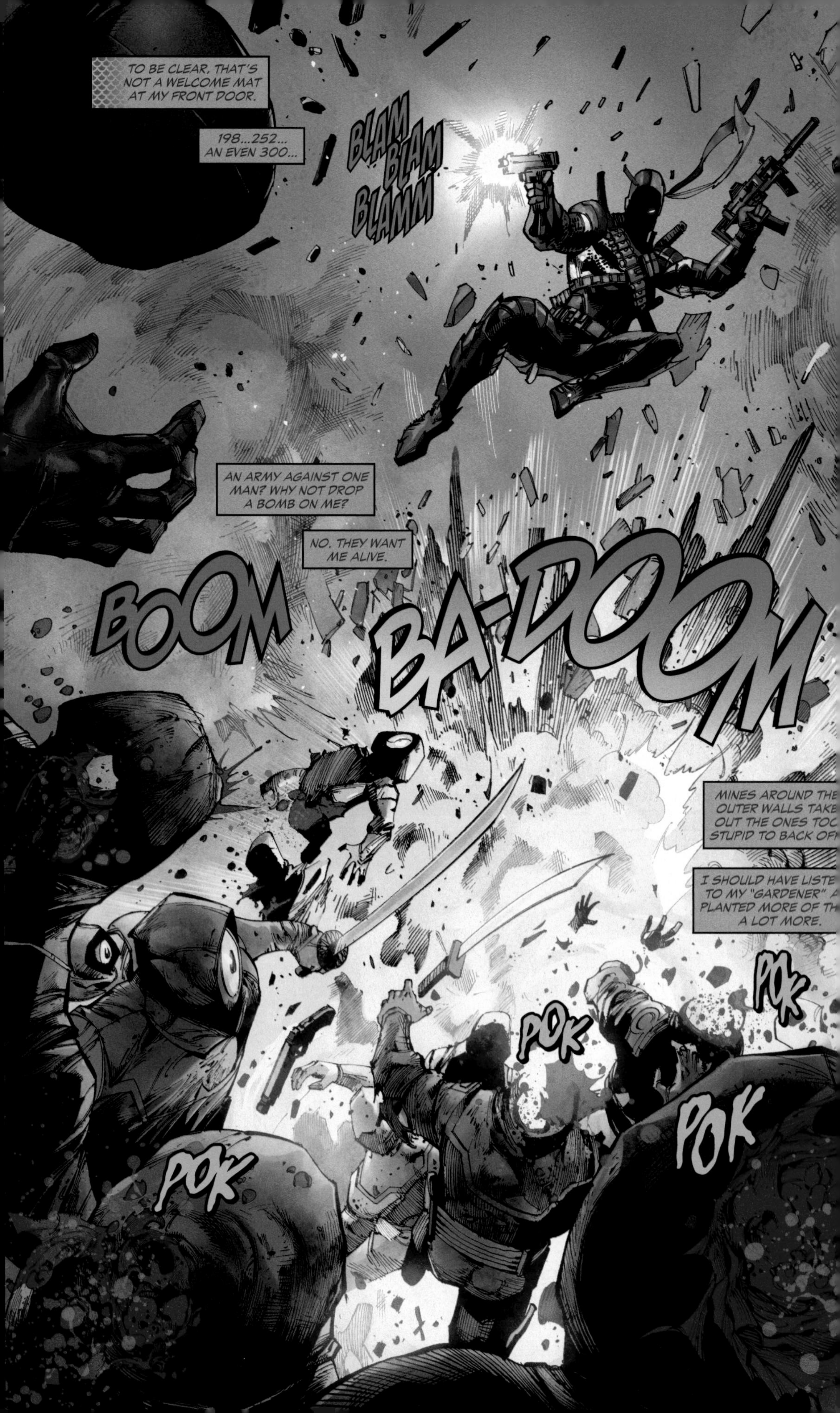
TO BE CLEAR, THAT'S NOT A WELCOME MAT AT MY FRONT DOOR.
198...252... AN EVEN 300...
BLAM BLAM BLAMM
AN ARMY AGAINST ONE MAN? WHY NOT DROP A BOMB ON ME?
NO. THEY WANT ME ALIVE.
BOOM
BA-DOOM
MINES AROUND THE OUTER WALLS TAKE OUT THE ONES TOO STUPID TO BACK OFF
I SHOULD HAVE LISTE TO MY "GARDENER" A PLANTED MORE OF TH A LOT MORE.
POK
POK
POK
POK

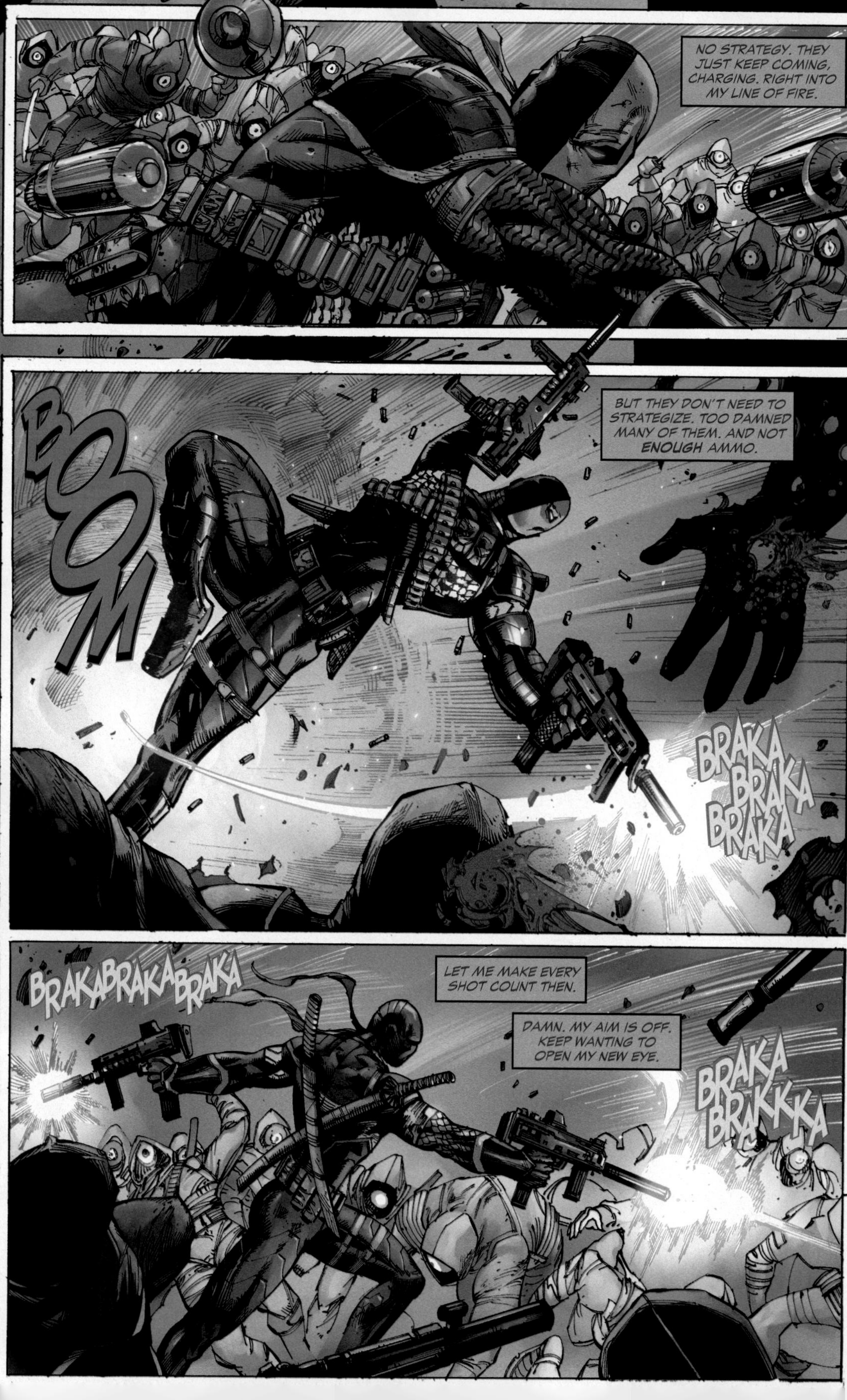
NO STRATEGY. THEY JUST KEEP COMING, CHARGING. RIGHT INTO MY LINE OF FIRE.
BOOM
BUT THEY DON'T NEED TO STRATEGIZE. TOO DAMNED MANY OF THEM. AND NOT ENOUGH AMMO.
BRAKA BRAKA BRAKA
BRAKABRAKABRAKA
LET ME MAKE EVERY SHOT COUNT THEN.
DAMN. MY AIM IS OFF. KEEP WANTING TO OPEN MY NEW EYE.
BRAKA BRAKKKA

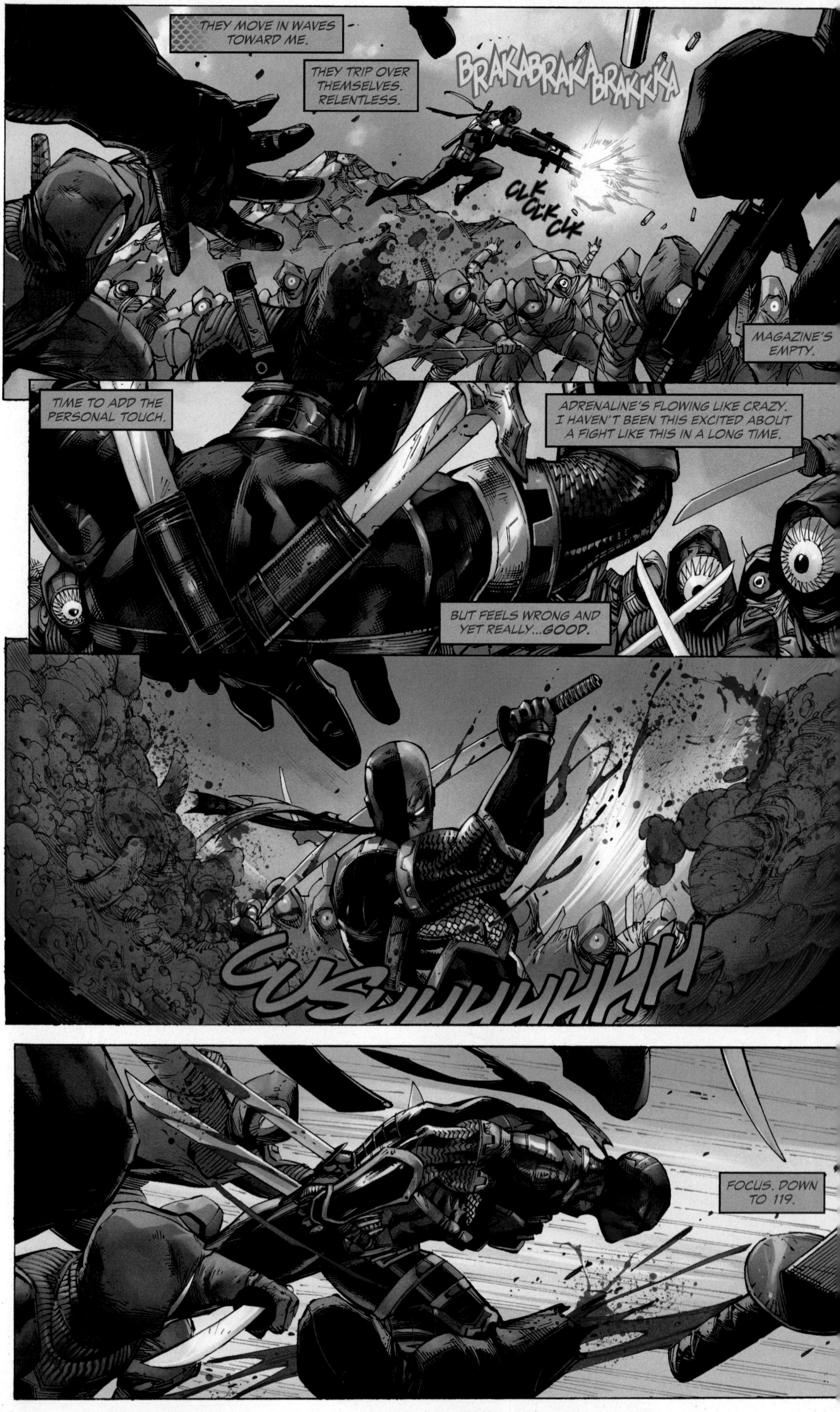
THEY MOVE IN WAVES TOWARD ME.
THEY TRIP OVER THEMSELVES. RELENTLESS.
BRAKABRAKABRAKKKA
CLK CLK CLK
MAGAZINE'S EMPTY.
TIME TO ADD THE PERSONAL TOUCH.
ADRENALINE'S FLOWING LIKE CRAZY. I HAVEN'T BEEN THIS EXCITED ABOUT A FIGHT LIKE THIS IN A LONG TIME.
BUT FEELS WRONG AND YET REALLY...GOOD.
CHSHHHHHHHH
FOCUS. DOWN TO 119.

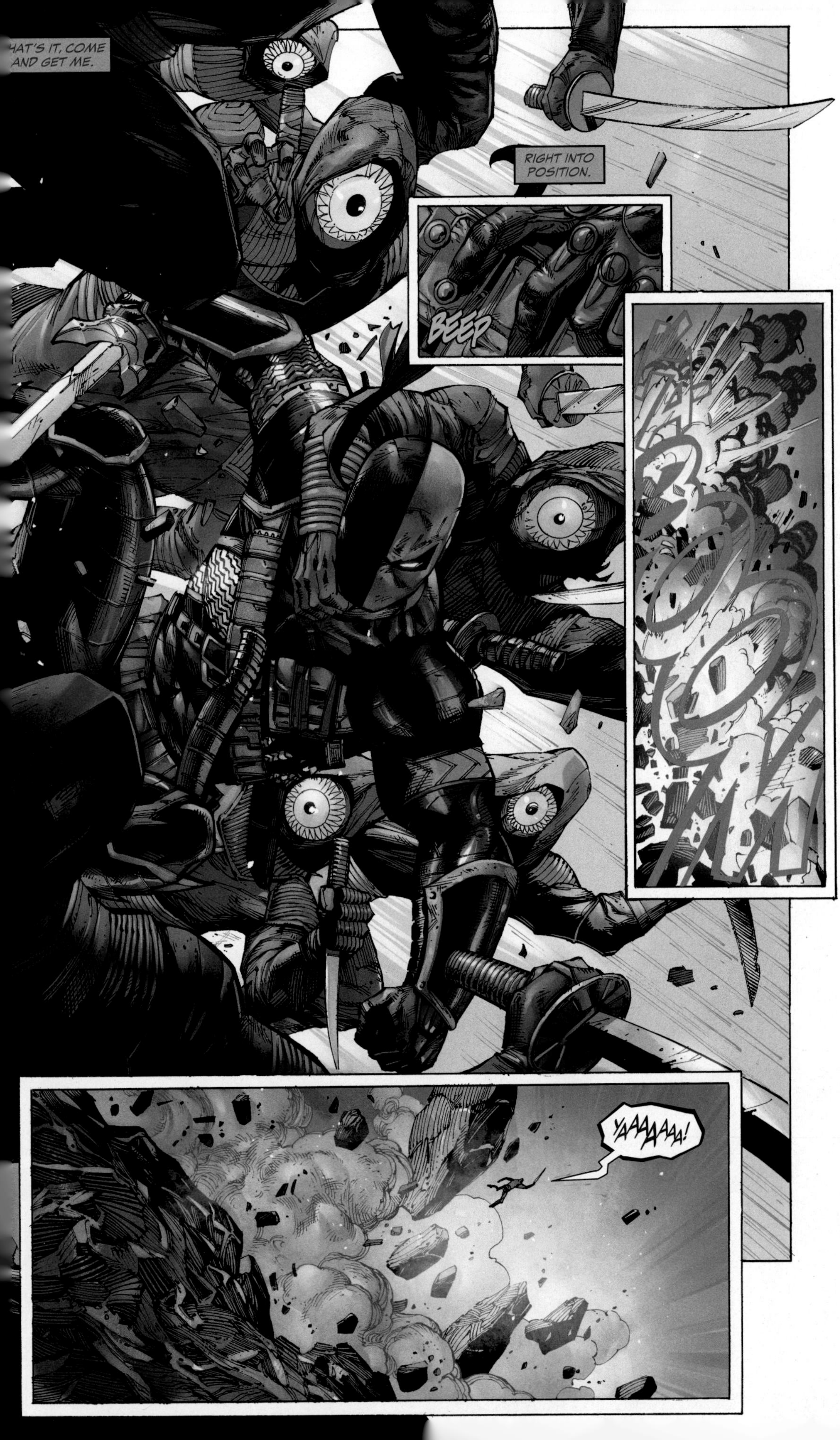

HAT'S IT, COME AND GET ME.
RIGHT INTO POSITION.
BEEP
YAAAAAAA!

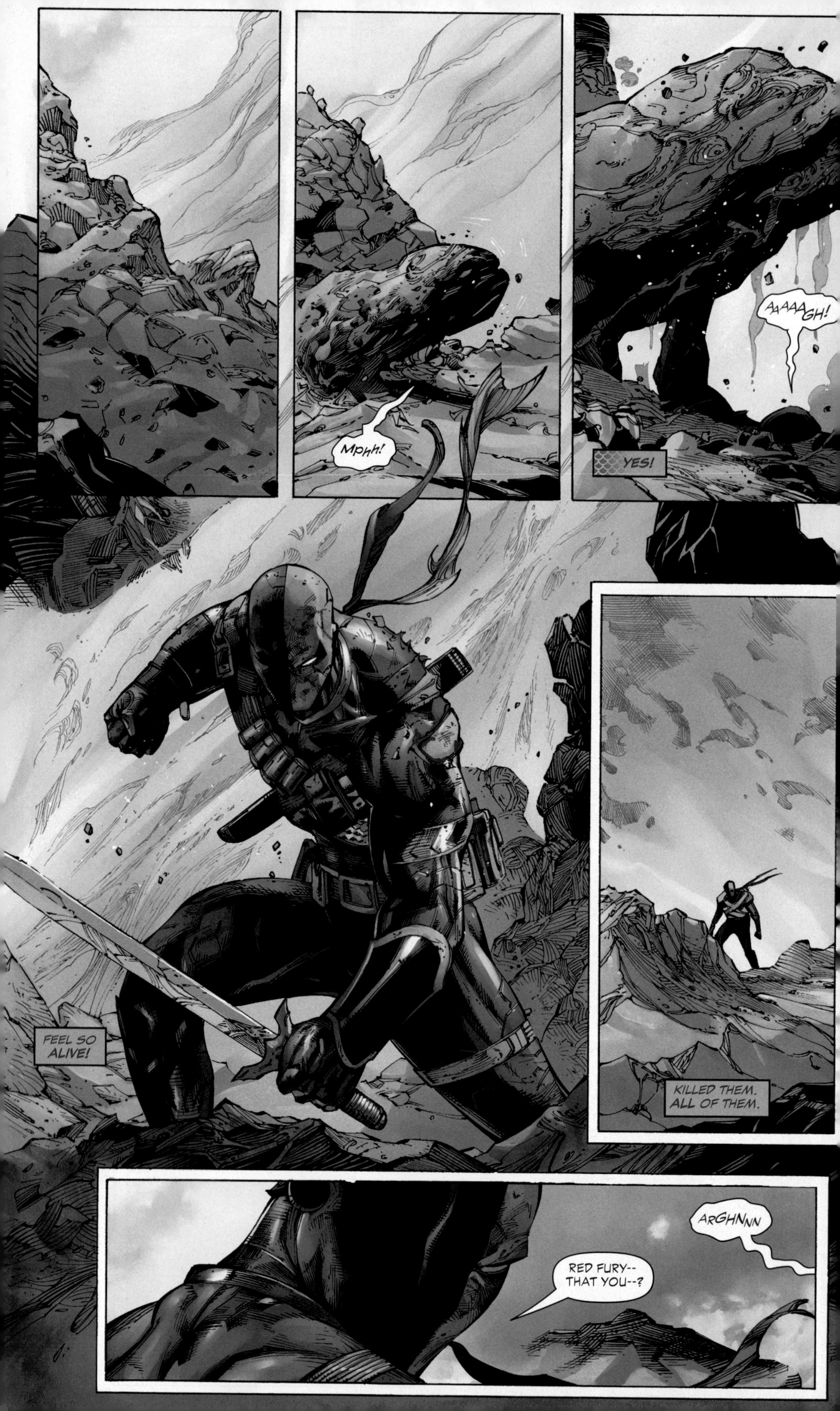

Mphh!
AAAAAGH!
YES!
FEEL SO ALIVE!
KILLED THEM. ALL OF THEM.
RED FURY-- THAT YOU--?
ARGHNNN

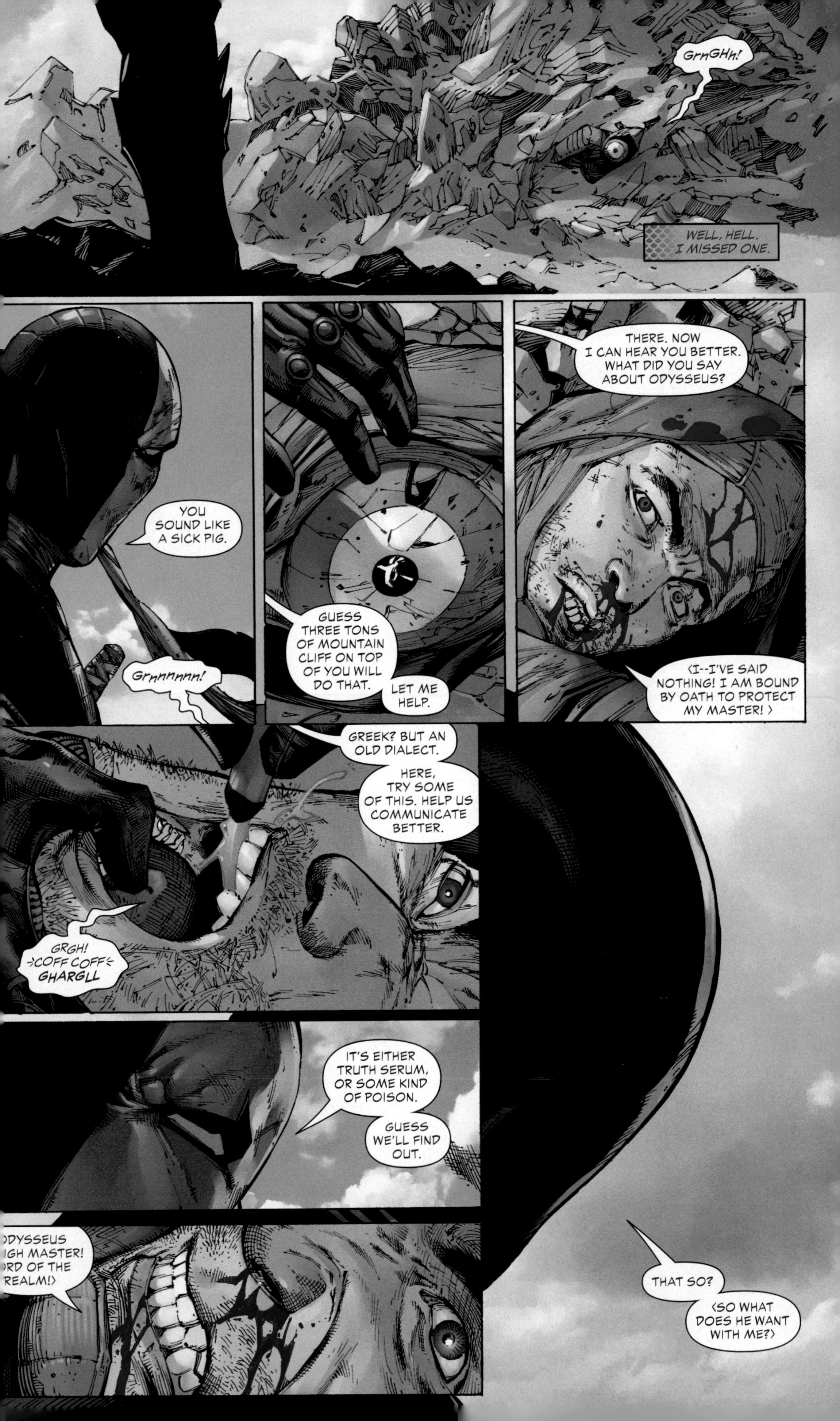
GrnGHh!
WELL, HELL. I MISSED ONE.
YOU SOUND LIKE A SICK PIG.
Grnnnnnn!
GUESS THREE TONS OF MOUNTAIN CLIFF ON TOP OF YOU WILL DO THAT.
LET ME HELP.
THERE. NOW I CAN HEAR YOU BETTER. WHAT DID YOU SAY ABOUT ODYSSEUS?
<I--I'VE SAID NOTHING! I AM BOUND BY OATH TO PROTECT MY MASTER!>
GREEK? BUT AN OLD DIALECT.
HERE, TRY SOME OF THIS. HELP US COMMUNICATE BETTER.
GRGH! COFF COFF GHARGLL
IT'S EITHER TRUTH SERUM, OR SOME KIND OF POISON.
GUESS WE'LL FIND OUT.
THAT SO?
<SO WHAT DOES HE WANT WITH ME?>

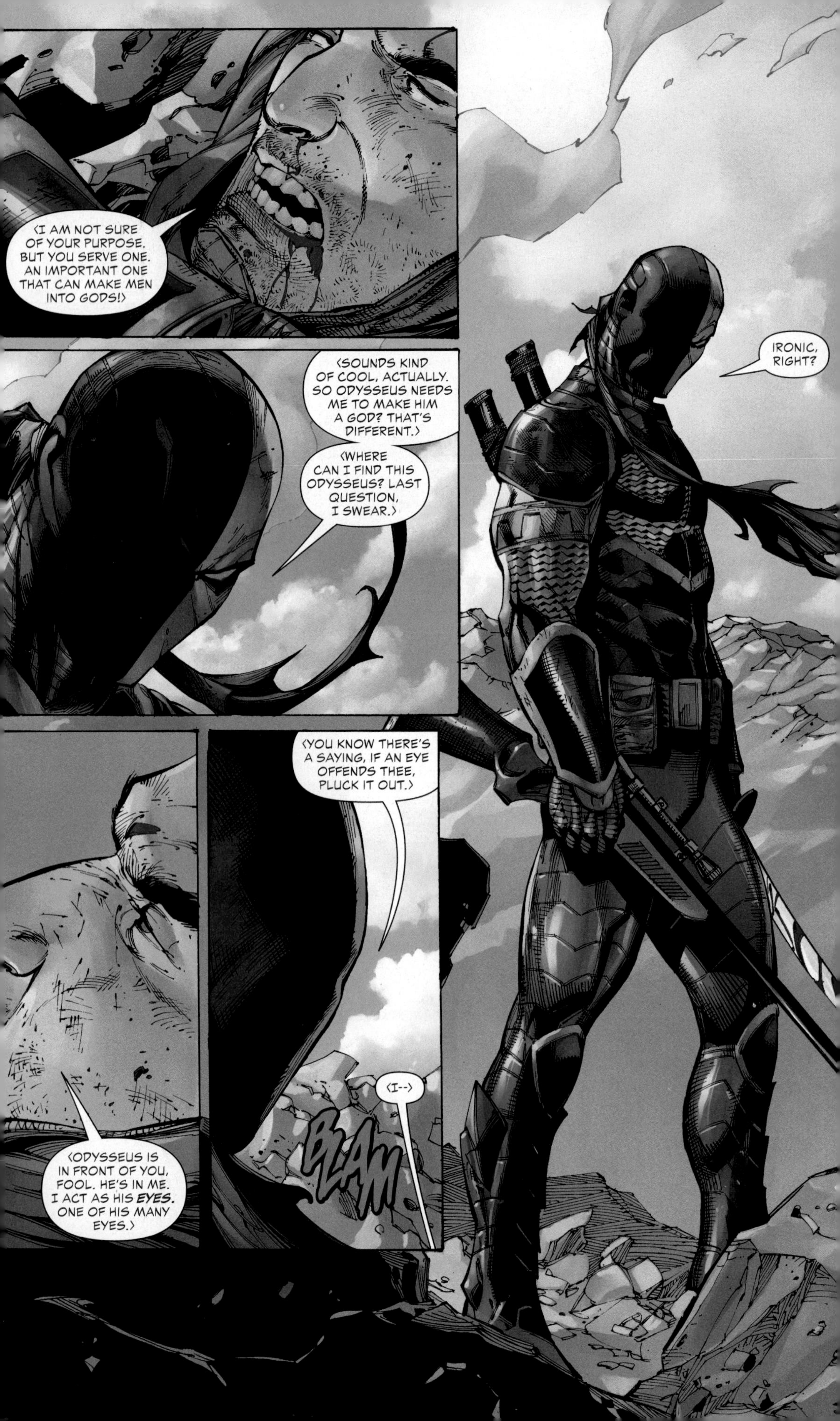

‹I AM NOT SURE OF YOUR PURPOSE. BUT YOU SERVE ONE. AN IMPORTANT ONE THAT CAN MAKE MEN INTO GODS!›
‹SOUNDS KIND OF COOL, ACTUALLY. SO ODYSSEUS NEEDS ME TO MAKE HIM A GOD? THAT'S DIFFERENT.›
‹WHERE CAN I FIND THIS ODYSSEUS? LAST QUESTION, I SWEAR.›
‹ODYSSEUS IS IN FRONT OF YOU, FOOL. HE'S IN ME. I ACT AS HIS *EYES*. ONE OF HIS MANY EYES.›
‹YOU KNOW THERE'S A SAYING, IF AN EYE OFFENDS THEE, PLUCK IT OUT.›
‹I--›
BLAM
IRONIC, RIGHT?

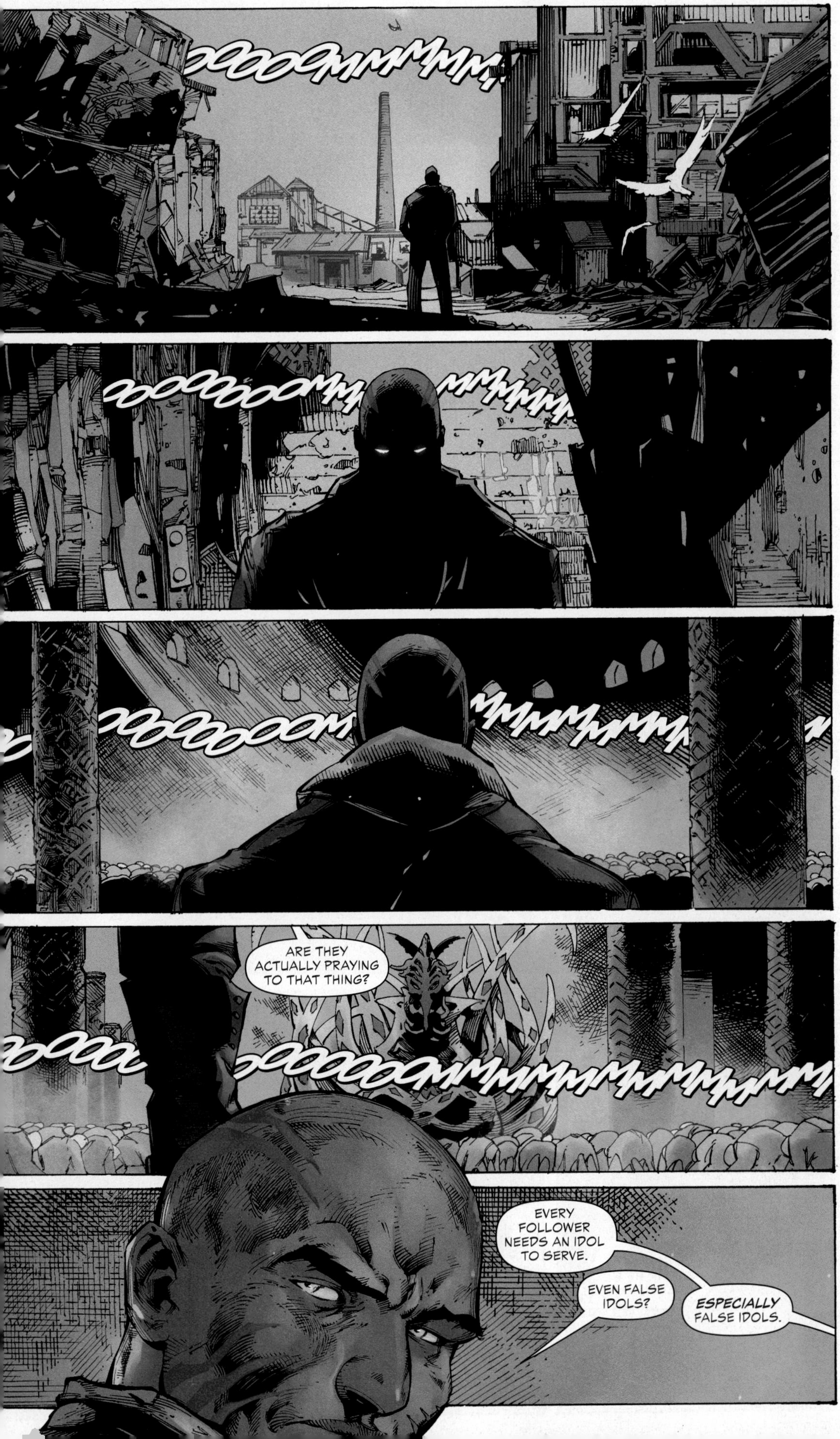
ARE THEY ACTUALLY PRAYING TO THAT THING?
EVERY FOLLOWER NEEDS AN IDOL TO SERVE.
EVEN FALSE IDOLS?
ESPECIALLY FALSE IDOLS.

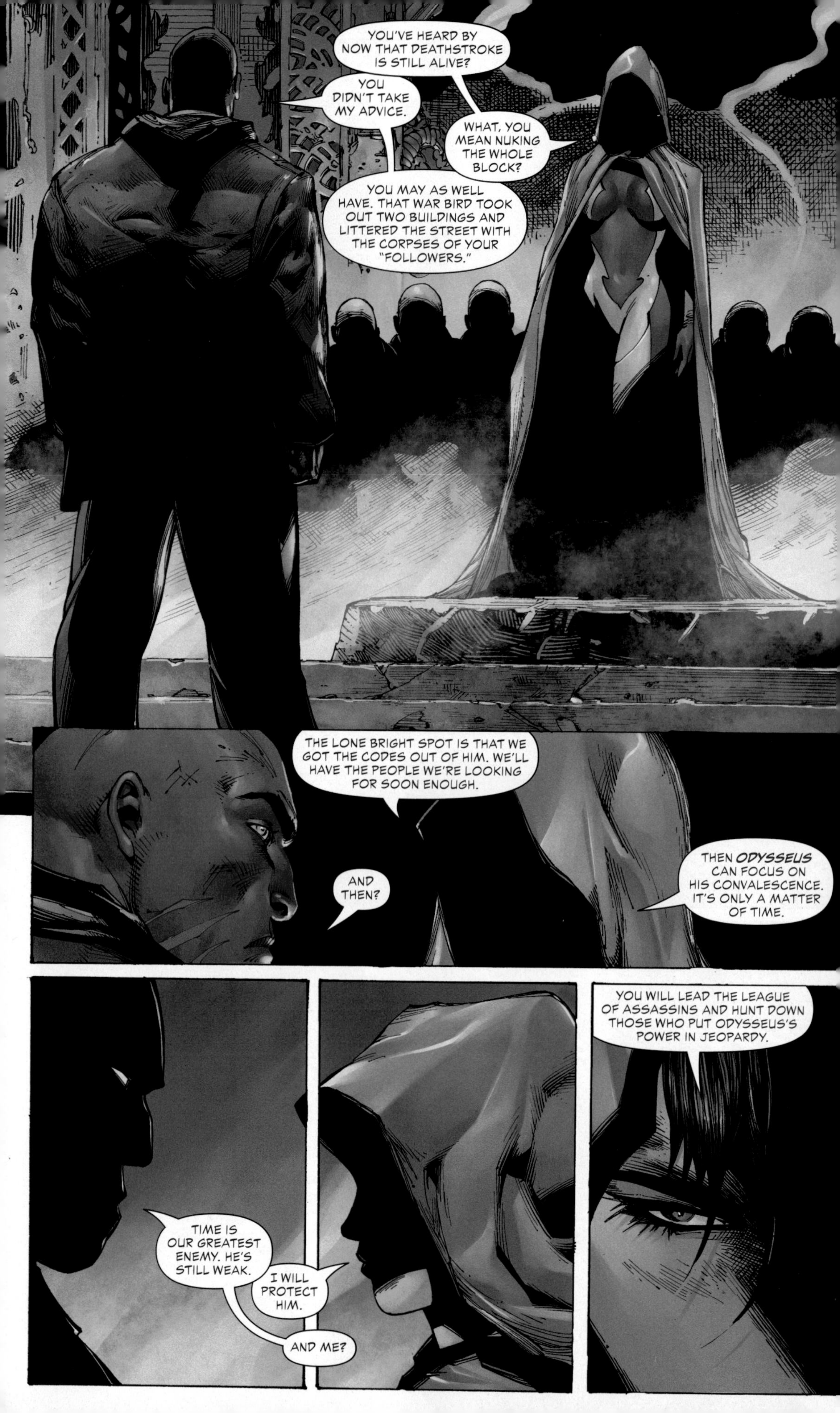
YOU'VE HEARD BY NOW THAT DEATHSTROKE IS STILL ALIVE?
YOU DIDN'T TAKE MY ADVICE.
WHAT, YOU MEAN NUKING THE WHOLE BLOCK?
YOU MAY AS WELL HAVE. THAT WAR BIRD TOOK OUT TWO BUILDINGS AND LITTERED THE STREET WITH THE CORPSES OF YOUR "FOLLOWERS."
THE LONE BRIGHT SPOT IS THAT WE GOT THE CODES OUT OF HIM. WE'LL HAVE THE PEOPLE WE'RE LOOKING FOR SOON ENOUGH.
AND THEN?
THEN *ODYSSEUS* CAN FOCUS ON HIS CONVALESCENCE. IT'S ONLY A MATTER OF TIME.
TIME IS OUR GREATEST ENEMY. HE'S STILL WEAK.
I WILL PROTECT HIM.
AND ME?
YOU WILL LEAD THE LEAGUE OF ASSASSINS AND HUNT DOWN THOSE WHO PUT ODYSSEUS'S POWER IN JEOPARDY.

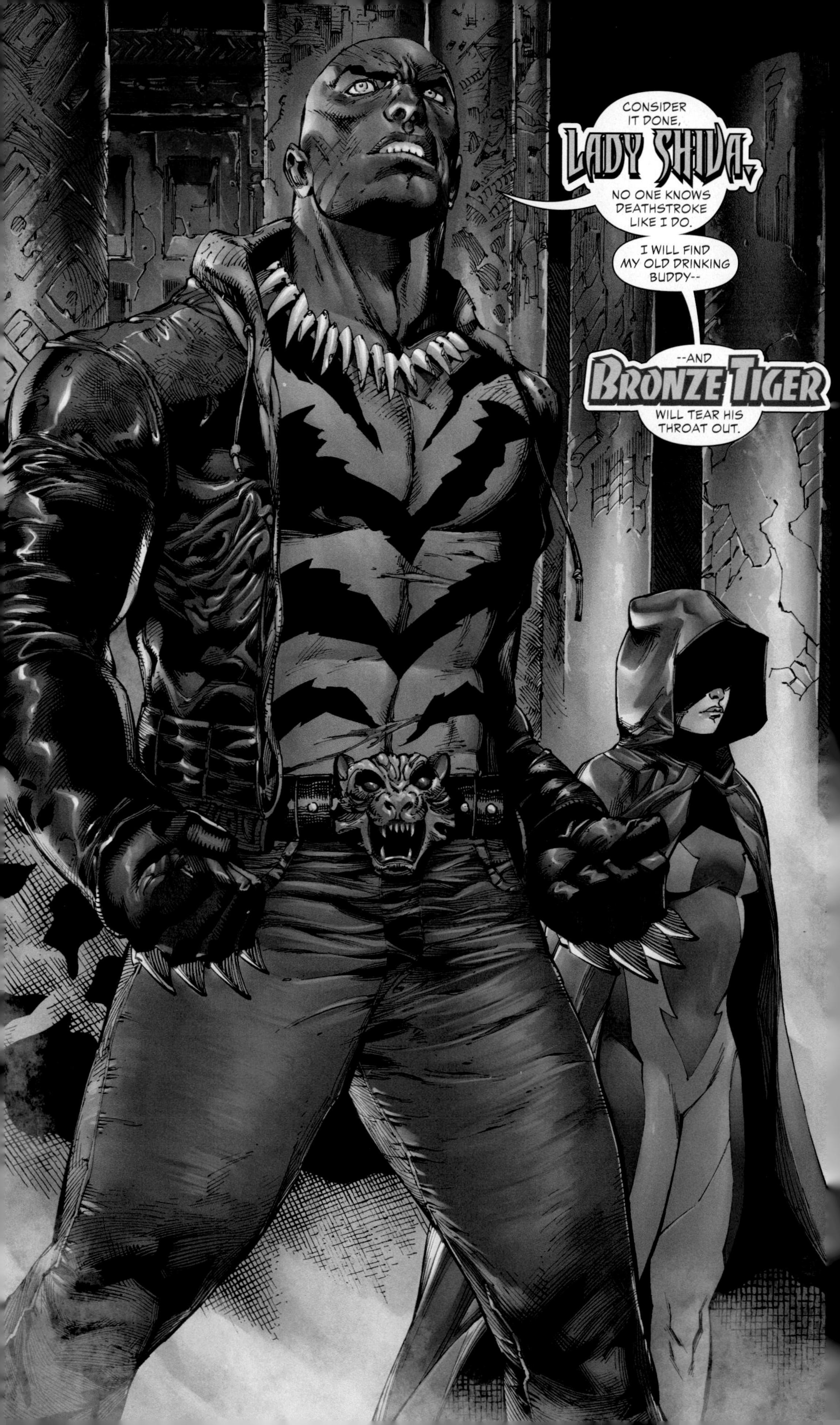

CONSIDER IT DONE, LADY SHIVA. NO ONE KNOWS DEATHSTROKE LIKE I DO.
I WILL FIND MY OLD DRINKING BUDDY--
--AND BRONZE TIGER WILL TEAR HIS THROAT OUT.

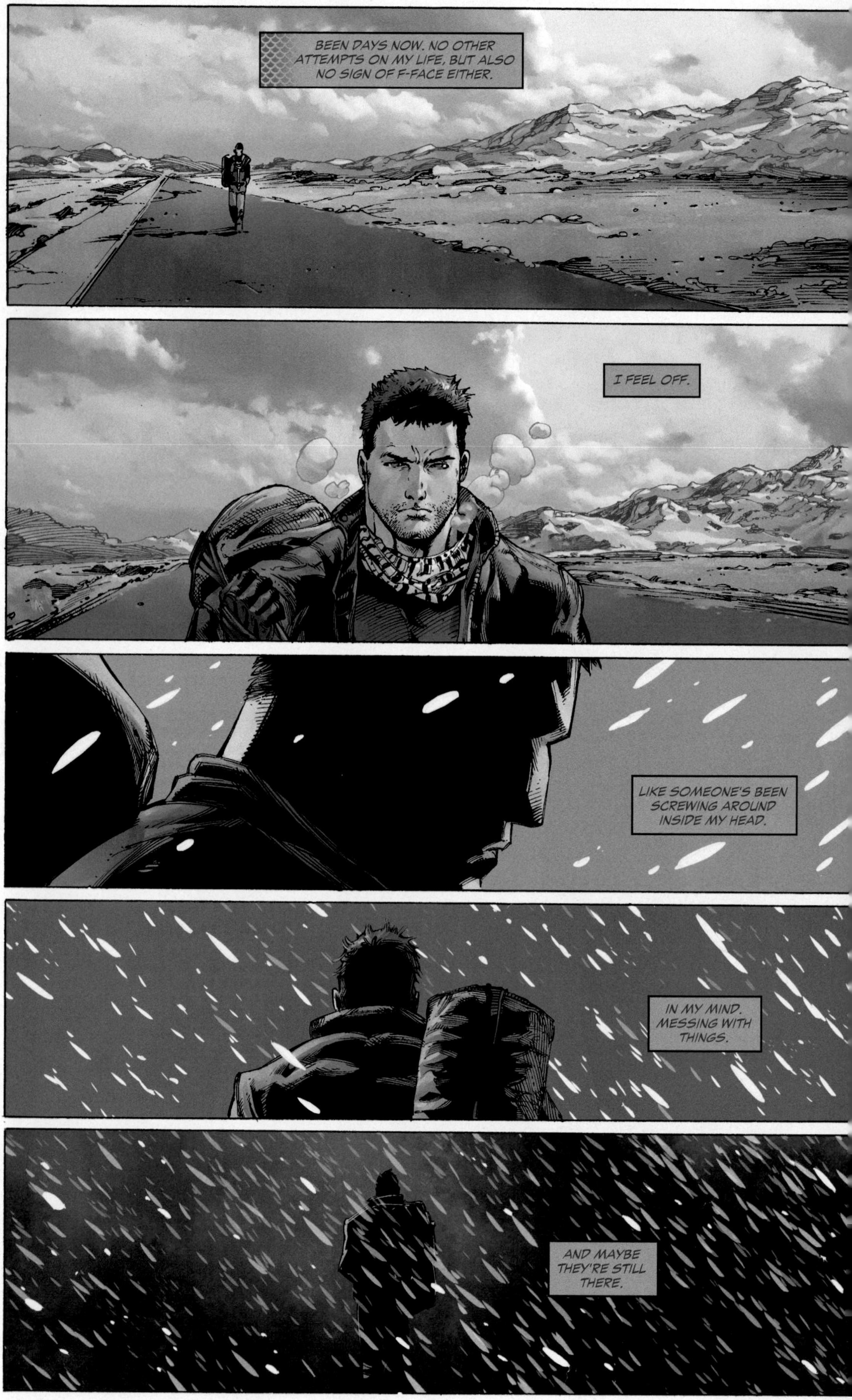
BEEN DAYS NOW. NO OTHER ATTEMPTS ON MY LIFE, BUT ALSO NO SIGN OF F-FACE EITHER.
I FEEL OFF.
LIKE SOMEONE'S BEEN SCREWING AROUND INSIDE MY HEAD.
IN MY MIND. MESSING WITH THINGS.
AND MAYBE THEY'RE STILL THERE.

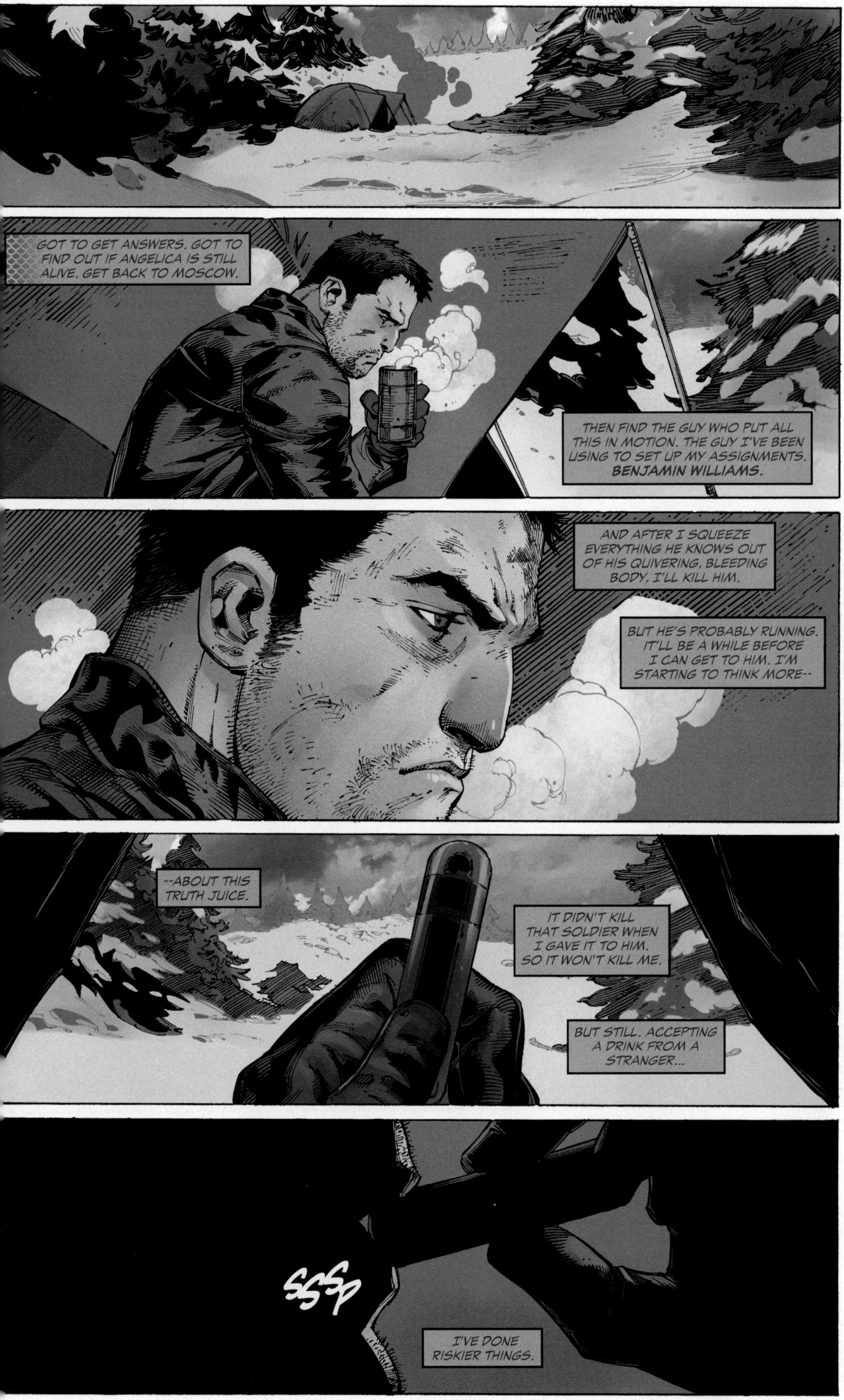
GOT TO GET ANSWERS. GOT TO FIND OUT IF ANGELICA IS STILL ALIVE. GET BACK TO MOSCOW.
THEN FIND THE GUY WHO PUT ALL THIS IN MOTION. THE GUY I'VE BEEN USING TO SET UP MY ASSIGNMENTS. BENJAMIN WILLIAMS.
AND AFTER I SQUEEZE EVERYTHING HE KNOWS OUT OF HIS QUIVERING, BLEEDING BODY, I'LL KILL HIM.
BUT HE'S PROBABLY RUNNING. IT'LL BE A WHILE BEFORE I CAN GET TO HIM. I'M STARTING TO THINK MORE--
--ABOUT THIS TRUTH JUICE.
IT DIDN'T KILL THAT SOLDIER WHEN I GAVE IT TO HIM. SO IT WON'T KILL ME.
BUT STILL. ACCEPTING A DRINK FROM A STRANGER...
SSSP
I'VE DONE RISKIER THINGS.

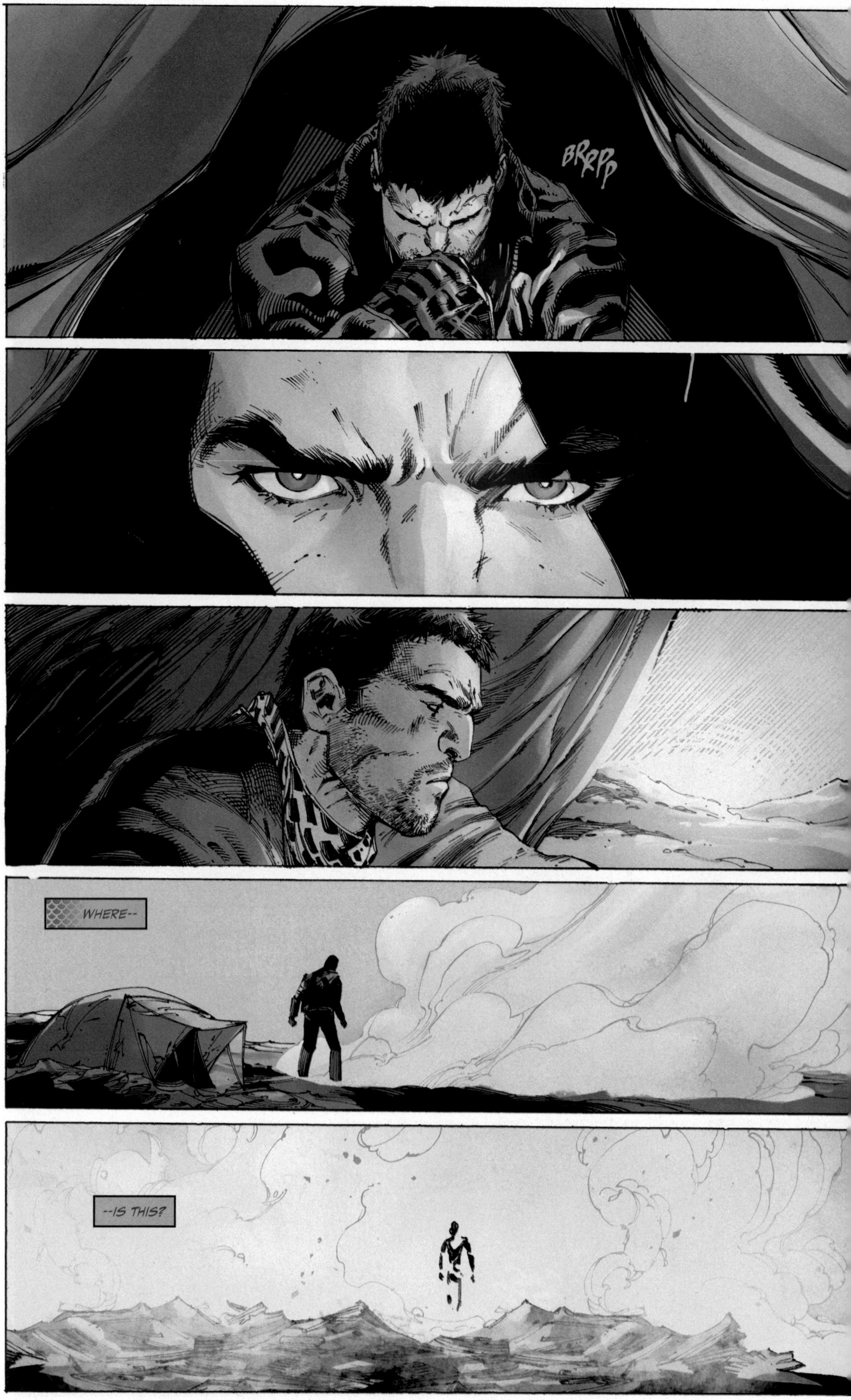
BRRPP
WHERE--
--IS THIS?

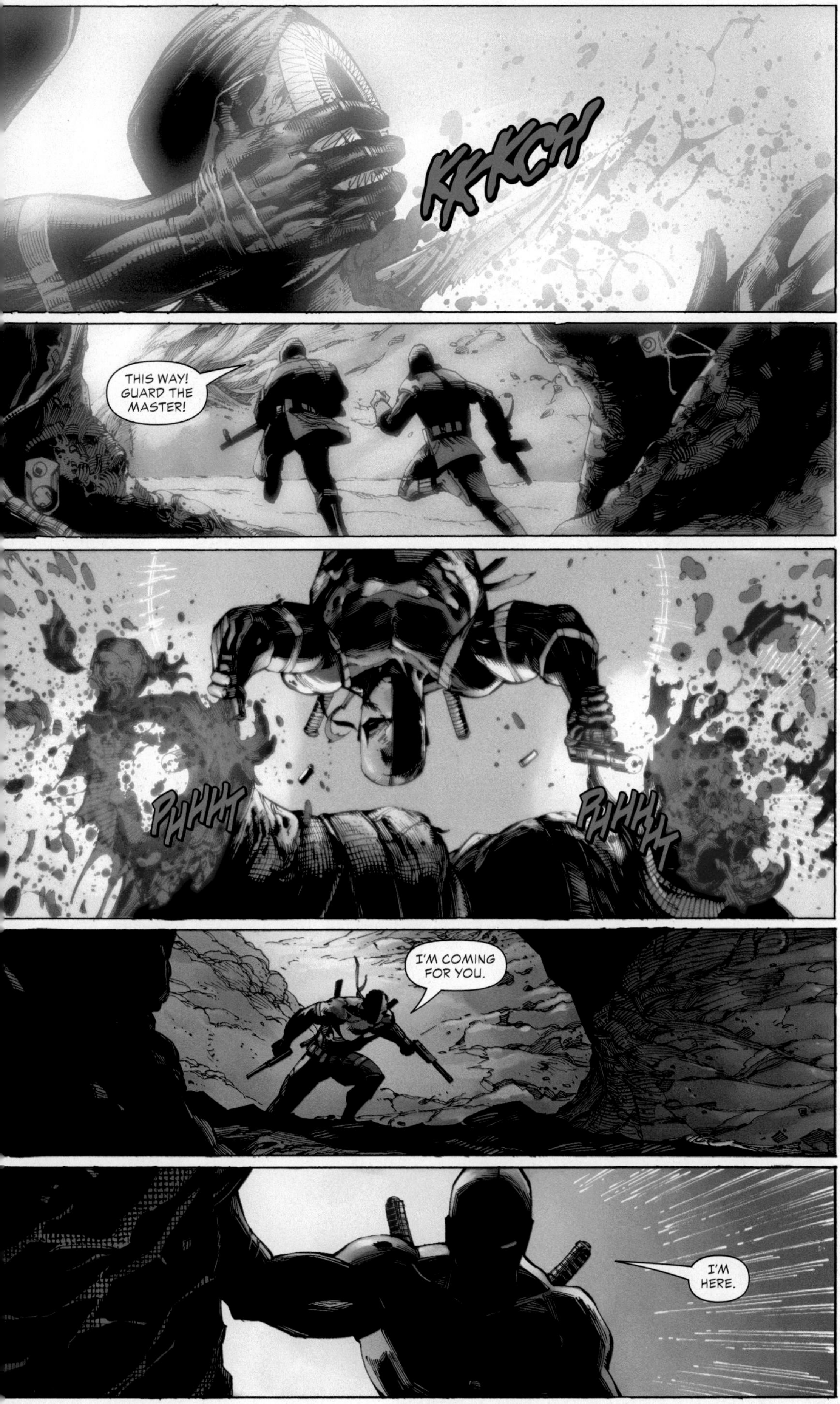
KKKCH
THIS WAY! GUARD THE MASTER!
PHHHT
PHHHHT
I'M COMING FOR YOU.
I'M HERE.

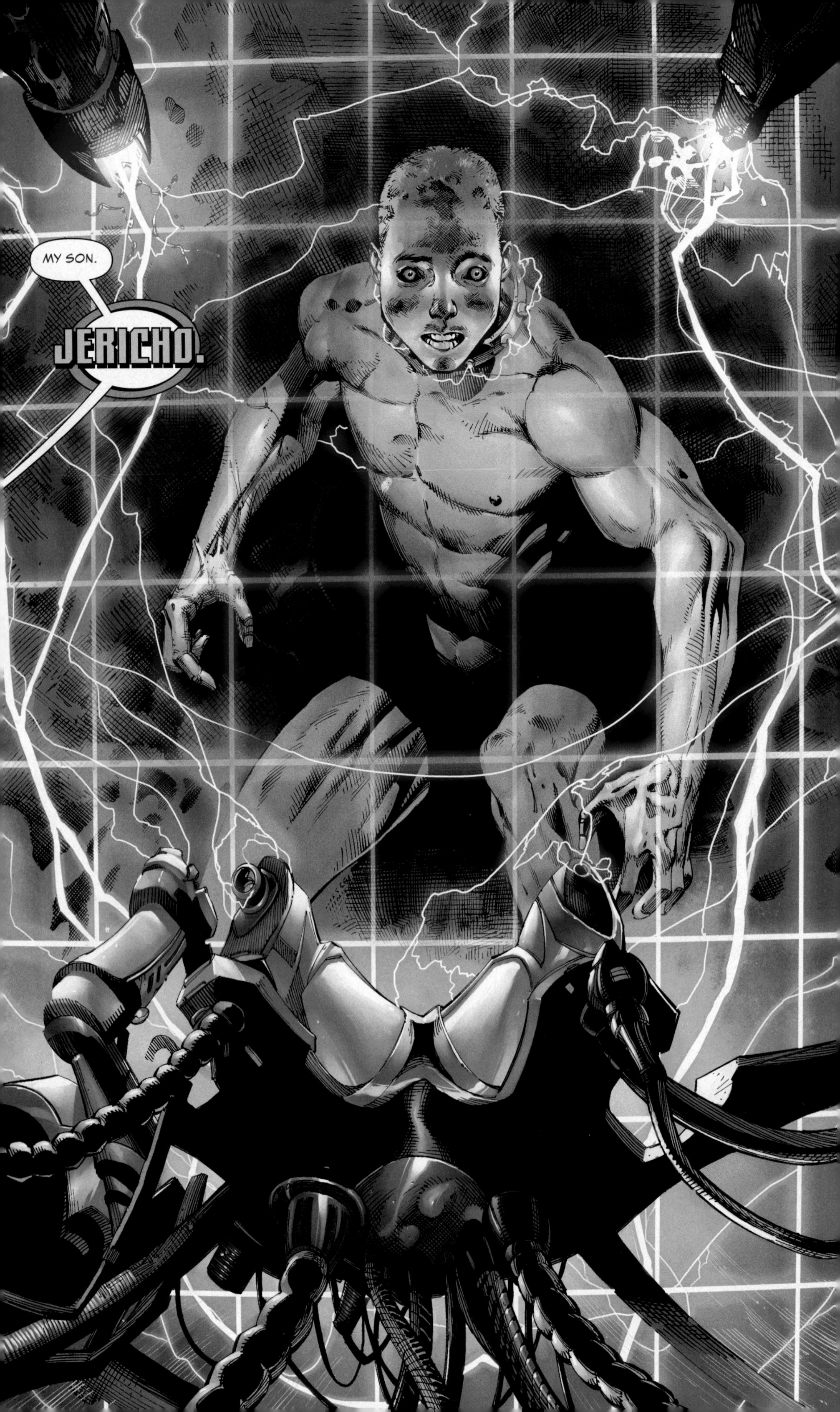
MY SON.
JERICHO.

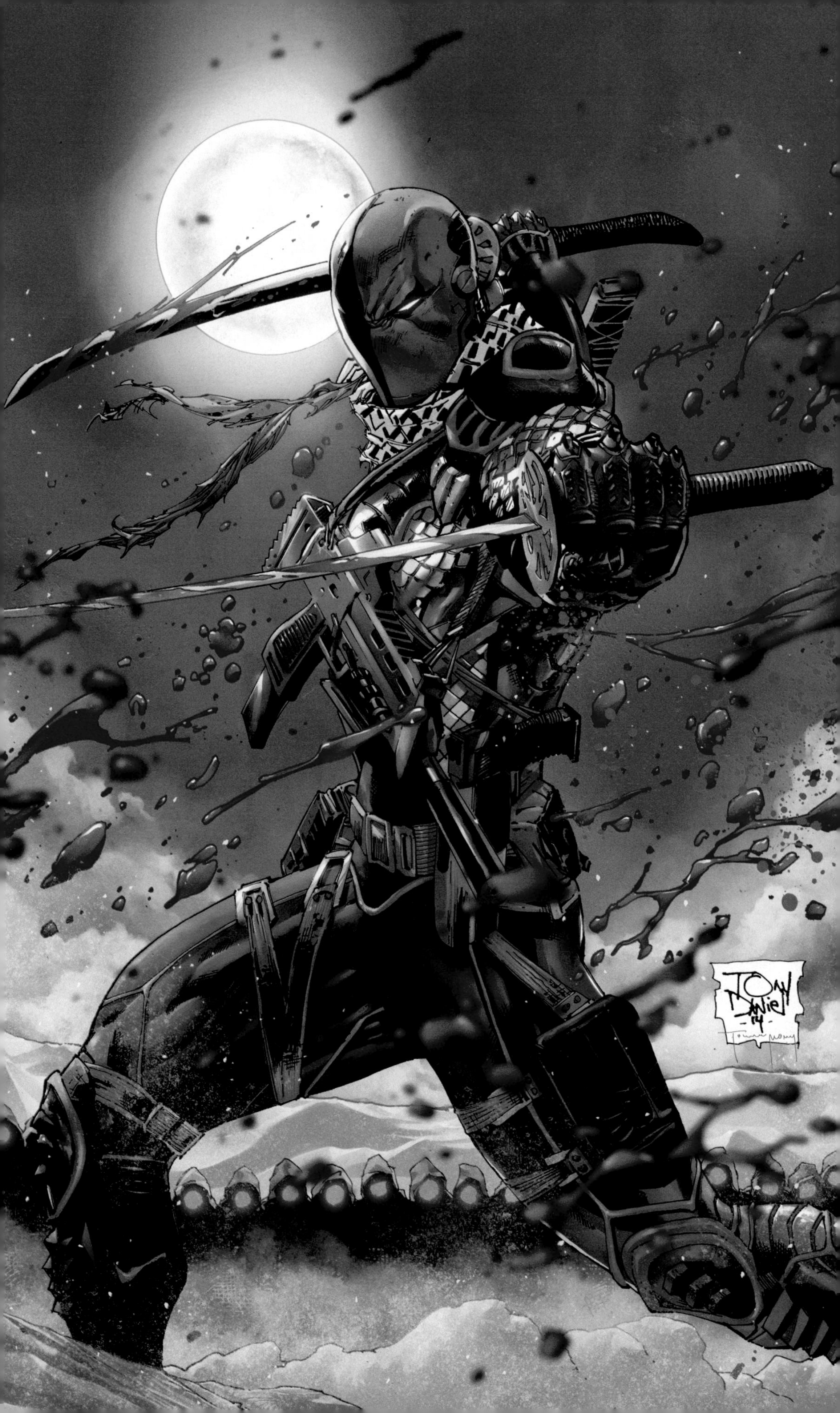

Variant cover by **TONY S. DANIEL & TOMEU MOREY**

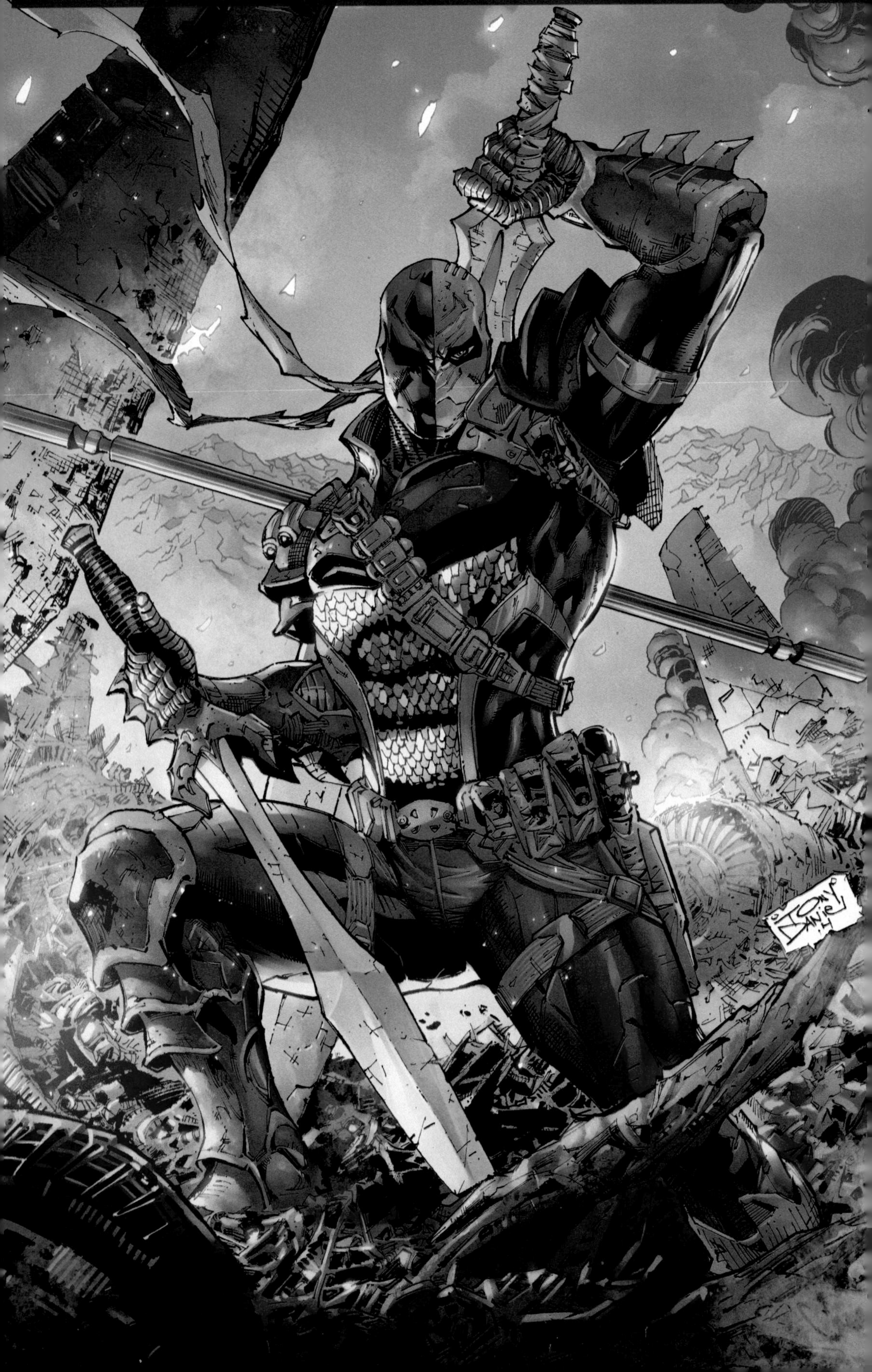

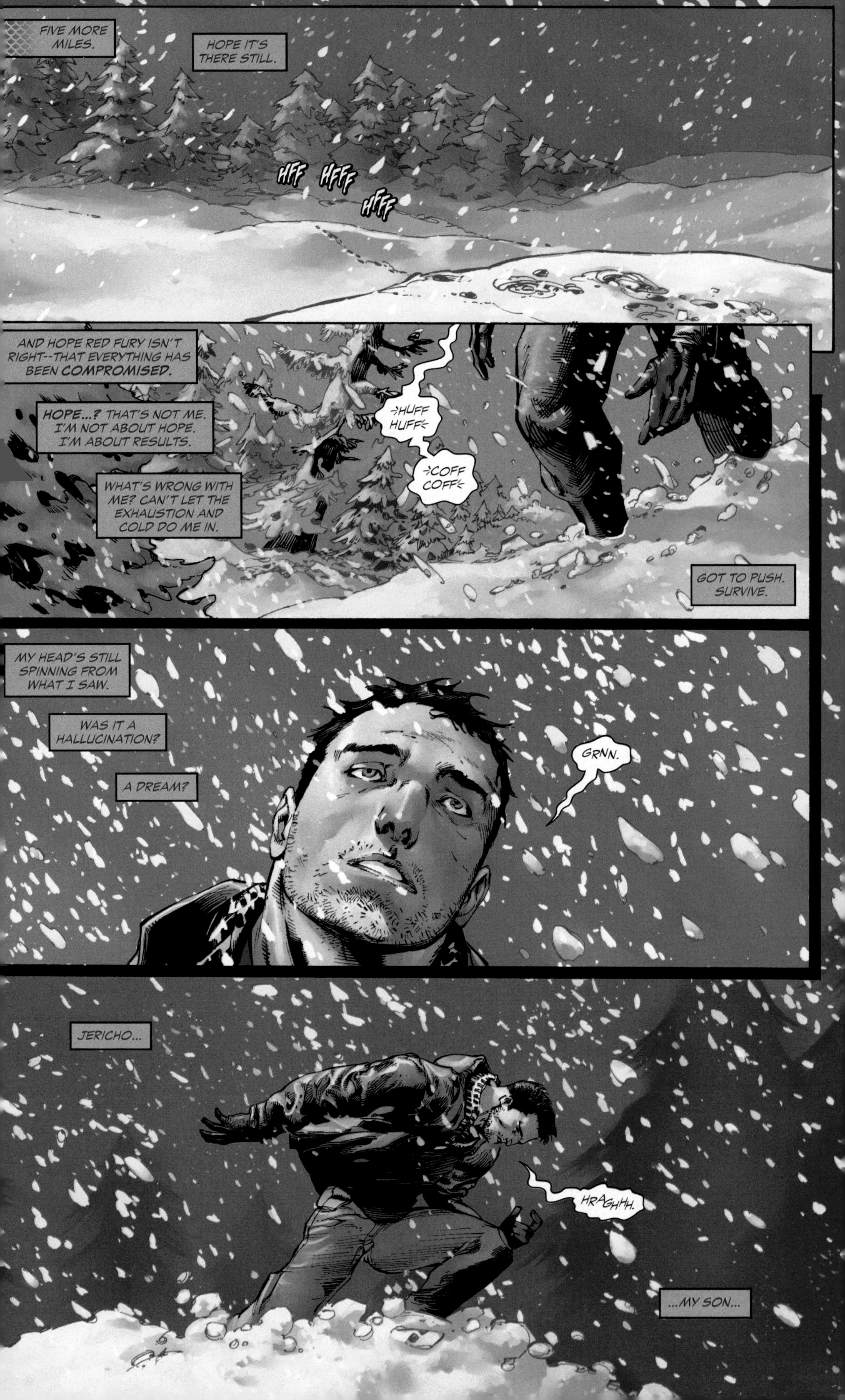
FIVE MORE MILES.
HOPE IT'S THERE STILL.
HFF HFFF HFFF
AND HOPE RED FURY ISN'T RIGHT--THAT EVERYTHING HAS BEEN COMPROMISED.
HOPE...? THAT'S NOT ME. I'M NOT ABOUT HOPE. I'M ABOUT RESULTS.
WHAT'S WRONG WITH ME? CAN'T LET THE EXHAUSTION AND COLD DO ME IN.
HUFF HUFF
COFF COFF
GOT TO PUSH. SURVIVE.
MY HEAD'S STILL SPINNING FROM WHAT I SAW.
WAS IT A HALLUCINATION?
A DREAM?
GRNN.
JERICHO...
HRAGHHH.
...MY SON...

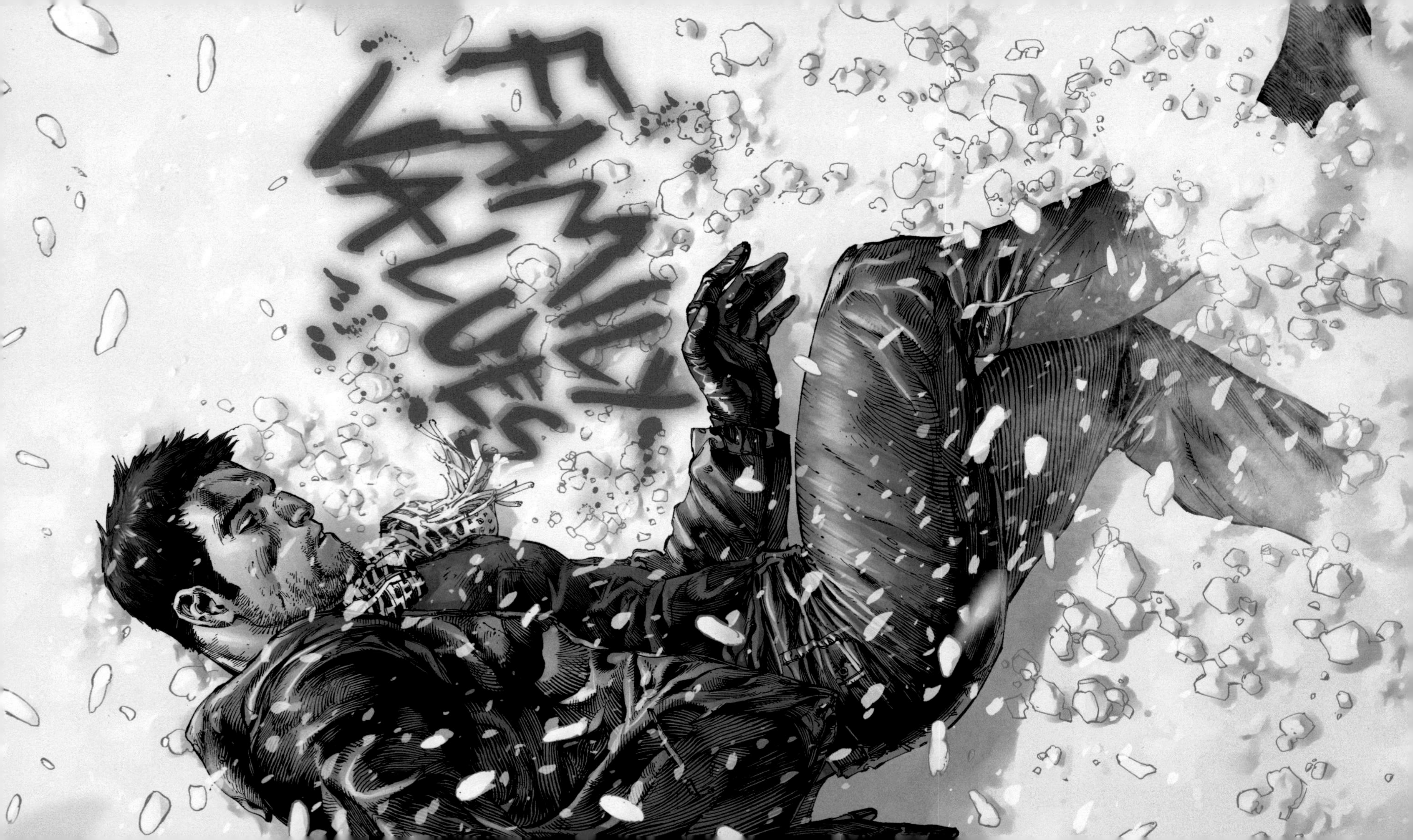
FAMILY VALUES

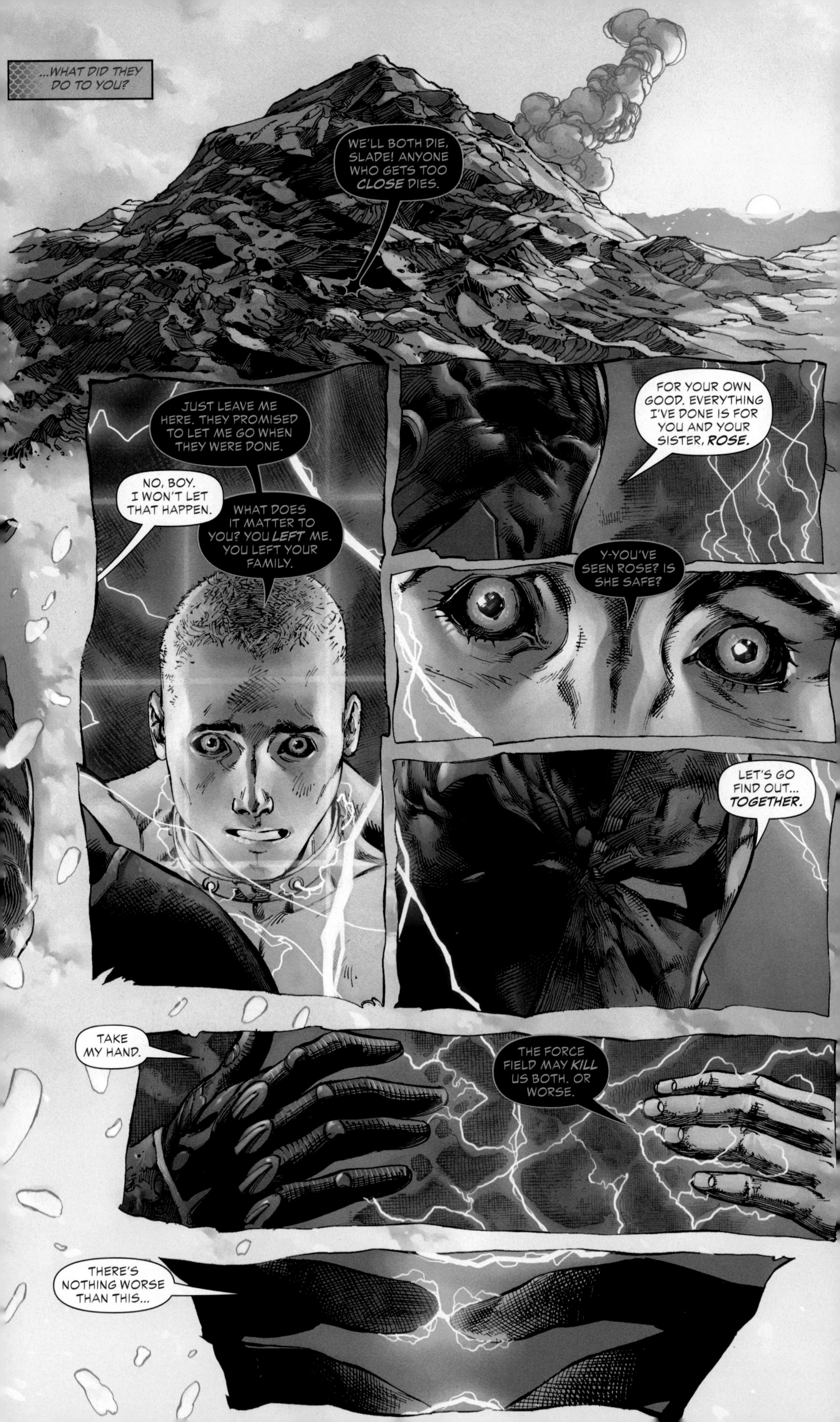
...WHAT DID THEY DO TO YOU?
WE'LL BOTH DIE, SLADE! ANYONE WHO GETS TOO CLOSE DIES.
JUST LEAVE ME HERE. THEY PROMISED TO LET ME GO WHEN THEY WERE DONE.
NO, BOY. I WON'T LET THAT HAPPEN.
WHAT DOES IT MATTER TO YOU? YOU LEFT ME. YOU LEFT YOUR FAMILY.
FOR YOUR OWN GOOD. EVERYTHING I'VE DONE IS FOR YOU AND YOUR SISTER, ROSE.
Y-YOU'VE SEEN ROSE? IS SHE SAFE?
LET'S GO FIND OUT... TOGETHER.
TAKE MY HAND.
THE FORCE FIELD MAY KILL US BOTH. OR WORSE.
THERE'S NOTHING WORSE THAN THIS...

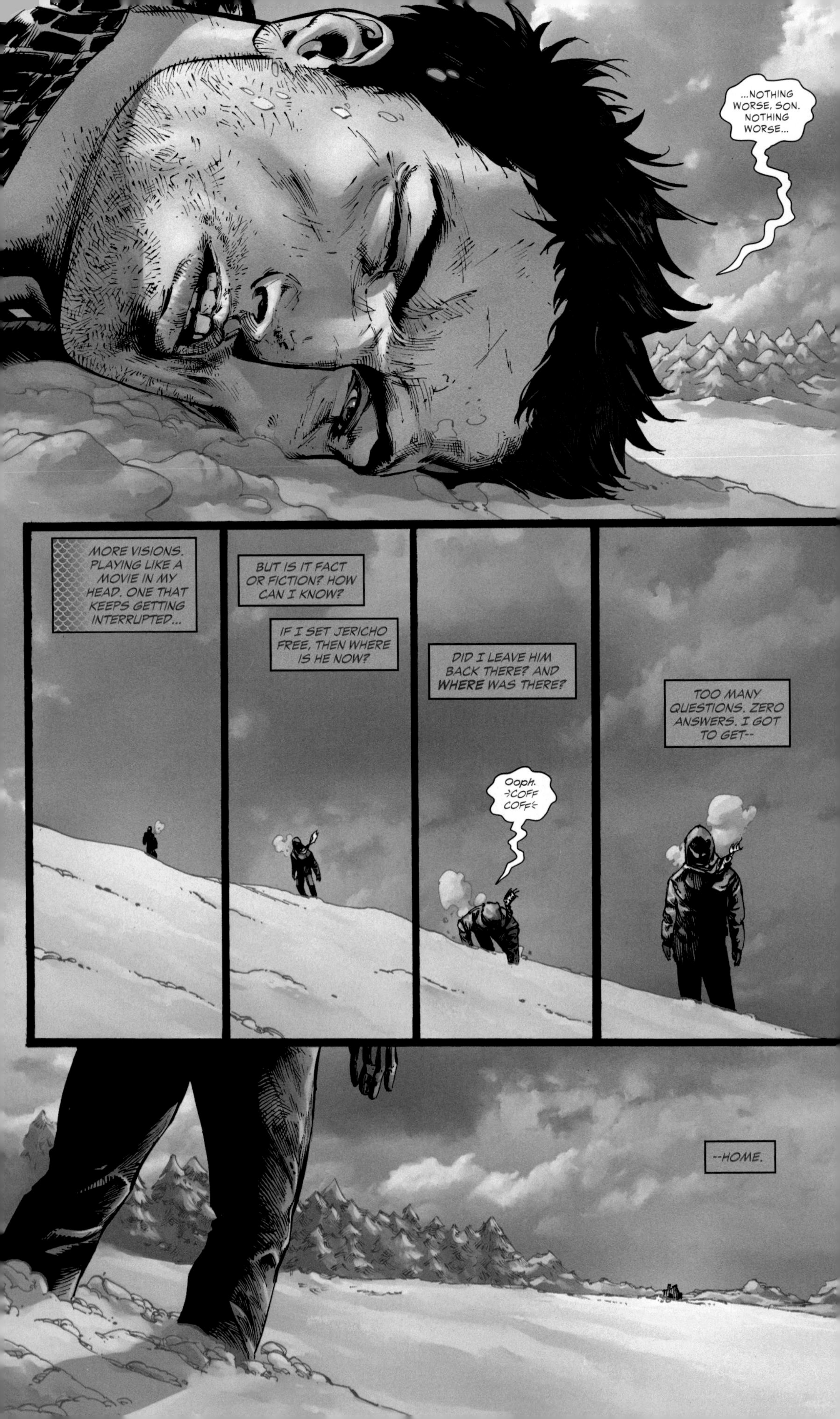
...NOTHING WORSE, SON. NOTHING WORSE...
MORE VISIONS. PLAYING LIKE A MOVIE IN MY HEAD. ONE THAT KEEPS GETTING INTERRUPTED...
BUT IS IT FACT OR FICTION? HOW CAN I KNOW?
IF I SET JERICHO FREE, THEN WHERE IS HE NOW?
DID I LEAVE HIM BACK THERE? AND WHERE WAS THERE?
Ooph. COFF COFF
TOO MANY QUESTIONS. ZERO ANSWERS. I GOT TO GET--
--HOME.

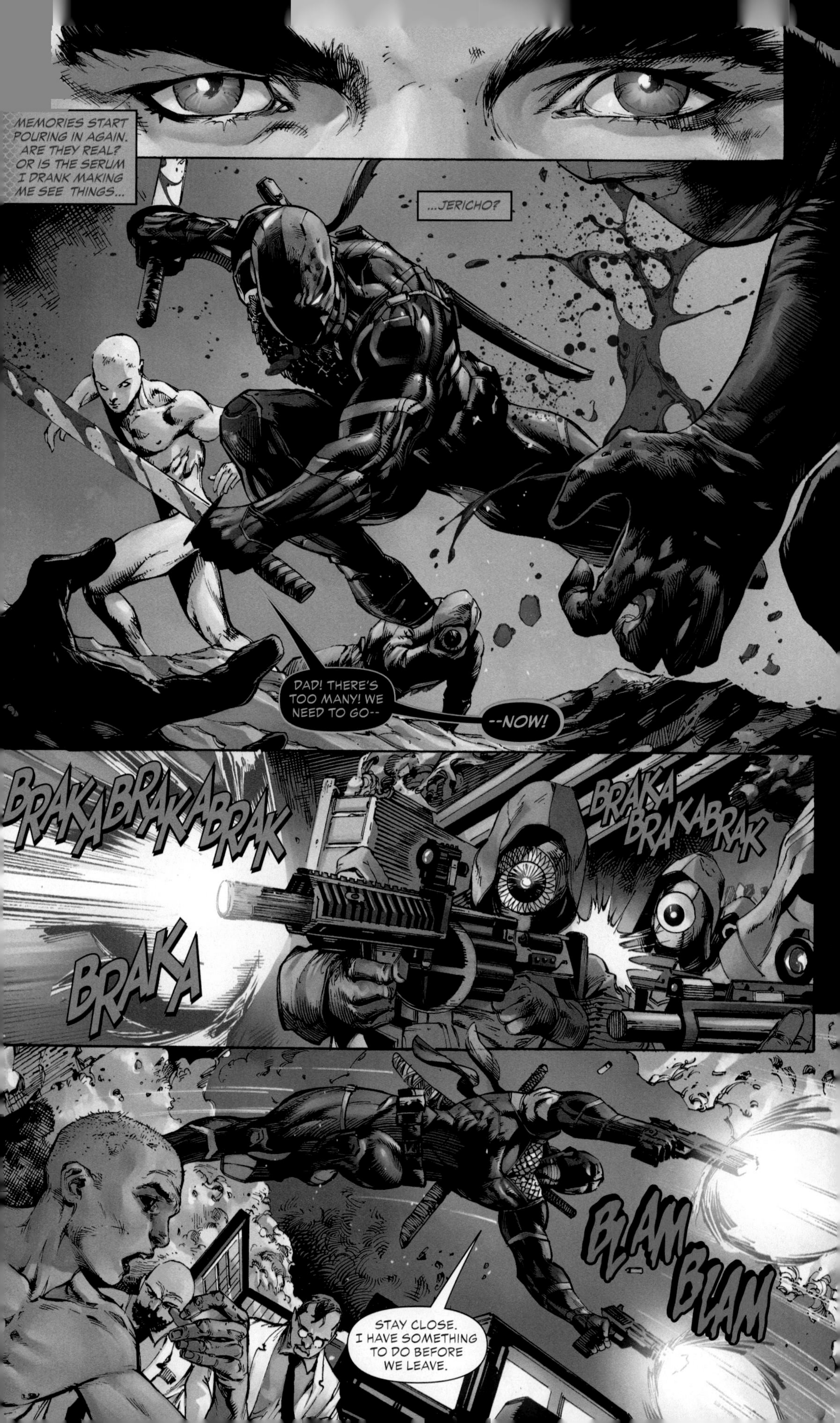
MEMORIES START POURING IN AGAIN. ARE THEY REAL? OR IS THE SERUM I DRANK MAKING ME SEE THINGS...
...JERICHO?
DAD! THERE'S TOO MANY! WE NEED TO GO--
--NOW!
BRAKABRAKABRAK
BRAKA BRAKABRAK
BRAKA
BLAM BLAM
STAY CLOSE. I HAVE SOMETHING TO DO BEFORE WE LEAVE.

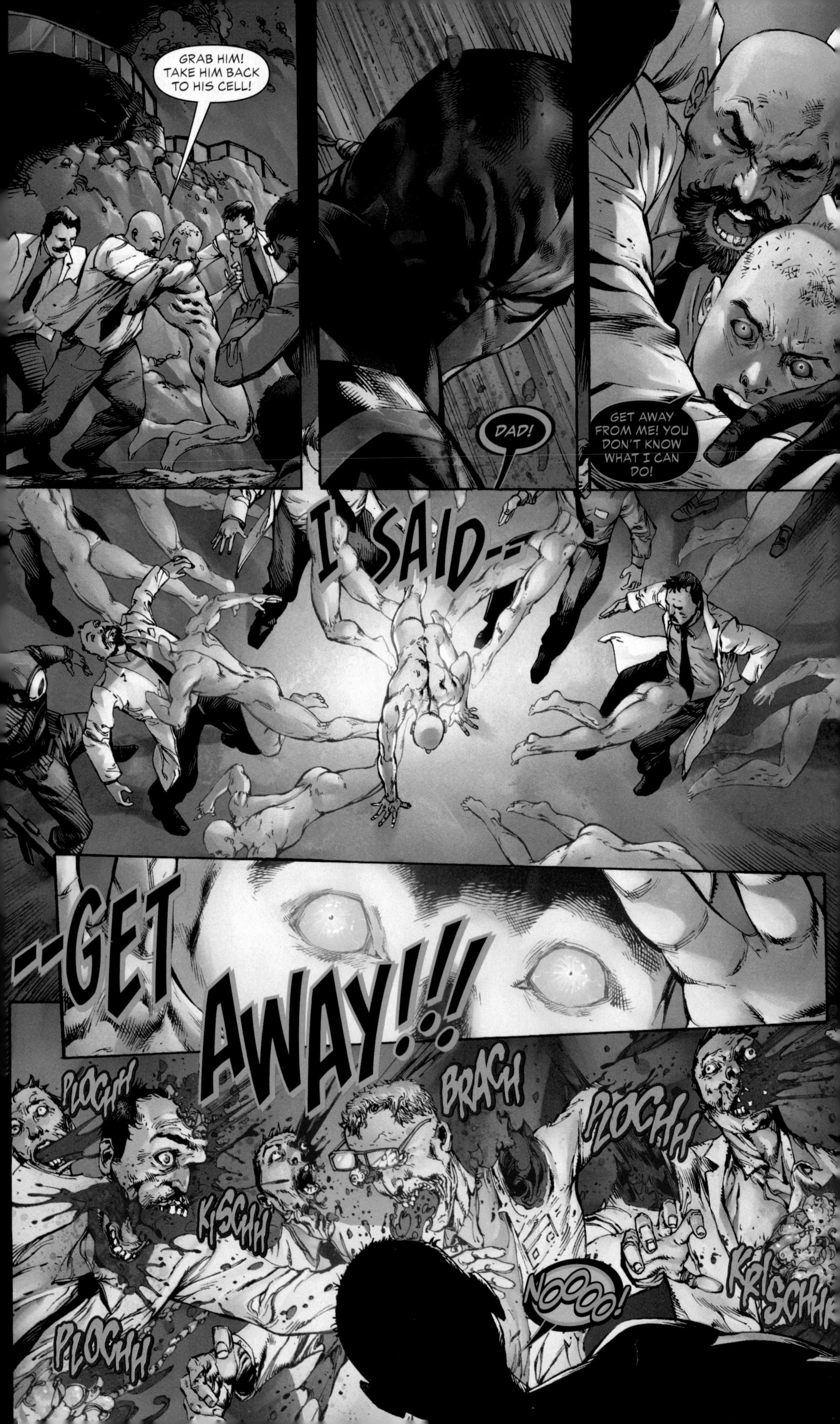
GRAB HIM! TAKE HIM BACK TO HIS CELL!
DAD!
GET AWAY FROM ME! YOU DON'T KNOW WHAT I CAN DO!
I SAID--
--GET AWAY!!!
PLOCHH
BRACH
PLOCHH
KISCHH
NOOOO!
KRISCHHR
PLOCHH

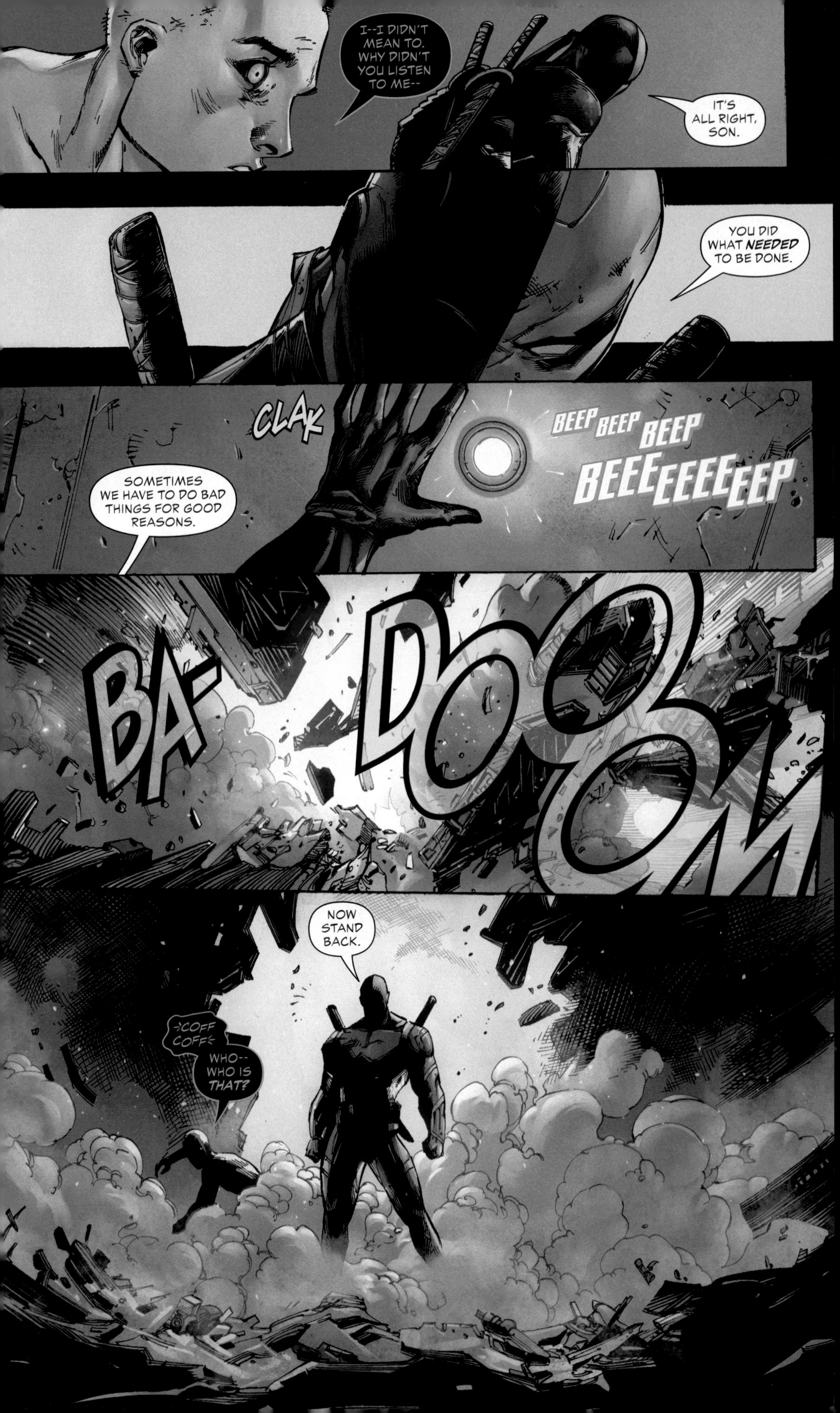
I--I DIDN'T MEAN TO. WHY DIDN'T YOU LISTEN TO ME--
IT'S ALL RIGHT, SON.
YOU DID WHAT NEEDED TO BE DONE.
CLAK
SOMETIMES WE HAVE TO DO BAD THINGS FOR GOOD REASONS.
BEEP BEEP BEEP BEEEEEEEEEP
BA-DOOOM
NOW STAND BACK.
COFF COFF
WHO-- WHO IS THAT?

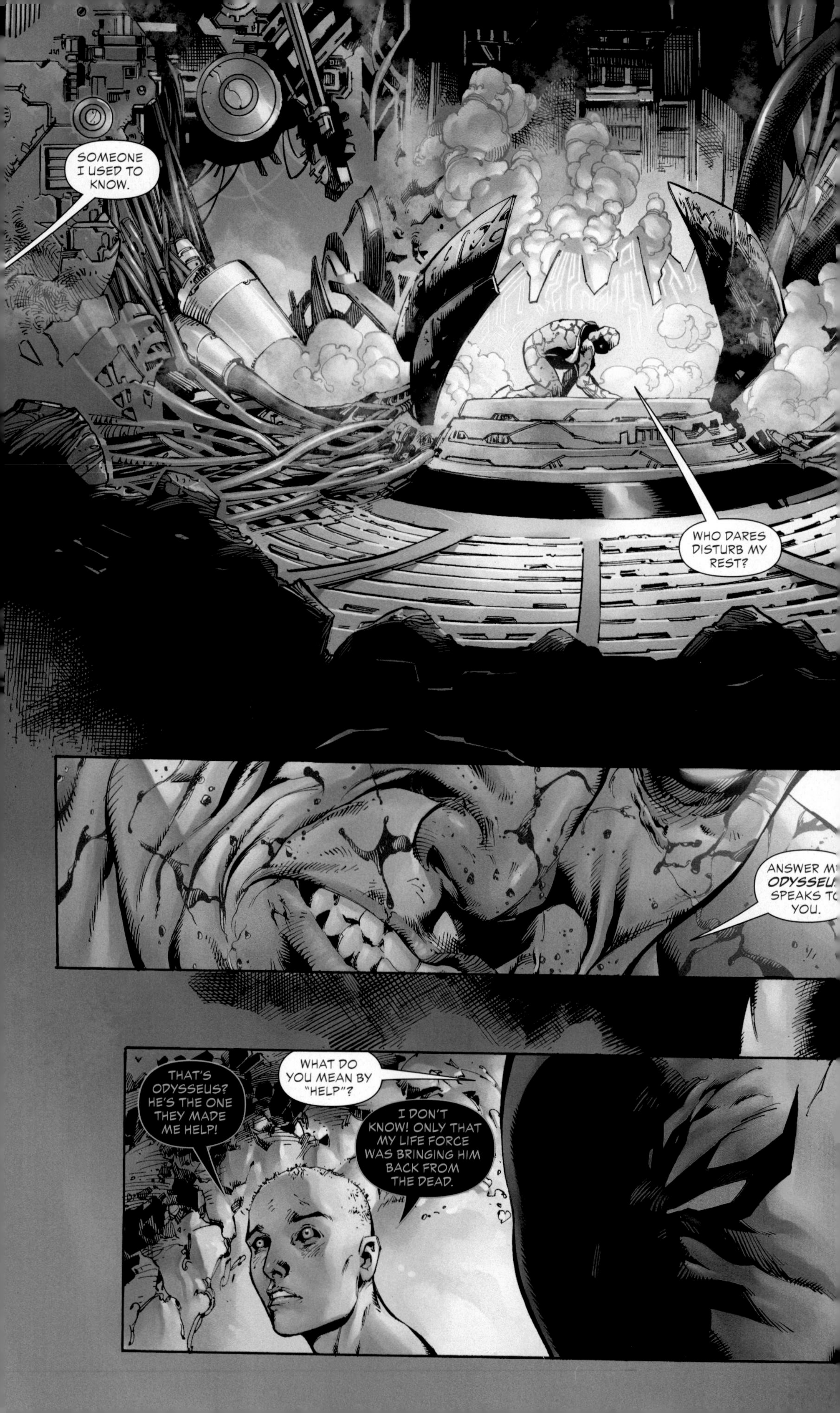

SOMEONE I USED TO KNOW.
WHO DARES DISTURB MY REST?
ANSWER M ODYSSEU SPEAKS T YOU.
THAT'S ODYSSEUS? HE'S THE ONE THEY MADE ME HELP!
WHAT DO YOU MEAN BY "HELP"?
I DON'T KNOW! ONLY THAT MY LIFE FORCE WAS BRINGING HIM BACK FROM THE DEAD.

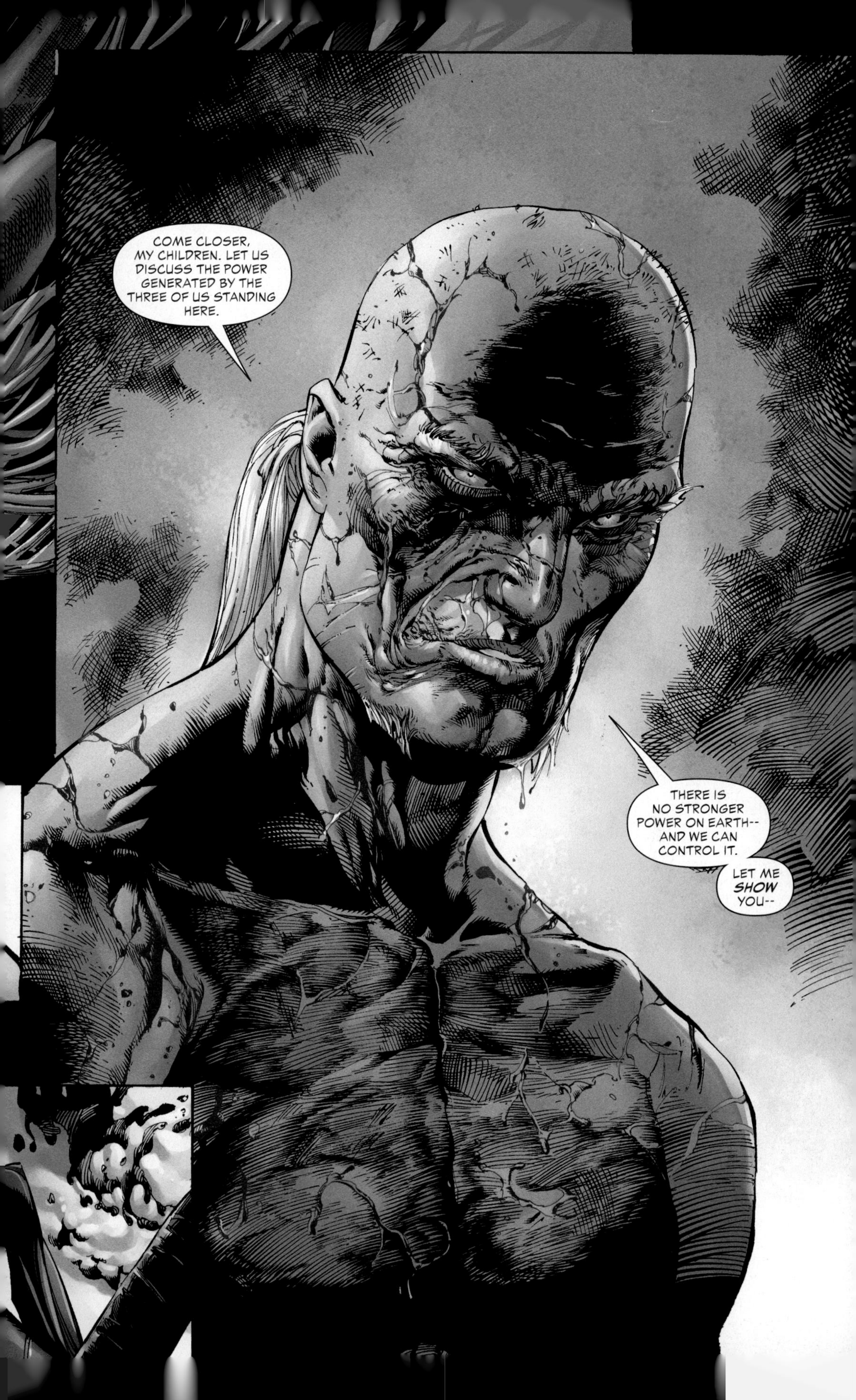

COME CLOSER, MY CHILDREN. LET US DISCUSS THE POWER GENERATED BY THE THREE OF US STANDING HERE.
THERE IS NO STRONGER POWER ON EARTH-- AND WE CAN CONTROL IT.
LET ME SHOW YOU--

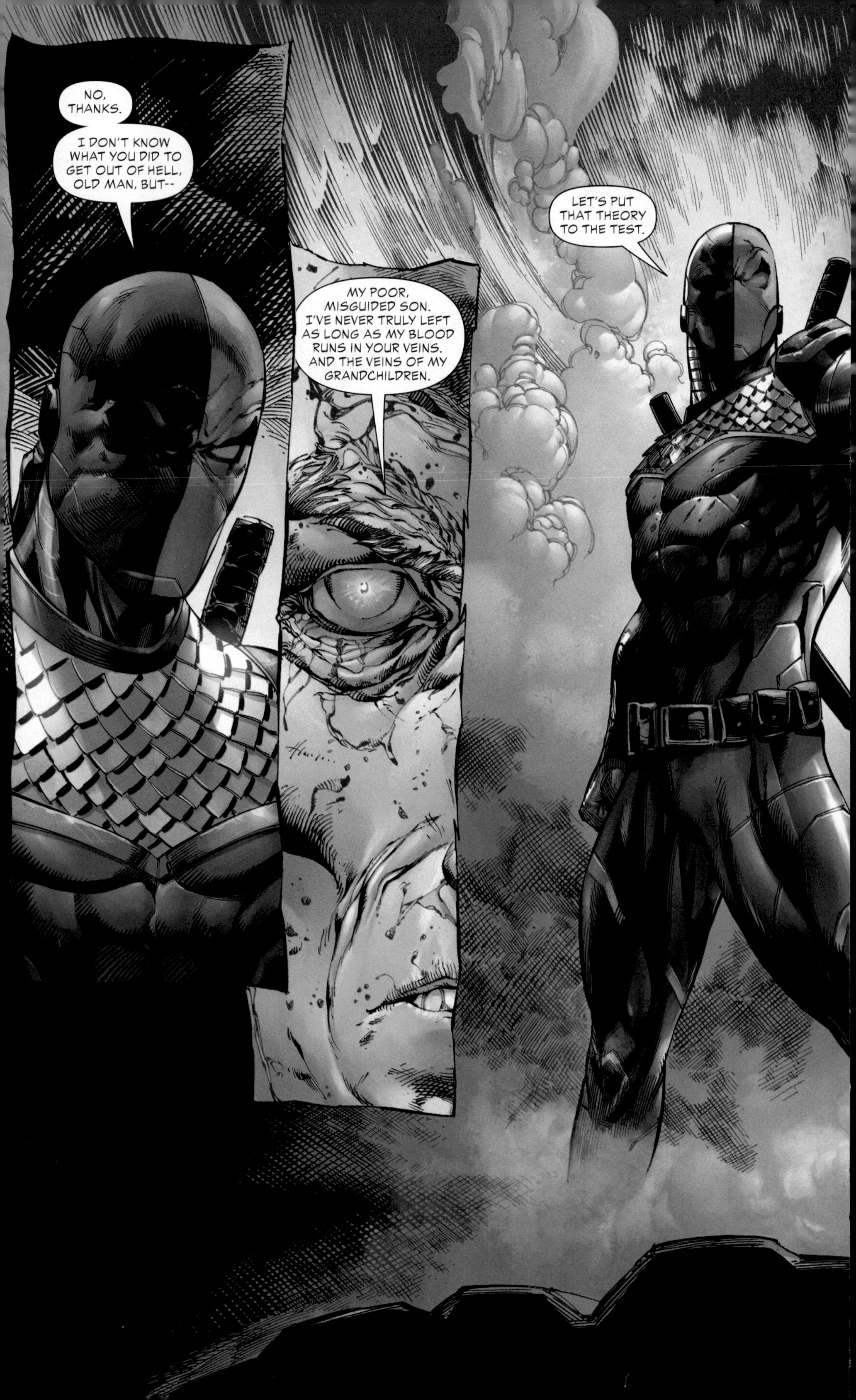
NO, THANKS.
I DON'T KNOW WHAT YOU DID TO GET OUT OF HELL, OLD MAN, BUT--
MY POOR, MISGUIDED SON. I'VE NEVER TRULY LEFT AS LONG AS MY BLOOD RUNS IN YOUR VEINS. AND THE VEINS OF MY GRANDCHILDREN.
LET'S PUT THAT THEORY TO THE TEST.

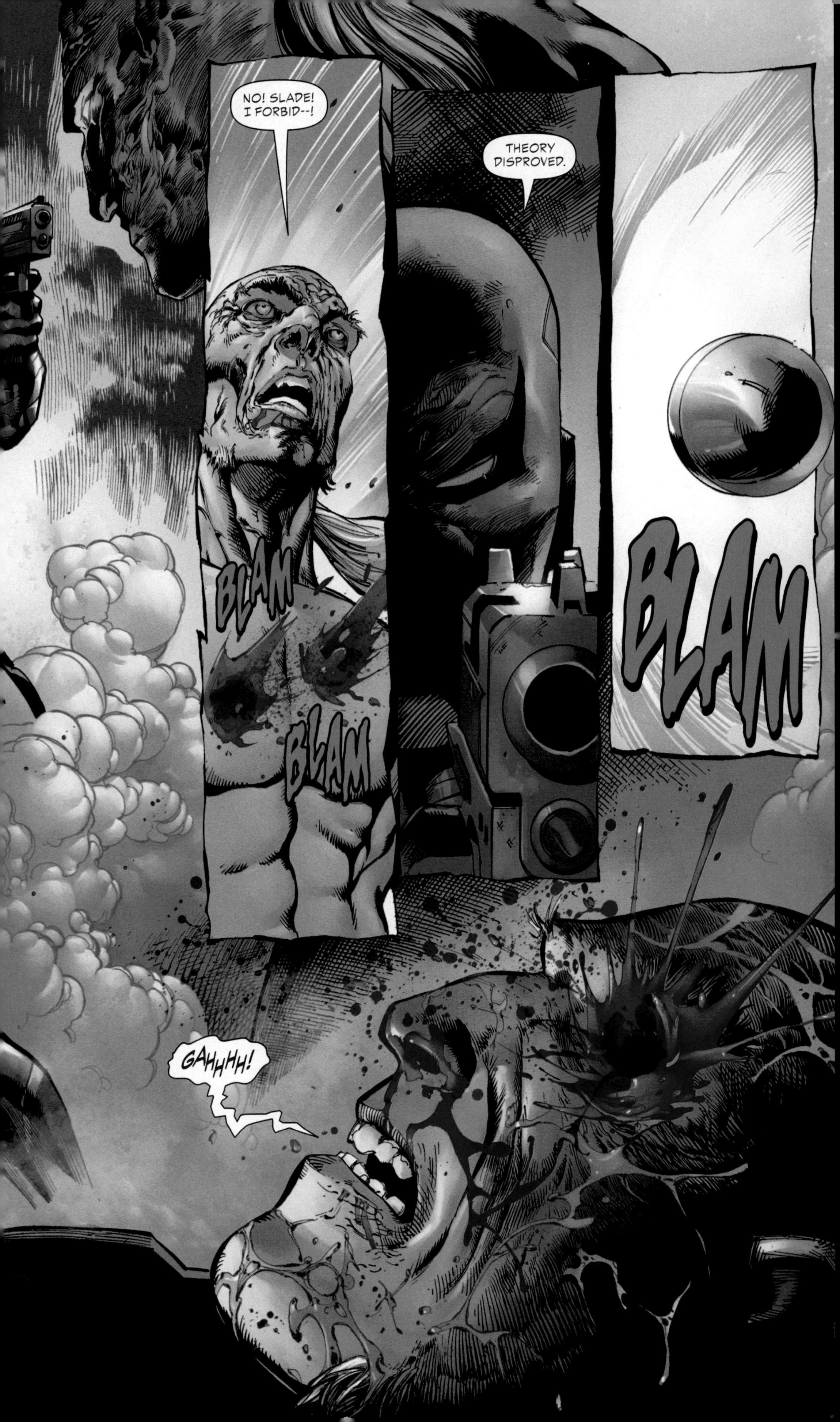
NO! SLADE! I FORBID--!
BLAM
BLAM
THEORY DISPROVED.
BLAM
GAHHHH!

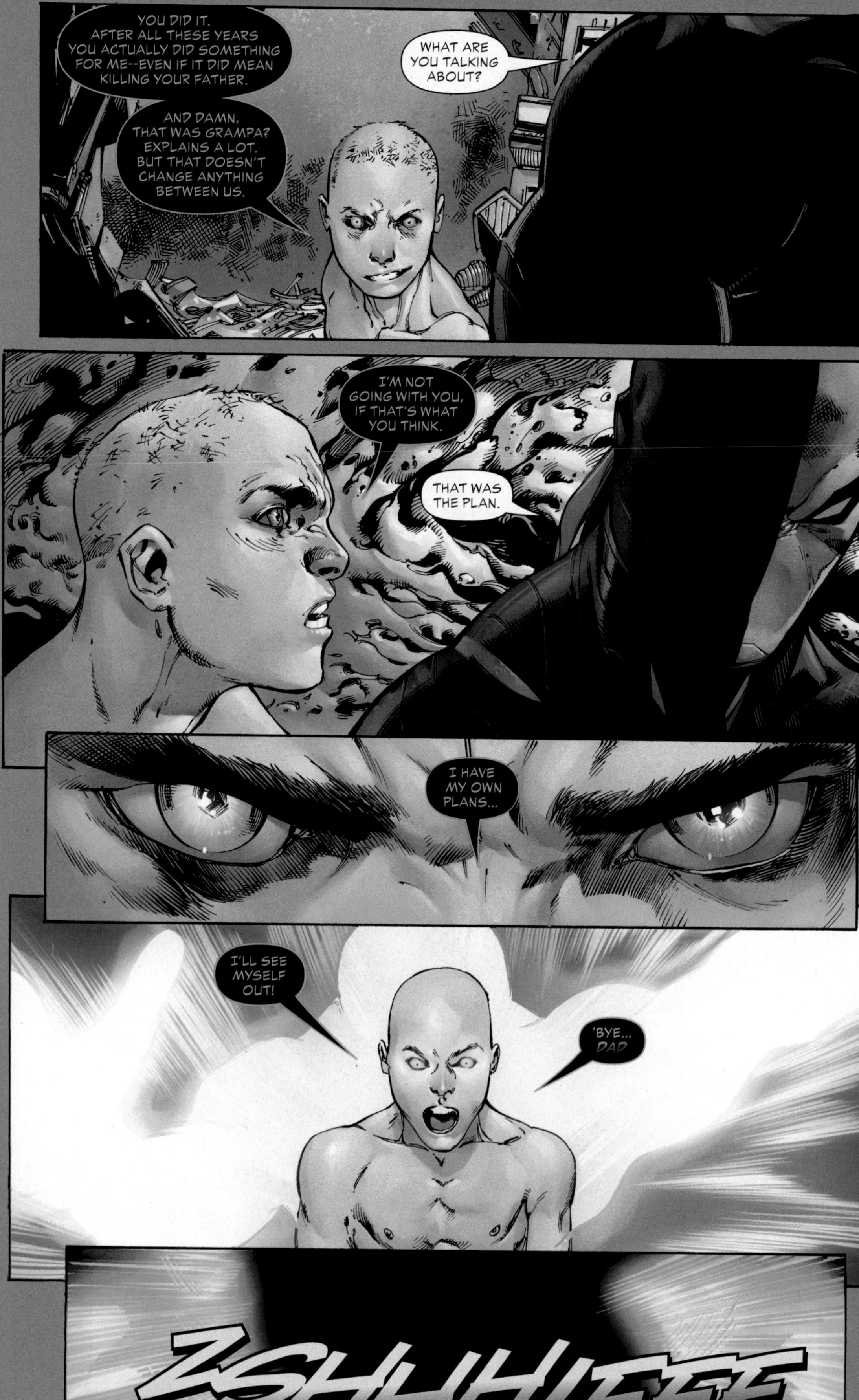
YOU DID IT. AFTER ALL THESE YEARS YOU ACTUALLY DID SOMETHING FOR ME--EVEN IF IT DID MEAN KILLING YOUR FATHER.
WHAT ARE YOU TALKING ABOUT?
AND DAMN, THAT WAS GRAMPA? EXPLAINS A LOT. BUT THAT DOESN'T CHANGE ANYTHING BETWEEN US.
I'M NOT GOING WITH YOU, IF THAT'S WHAT YOU THINK.
THAT WAS THE PLAN.
I HAVE MY OWN PLANS...
I'LL SEE MYSELF OUT!
'BYE... DAD.
ZSHHHIFFF

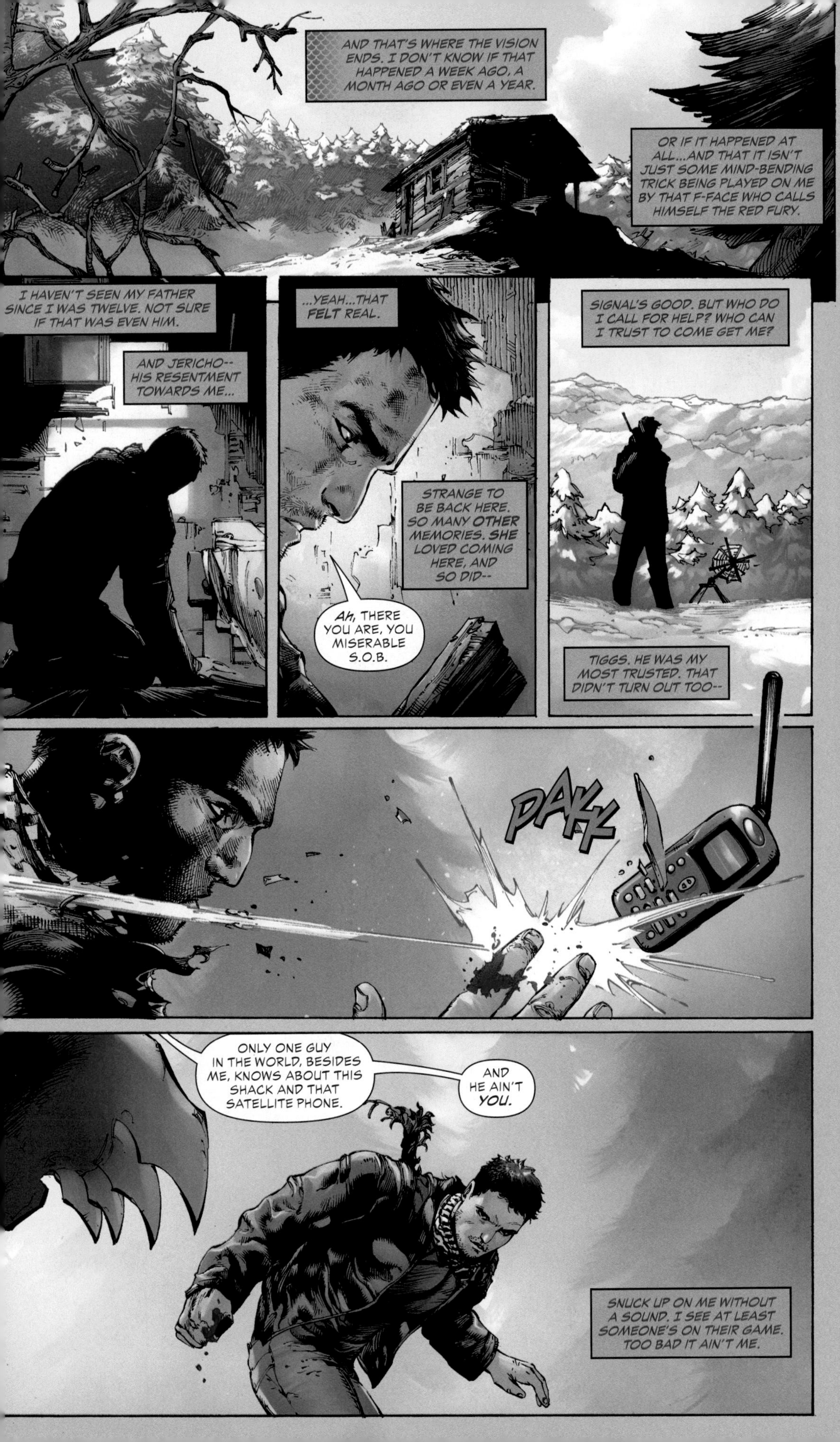
AND THAT'S WHERE THE VISION ENDS. I DON'T KNOW IF THAT HAPPENED A WEEK AGO, A MONTH AGO OR EVEN A YEAR.
OR IF IT HAPPENED AT ALL...AND THAT IT ISN'T JUST SOME MIND-BENDING TRICK BEING PLAYED ON ME BY THAT F-FACE WHO CALLS HIMSELF THE RED FURY.
I HAVEN'T SEEN MY FATHER SINCE I WAS TWELVE. NOT SURE IF THAT WAS EVEN HIM.
AND JERICHO-- HIS RESENTMENT TOWARDS ME...
...YEAH...THAT FELT REAL.
STRANGE TO BE BACK HERE. SO MANY OTHER MEMORIES. SHE LOVED COMING HERE, AND SO DID--
AH, THERE YOU ARE, YOU MISERABLE S.O.B.
SIGNAL'S GOOD. BUT WHO DO I CALL FOR HELP? WHO CAN I TRUST TO COME GET ME?
TIGGS. HE WAS MY MOST TRUSTED. THAT DIDN'T TURN OUT TOO--
DAKK
ONLY ONE GUY IN THE WORLD, BESIDES ME, KNOWS ABOUT THIS SHACK AND THAT SATELLITE PHONE.
AND HE AIN'T YOU.
SNUCK UP ON ME WITHOUT A SOUND. I SEE AT LEAST SOMEONE'S ON THEIR GAME. TOO BAD IT AIN'T ME.

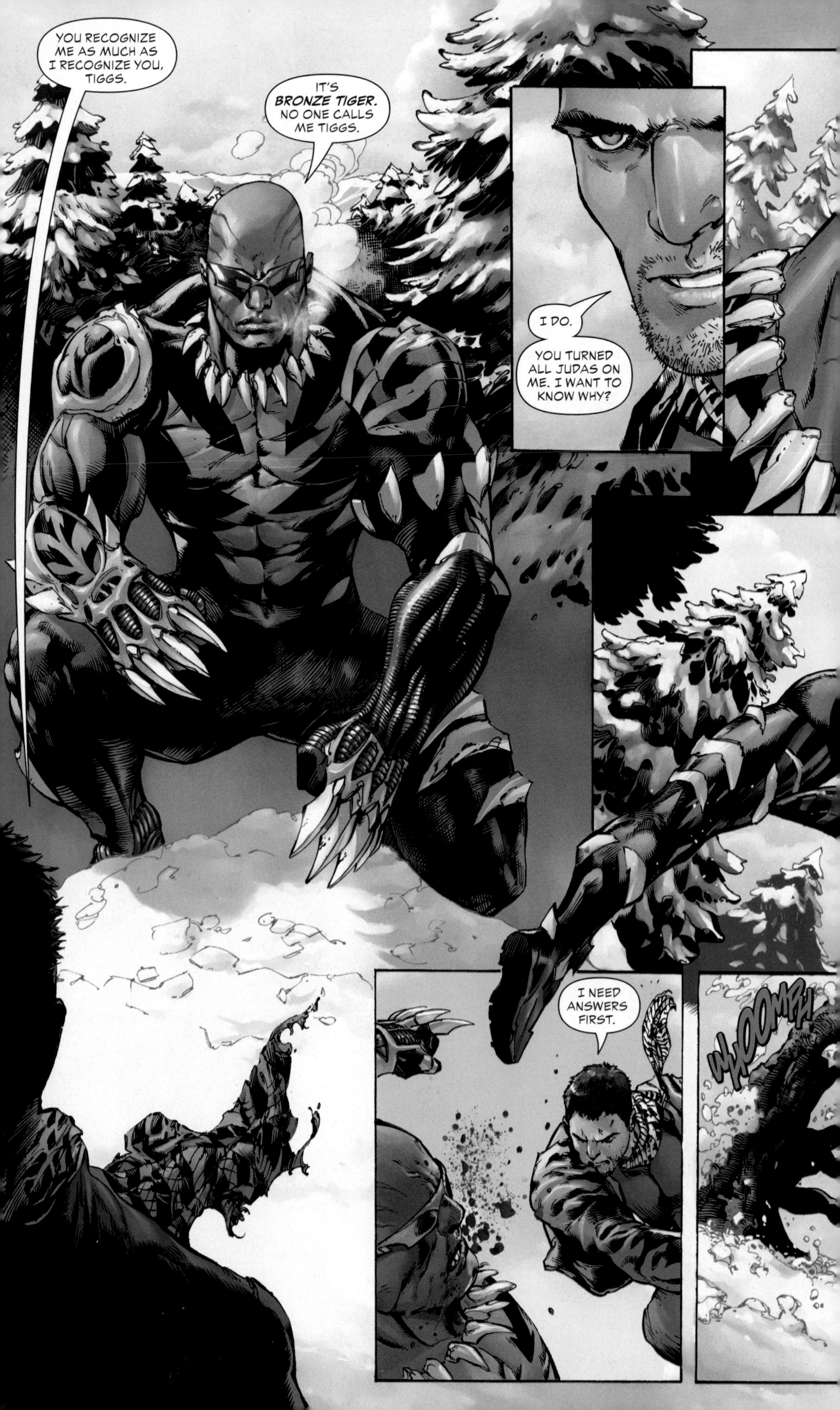

YOU RECOGNIZE ME AS MUCH AS I RECOGNIZE YOU, TIGGS.
IT'S BRONZE TIGER. NO ONE CALLS ME TIGGS.
I DO.
YOU TURNED ALL JUDAS ON ME. I WANT TO KNOW WHY?
I NEED ANSWERS FIRST.
WHOOMPH

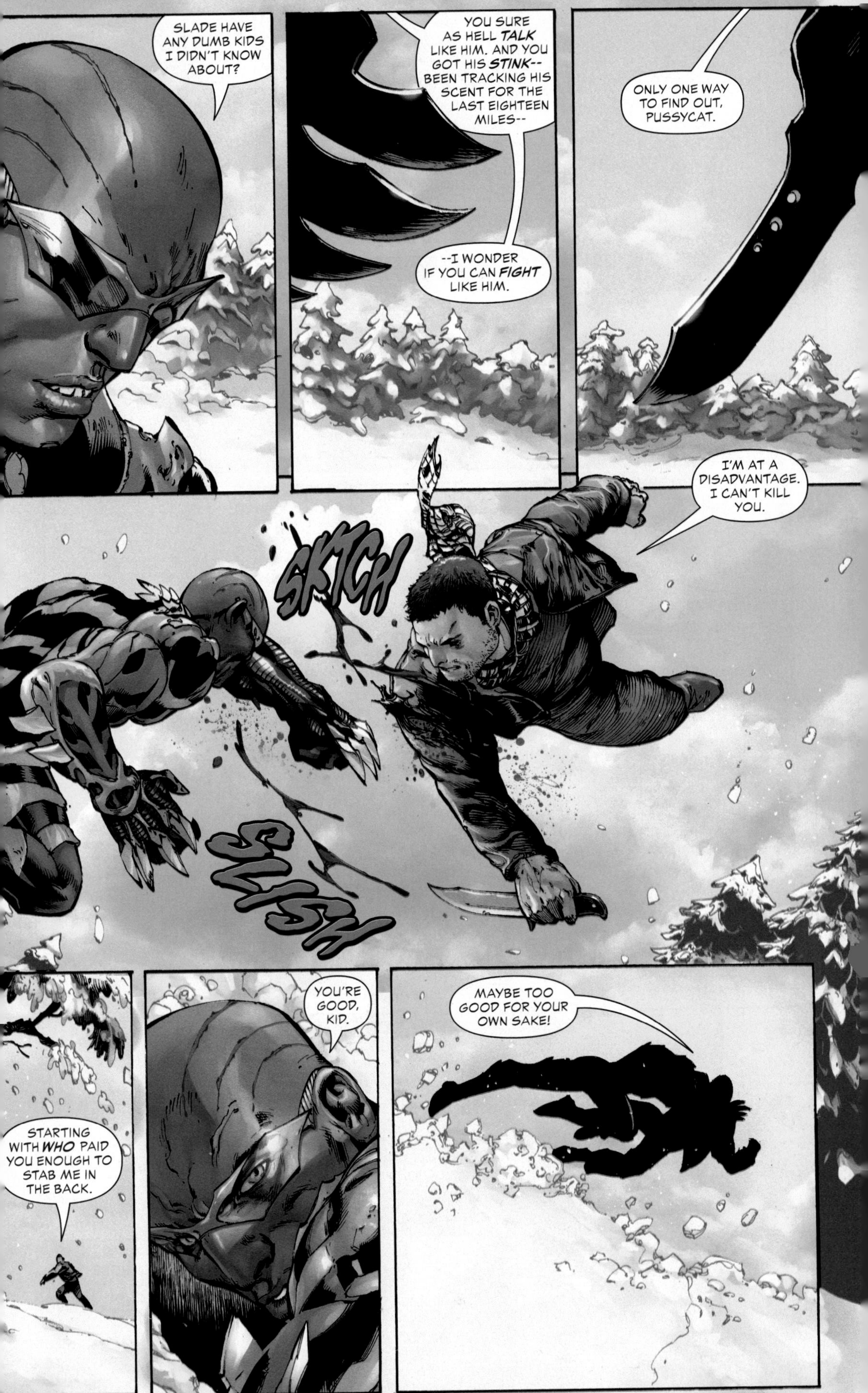
SLADE HAVE ANY DUMB KIDS I DIDN'T KNOW ABOUT?
YOU SURE AS HELL *TALK* LIKE HIM. AND YOU GOT HIS *STINK*-- BEEN TRACKING HIS SCENT FOR THE LAST EIGHTEEN MILES--
--I WONDER IF YOU CAN *FIGHT* LIKE HIM.
ONLY ONE WAY TO FIND OUT, PUSSYCAT.
I'M AT A DISADVANTAGE. I CAN'T KILL YOU.
SKTCH
SLISH
STARTING WITH *WHO* PAID YOU ENOUGH TO STAB ME IN THE BACK.
YOU'RE GOOD, KID.
MAYBE TOO GOOD FOR YOUR OWN SAKE!

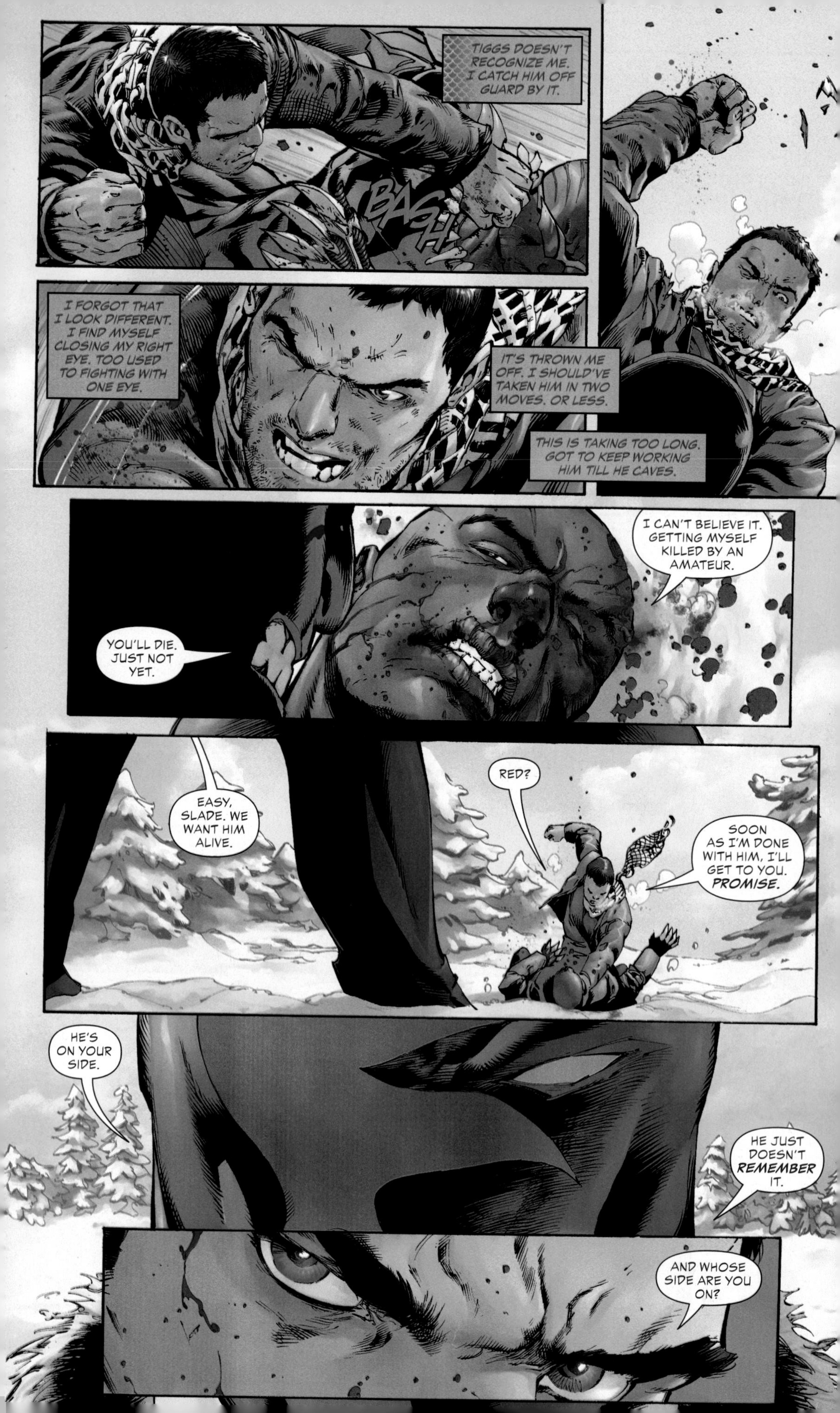
TIGGS DOESN'T RECOGNIZE ME. I CATCH HIM OFF GUARD BY IT.
BASH
I FORGOT THAT I LOOK DIFFERENT. I FIND MYSELF CLOSING MY RIGHT EYE. TOO USED TO FIGHTING WITH ONE EYE.
IT'S THROWN ME OFF. I SHOULD'VE TAKEN HIM IN TWO MOVES. OR LESS.
THIS IS TAKING TOO LONG. GOT TO KEEP WORKING HIM TILL HE CAVES.
I CAN'T BELIEVE IT. GETTING MYSELF KILLED BY AN AMATEUR.
YOU'LL DIE. JUST NOT YET.
EASY, SLADE. WE WANT HIM ALIVE.
RED?
SOON AS I'M DONE WITH HIM, I'LL GET TO YOU. PROMISE.
HE'S ON YOUR SIDE.
HE JUST DOESN'T REMEMBER IT.
AND WHOSE SIDE ARE YOU ON?

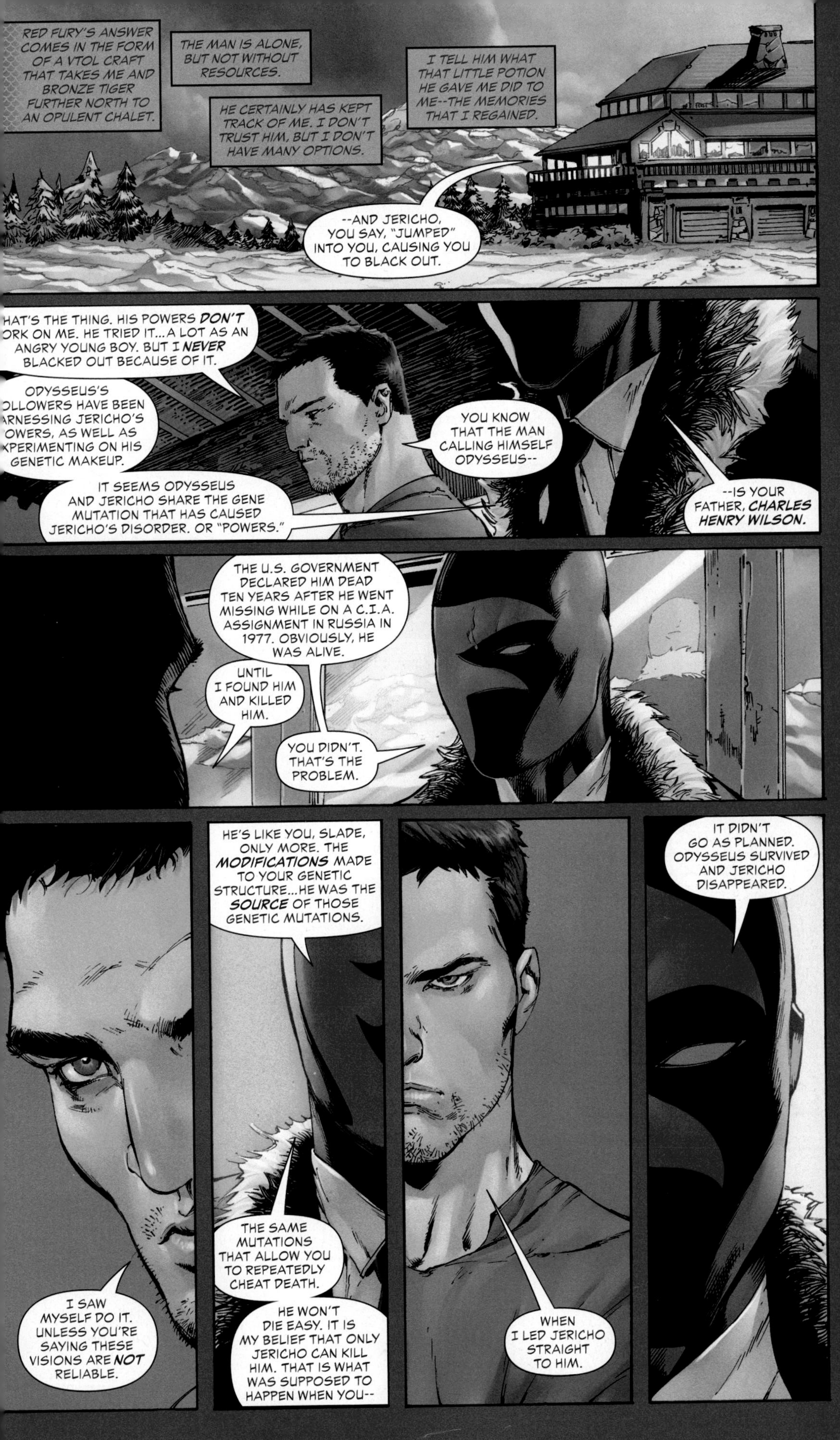
RED FURY'S ANSWER COMES IN THE FORM OF A VTOL CRAFT THAT TAKES ME AND BRONZE TIGER FURTHER NORTH TO AN OPULENT CHALET.
THE MAN IS ALONE, BUT NOT WITHOUT RESOURCES.
HE CERTAINLY HAS KEPT TRACK OF ME. I DON'T TRUST HIM, BUT I DON'T HAVE MANY OPTIONS.
I TELL HIM WHAT THAT LITTLE POTION HE GAVE ME DID TO ME--THE MEMORIES THAT I REGAINED.
--AND JERICHO, YOU SAY, "JUMPED" INTO YOU, CAUSING YOU TO BLACK OUT.
HAT'S THE THING. HIS POWERS DON'T ORK ON ME. HE TRIED IT...A LOT AS AN ANGRY YOUNG BOY. BUT I NEVER BLACKED OUT BECAUSE OF IT.
ODYSSEUS'S OLLOWERS HAVE BEEN ARNESSING JERICHO'S OWERS, AS WELL AS XPERIMENTING ON HIS GENETIC MAKEUP.
IT SEEMS ODYSSEUS AND JERICHO SHARE THE GENE MUTATION THAT HAS CAUSED JERICHO'S DISORDER. OR "POWERS."
YOU KNOW THAT THE MAN CALLING HIMSELF ODYSSEUS--
--IS YOUR FATHER, CHARLES HENRY WILSON.
THE U.S. GOVERNMENT DECLARED HIM DEAD TEN YEARS AFTER HE WENT MISSING WHILE ON A C.I.A. ASSIGNMENT IN RUSSIA IN 1977. OBVIOUSLY, HE WAS ALIVE.
UNTIL I FOUND HIM AND KILLED HIM.
YOU DIDN'T. THAT'S THE PROBLEM.
I SAW MYSELF DO IT. UNLESS YOU'RE SAYING THESE VISIONS ARE NOT RELIABLE.
HE'S LIKE YOU, SLADE, ONLY MORE. THE MODIFICATIONS MADE TO YOUR GENETIC STRUCTURE...HE WAS THE SOURCE OF THOSE GENETIC MUTATIONS.
THE SAME MUTATIONS THAT ALLOW YOU TO REPEATEDLY CHEAT DEATH.
HE WON'T DIE EASY. IT IS MY BELIEF THAT ONLY JERICHO CAN KILL HIM. THAT IS WHAT WAS SUPPOSED TO HAPPEN WHEN YOU--
WHEN I LED JERICHO STRAIGHT TO HIM.
IT DIDN'T GO AS PLANNED. ODYSSEUS SURVIVED AND JERICHO DISAPPEARED.

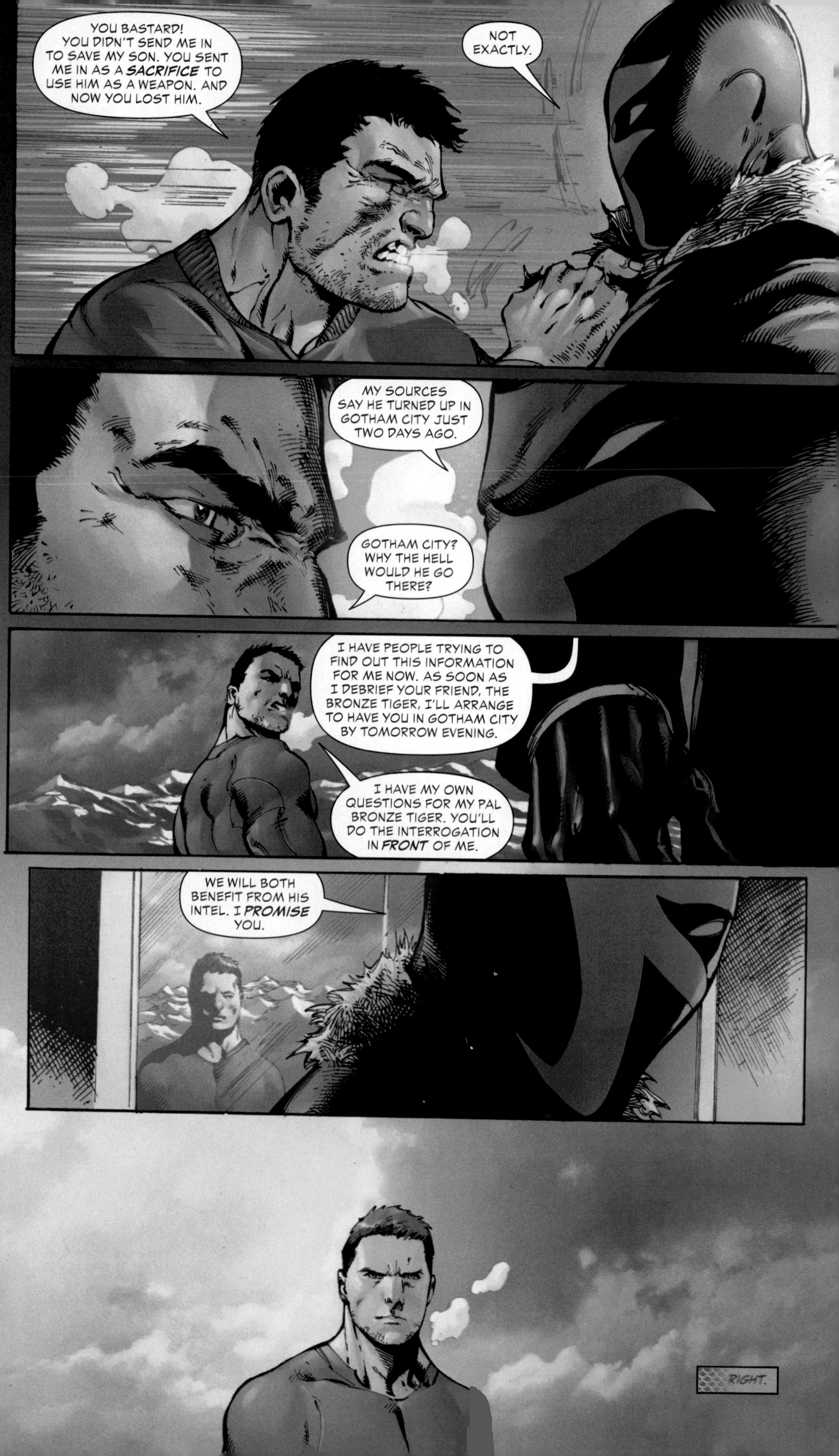
YOU BASTARD! YOU DIDN'T SEND ME IN TO SAVE MY SON. YOU SENT ME IN AS A *SACRIFICE* TO USE HIM AS A WEAPON. AND NOW YOU LOST HIM.
NOT EXACTLY.
MY SOURCES SAY HE TURNED UP IN GOTHAM CITY JUST TWO DAYS AGO.
GOTHAM CITY? WHY THE HELL WOULD HE GO THERE?
I HAVE PEOPLE TRYING TO FIND OUT THIS INFORMATION FOR ME NOW. AS SOON AS I DEBRIEF YOUR FRIEND, THE BRONZE TIGER, I'LL ARRANGE TO HAVE YOU IN GOTHAM CITY BY TOMORROW EVENING.
I HAVE MY OWN QUESTIONS FOR MY PAL BRONZE TIGER. YOU'LL DO THE INTERROGATION IN *FRONT* OF ME.
WE WILL BOTH BENEFIT FROM HIS INTEL. I *PROMISE* YOU.
RIGHT.

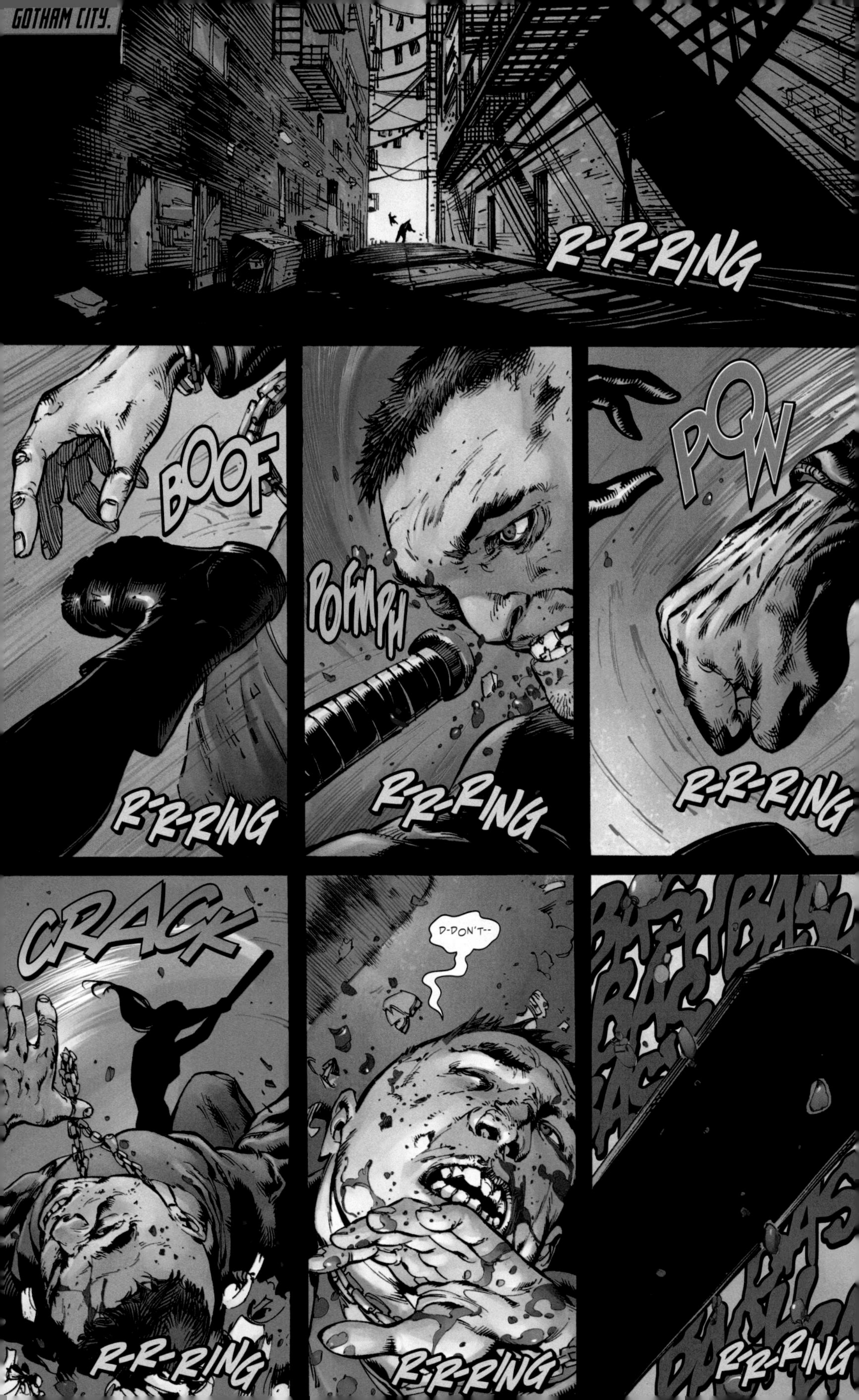
GOTHAM CITY.
R-R-RING
BOOF
R-R-RING
POFMPH
R-R-RING
POW
R-R-RING
CRACK
R-R-RING
D-DON'T--
R-R-RING
R-R-RING

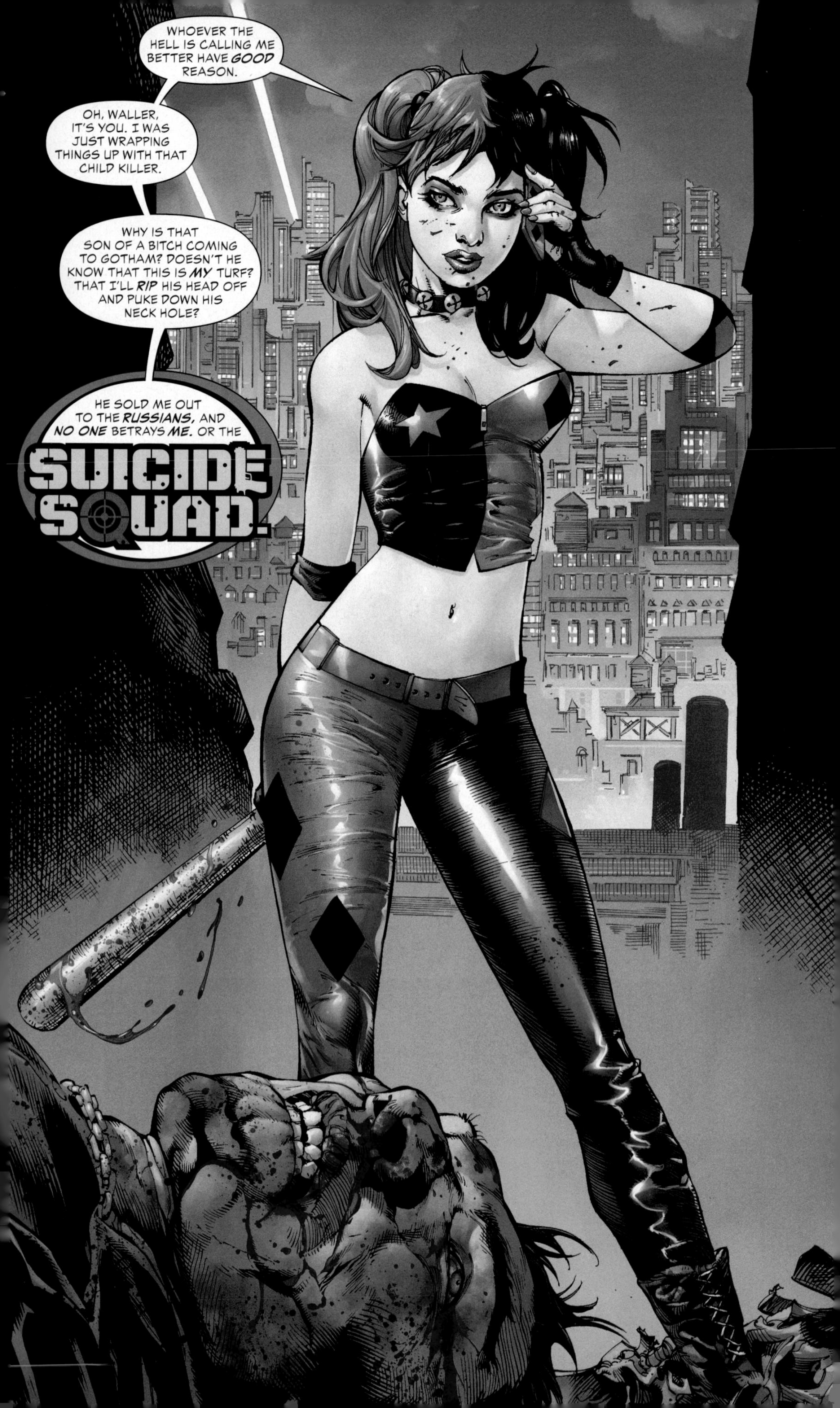
WHOEVER THE HELL IS CALLING ME BETTER HAVE GOOD REASON.
OH, WALLER, IT'S YOU. I WAS JUST WRAPPING THINGS UP WITH THAT CHILD KILLER.
WHY IS THAT SON OF A BITCH COMING TO GOTHAM? DOESN'T HE KNOW THAT THIS IS MY TURF? THAT I'LL RIP HIS HEAD OFF AND PUKE DOWN HIS NECK HOLE?
HE SOLD ME OUT TO THE RUSSIANS, AND NO ONE BETRAYS ME. OR THE
SUICIDE SQUAD.

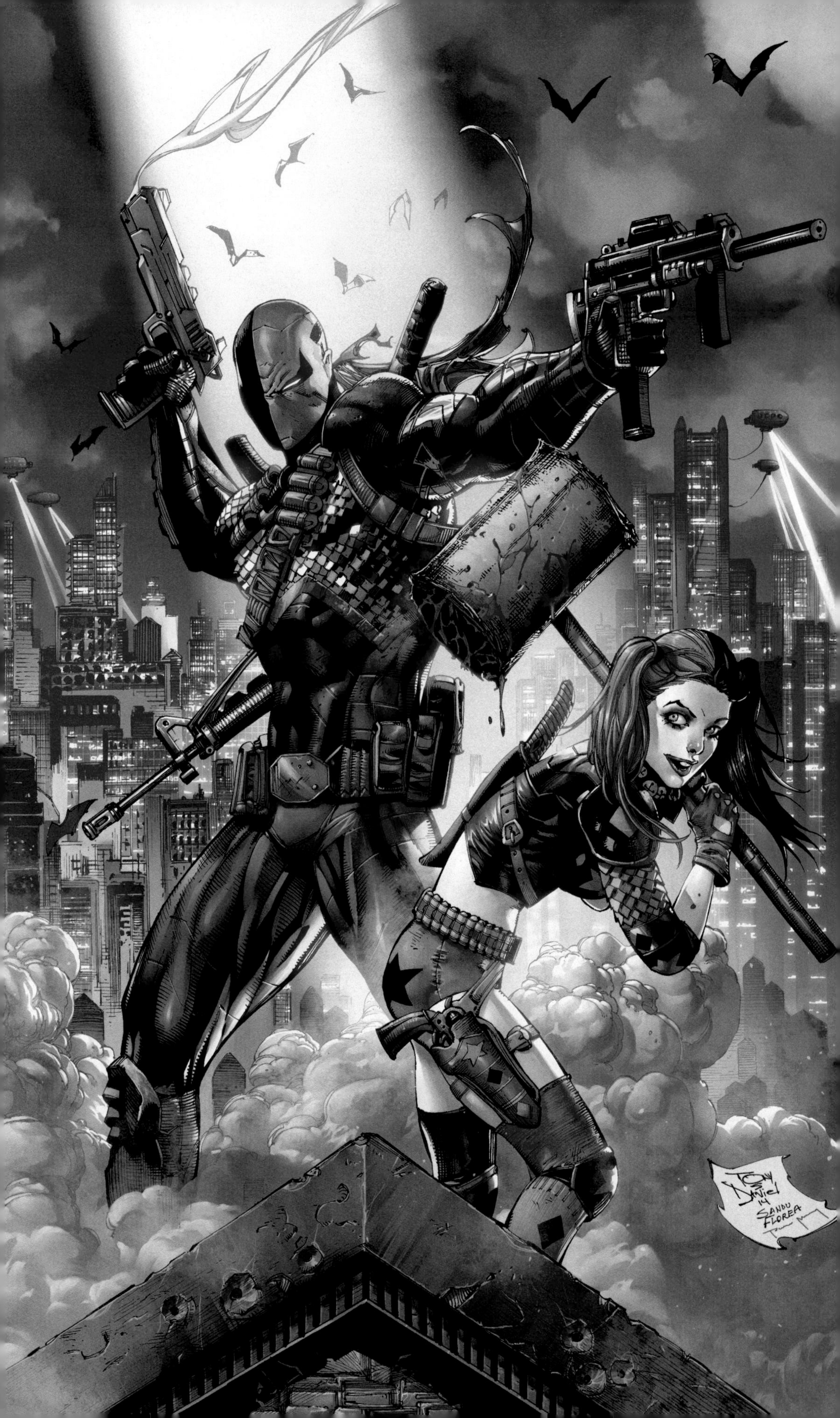
TONY S. DANIEL
14
SANDU FLOREA

Variant cover by MATTEO SCALERA & TOMEU MOREY

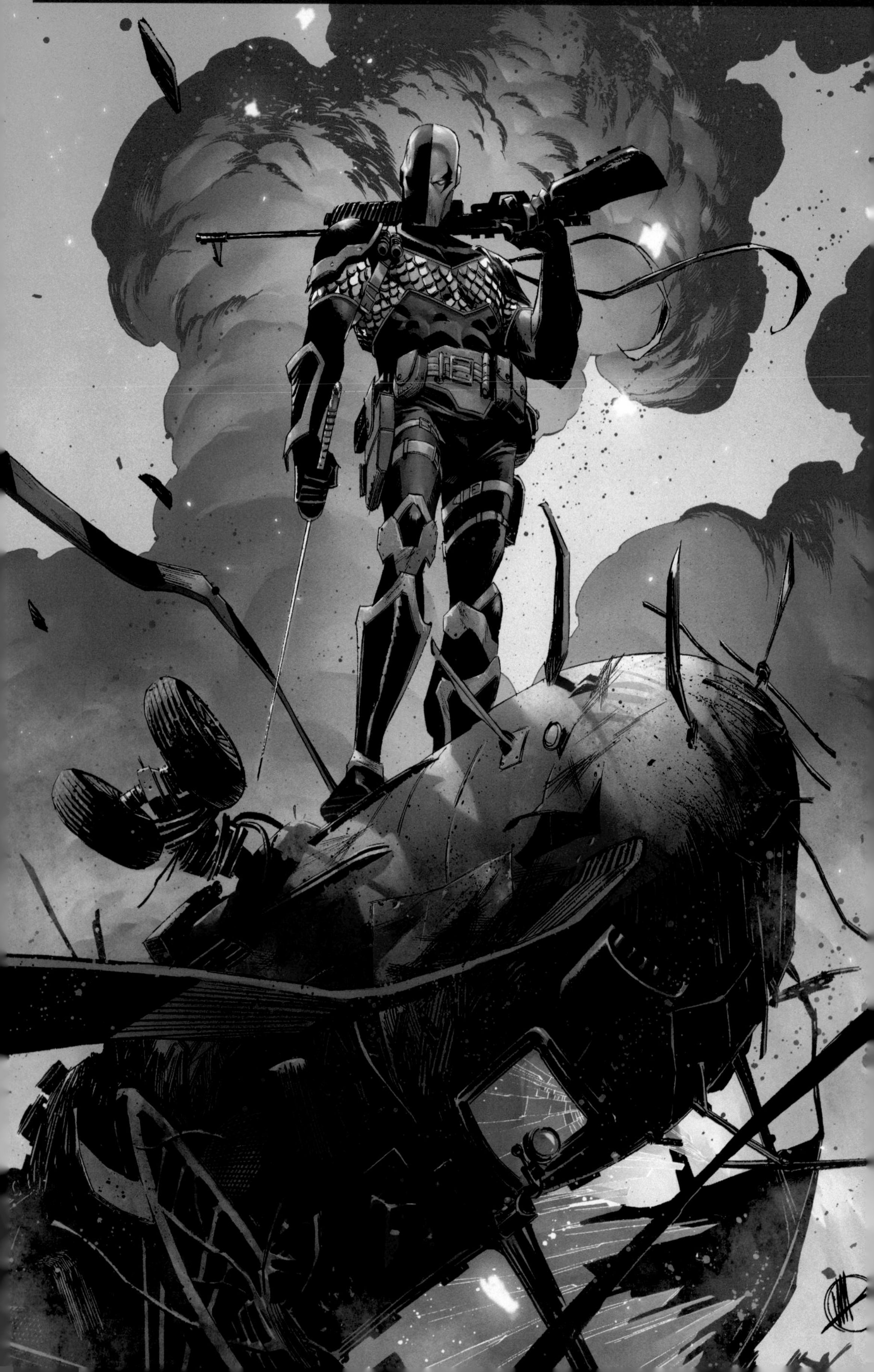

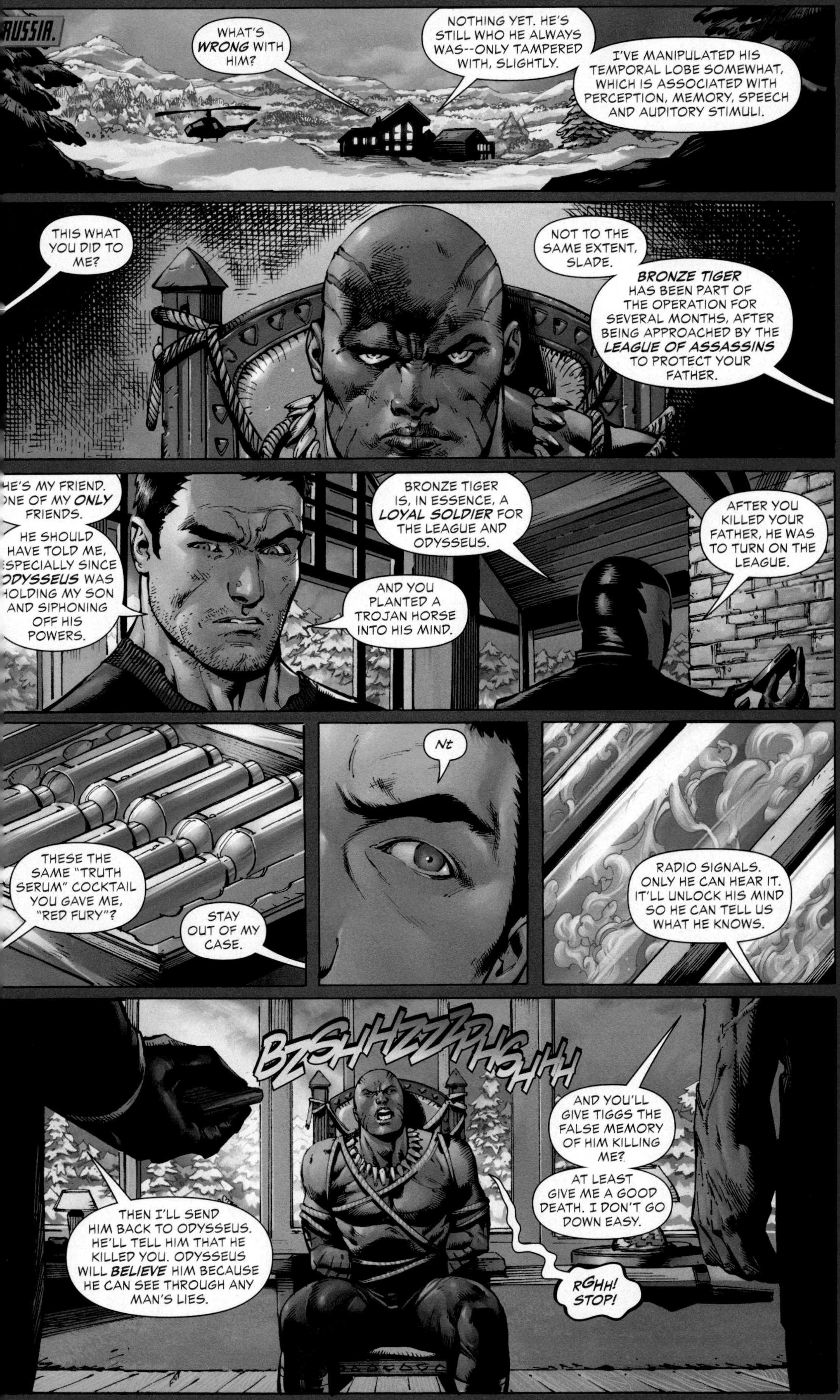
RUSSIA.
WHAT'S *WRONG* WITH HIM?
NOTHING YET. HE'S STILL WHO HE ALWAYS WAS--ONLY TAMPERED WITH, SLIGHTLY.
I'VE MANIPULATED HIS TEMPORAL LOBE SOMEWHAT, WHICH IS ASSOCIATED WITH PERCEPTION, MEMORY, SPEECH AND AUDITORY STIMULI.
THIS WHAT YOU DID TO ME?
NOT TO THE SAME EXTENT, SLADE.
BRONZE TIGER HAS BEEN PART OF THE OPERATION FOR SEVERAL MONTHS, AFTER BEING APPROACHED BY THE *LEAGUE OF ASSASSINS* TO PROTECT YOUR FATHER.
HE'S MY FRIEND. ONE OF MY *ONLY* FRIENDS.
HE SHOULD HAVE TOLD ME, ESPECIALLY SINCE *ODYSSEUS* WAS HOLDING MY SON AND SIPHONING OFF HIS POWERS.
BRONZE TIGER IS, IN ESSENCE, A *LOYAL SOLDIER* FOR THE LEAGUE AND ODYSSEUS.
AND YOU PLANTED A TROJAN HORSE INTO HIS MIND.
AFTER YOU KILLED YOUR FATHER, HE WAS TO TURN ON THE LEAGUE.
THESE THE SAME "TRUTH SERUM" COCKTAIL YOU GAVE ME, "RED FURY"?
STAY OUT OF MY CASE.
Nt
RADIO SIGNALS. ONLY HE CAN HEAR IT. IT'LL UNLOCK HIS MIND SO HE CAN TELL US WHAT HE KNOWS.
BZSHHZZZPHSHHH
THEN I'LL SEND HIM BACK TO ODYSSEUS. HE'LL TELL HIM THAT HE KILLED YOU. ODYSSEUS WILL *BELIEVE* HIM BECAUSE HE CAN SEE THROUGH ANY MAN'S LIES.
AND YOU'LL GIVE TIGGS THE FALSE MEMORY OF HIM KILLING ME?
AT LEAST GIVE ME A GOOD DEATH. I DON'T GO DOWN EASY.
RGHH! STOP!

GAHRGHHHHH!

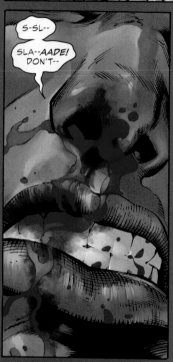

S-SL-- SLA--AADE! DON'T--

COME OUT OF THERE, TIGGS. TALK TO ME.

THIS IS NORMAL, RIGHT, RED?

K-KILL--

KILL, WHO? WHAT'S HAPPENING TO HIM?

I-I DON'T KNOW. HE'S HAVING TROUBLE COMING OUT OF IT.

K--RGHHHH!-- K-KILL--

HER!

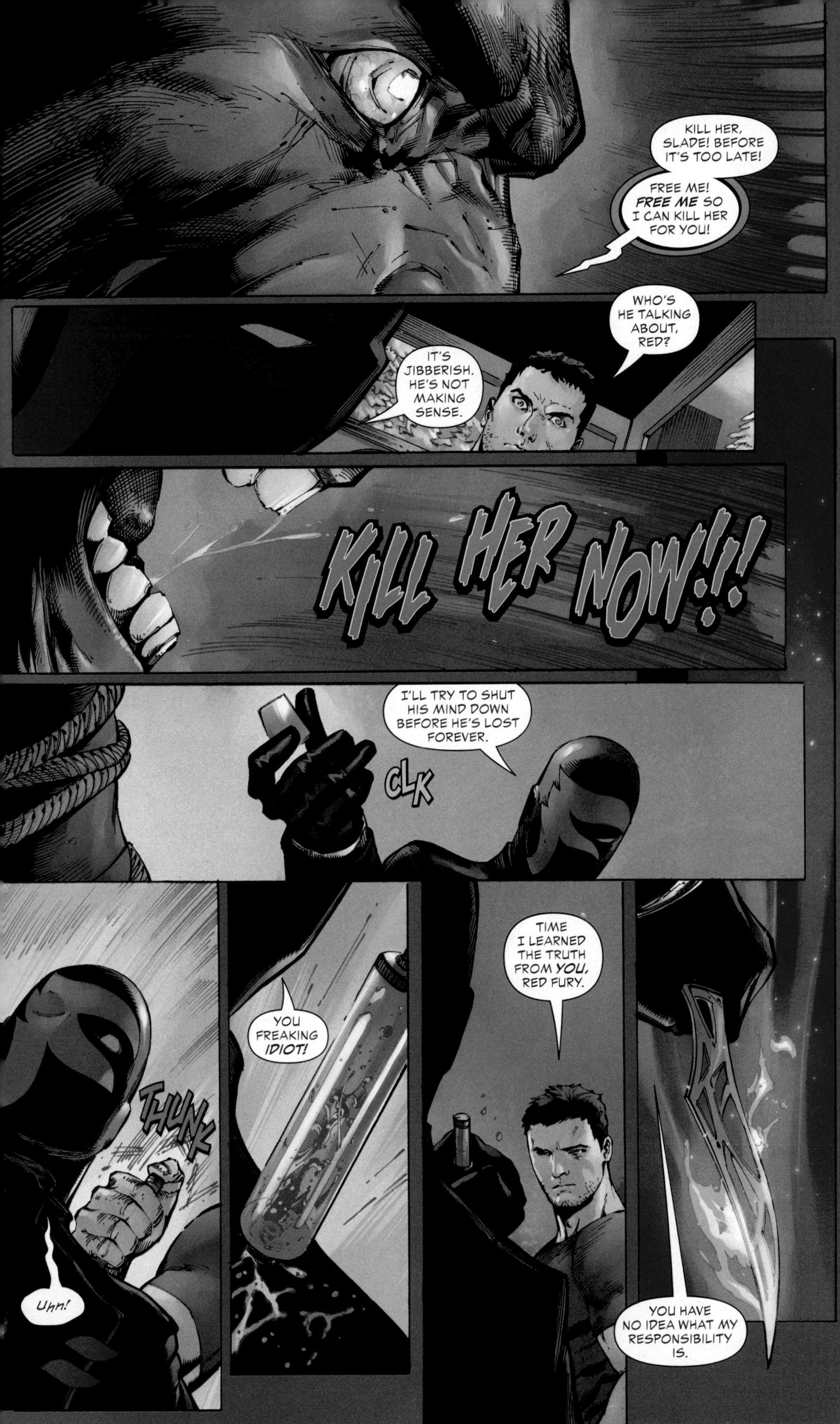
KILL HER, SLADE! BEFORE IT'S TOO LATE!
FREE ME! *FREE ME* SO I CAN KILL HER FOR YOU!
WHO'S HE TALKING ABOUT, RED?
IT'S JIBBERISH. HE'S NOT MAKING SENSE.
KILL HER NOW!!!
I'LL TRY TO SHUT HIS MIND DOWN BEFORE HE'S LOST FOREVER.
CLK
THUNK
Uhn!
YOU FREAKING *IDIOT!*
TIME I LEARNED THE TRUTH FROM *YOU,* RED FURY.
YOU HAVE NO IDEA WHAT MY RESPONSIBILITY IS.

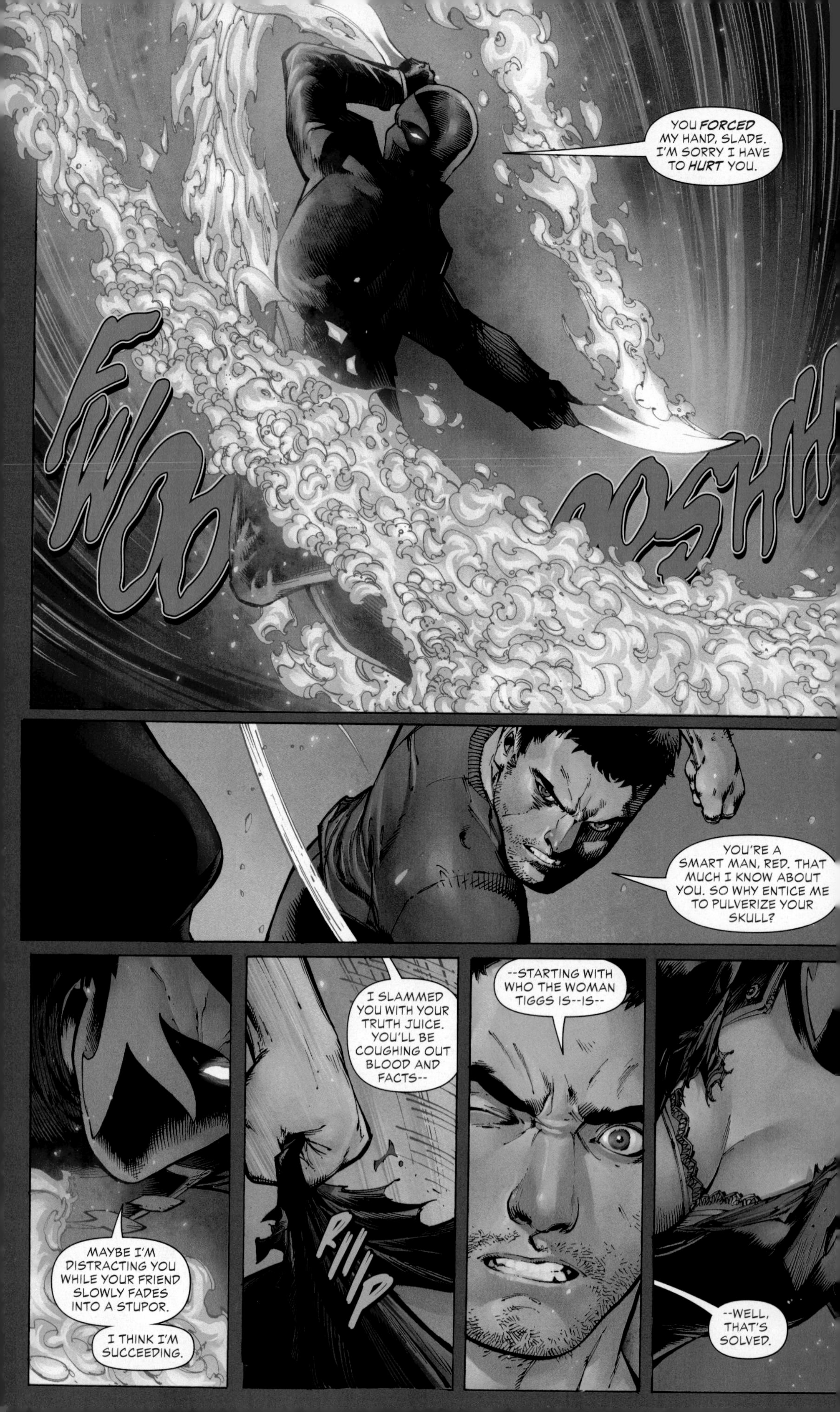
YOU *FORCED* MY HAND, SLADE. I'M SORRY I HAVE TO *HURT* YOU.
FWOOOSHH
YOU'RE A SMART MAN, RED. THAT MUCH I KNOW ABOUT YOU. SO WHY ENTICE ME TO PULVERIZE YOUR SKULL?
MAYBE I'M DISTRACTING YOU WHILE YOUR FRIEND SLOWLY FADES INTO A STUPOR.
I THINK I'M SUCCEEDING.
I SLAMMED YOU WITH YOUR TRUTH JUICE. YOU'LL BE COUGHING OUT BLOOD AND FACTS--
RIIIP
--STARTING WITH WHO THE WOMAN TIGGS IS--IS--
--WELL, THAT'S SOLVED.

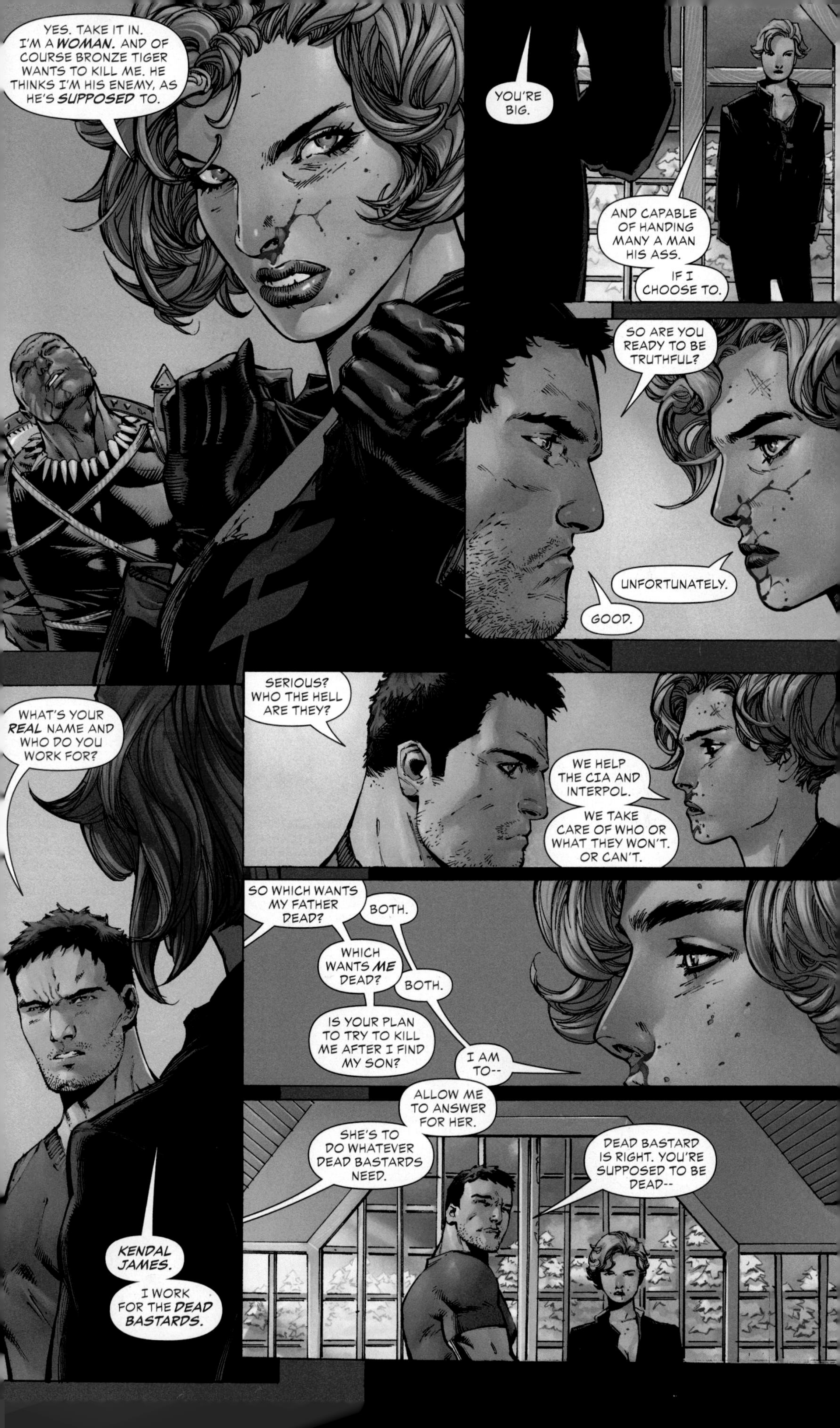

YES. TAKE IT IN. I'M A WOMAN. AND OF COURSE BRONZE TIGER WANTS TO KILL ME. HE THINKS I'M HIS ENEMY, AS HE'S SUPPOSED TO.
YOU'RE BIG.
AND CAPABLE OF HANDING MANY A MAN HIS ASS.
IF I CHOOSE TO.
SO ARE YOU READY TO BE TRUTHFUL?
UNFORTUNATELY.
GOOD.
WHAT'S YOUR REAL NAME AND WHO DO YOU WORK FOR?
KENDAL JAMES.
I WORK FOR THE DEAD BASTARDS.
SERIOUS? WHO THE HELL ARE THEY?
WE HELP THE CIA AND INTERPOL.
WE TAKE CARE OF WHO OR WHAT THEY WON'T. OR CAN'T.
SO WHICH WANTS MY FATHER DEAD?
BOTH.
WHICH WANTS ME DEAD?
BOTH.
IS YOUR PLAN TO TRY TO KILL ME AFTER I FIND MY SON?
I AM TO--
ALLOW ME TO ANSWER FOR HER.
SHE'S TO DO WHATEVER DEAD BASTARDS NEED.
DEAD BASTARD IS RIGHT. YOU'RE SUPPOSED TO BE DEAD--

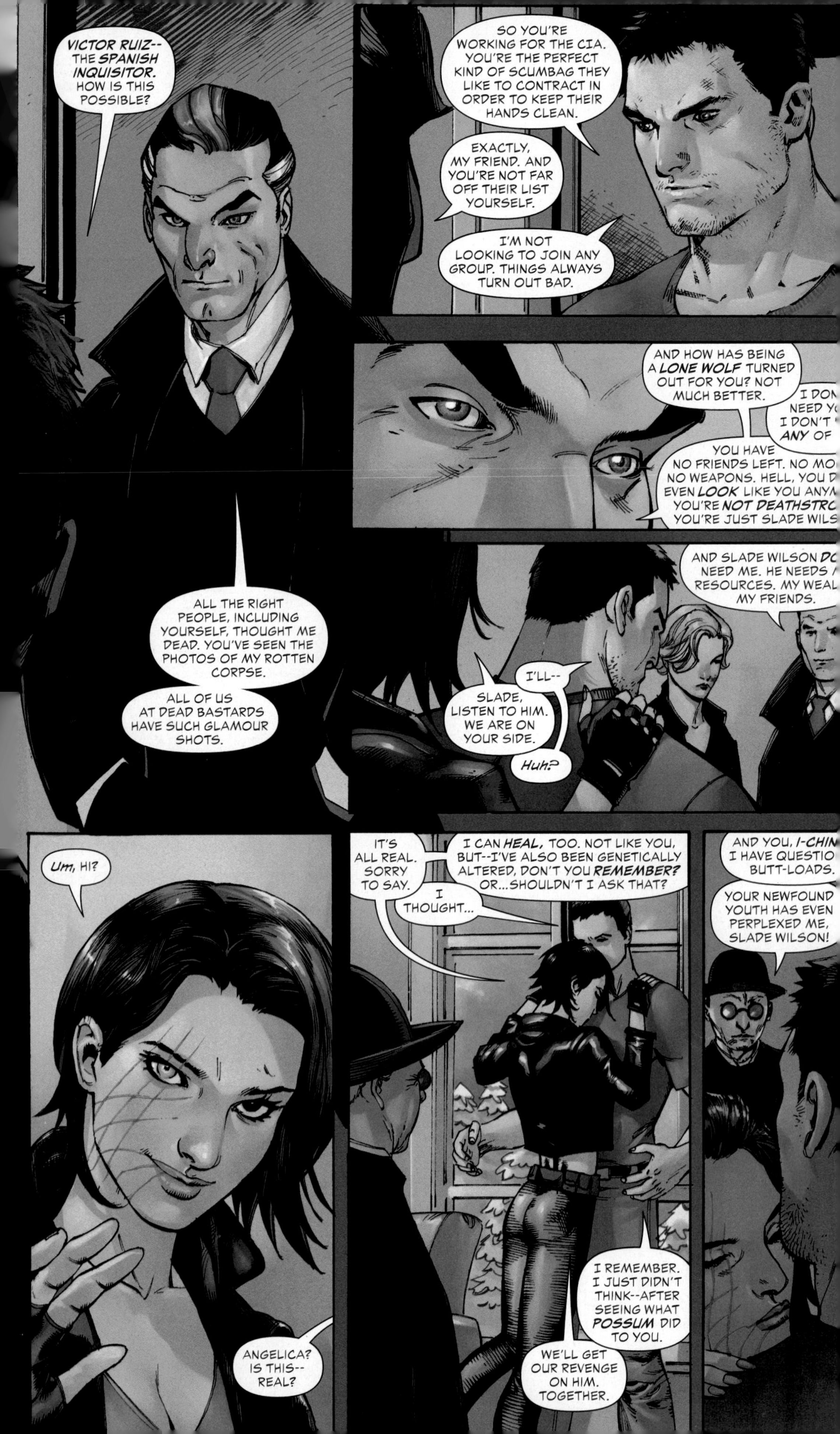

VICTOR RUIZ-- THE SPANISH INQUISITOR. HOW IS THIS POSSIBLE?
ALL THE RIGHT PEOPLE, INCLUDING YOURSELF, THOUGHT ME DEAD. YOU'VE SEEN THE PHOTOS OF MY ROTTEN CORPSE.
ALL OF US AT DEAD BASTARDS HAVE SUCH GLAMOUR SHOTS.
SO YOU'RE WORKING FOR THE CIA. YOU'RE THE PERFECT KIND OF SCUMBAG THEY LIKE TO CONTRACT IN ORDER TO KEEP THEIR HANDS CLEAN.
EXACTLY, MY FRIEND. AND YOU'RE NOT FAR OFF THEIR LIST YOURSELF.
I'M NOT LOOKING TO JOIN ANY GROUP. THINGS ALWAYS TURN OUT BAD.
AND HOW HAS BEING A LONE WOLF TURNED OUT FOR YOU? NOT MUCH BETTER.
I DON NEED YO I DON'T ANY OF
YOU HAVE NO FRIENDS LEFT. NO MO NO WEAPONS. HELL, YOU D EVEN LOOK LIKE YOU ANYM YOU'RE NOT DEATHSTRO YOU'RE JUST SLADE WILS
AND SLADE WILSON DO NEED ME. HE NEEDS RESOURCES. MY WEAL MY FRIENDS.
I'LL--
SLADE, LISTEN TO HIM. WE ARE ON YOUR SIDE.
Huh?
Um, HI?
ANGELICA? IS THIS-- REAL?
IT'S ALL REAL. SORRY TO SAY.
I THOUGHT...
I CAN HEAL, TOO. NOT LIKE YOU, BUT--I'VE ALSO BEEN GENETICALLY ALTERED, DON'T YOU REMEMBER? OR...SHOULDN'T I ASK THAT?
I REMEMBER. I JUST DIDN'T THINK--AFTER SEEING WHAT POSSUM DID TO YOU.
WE'LL GET OUR REVENGE ON HIM. TOGETHER.
AND YOU, I-CHIN I HAVE QUESTIO BUTT-LOADS.
YOUR NEWFOUND YOUTH HAS EVEN PERPLEXED ME, SLADE WILSON!

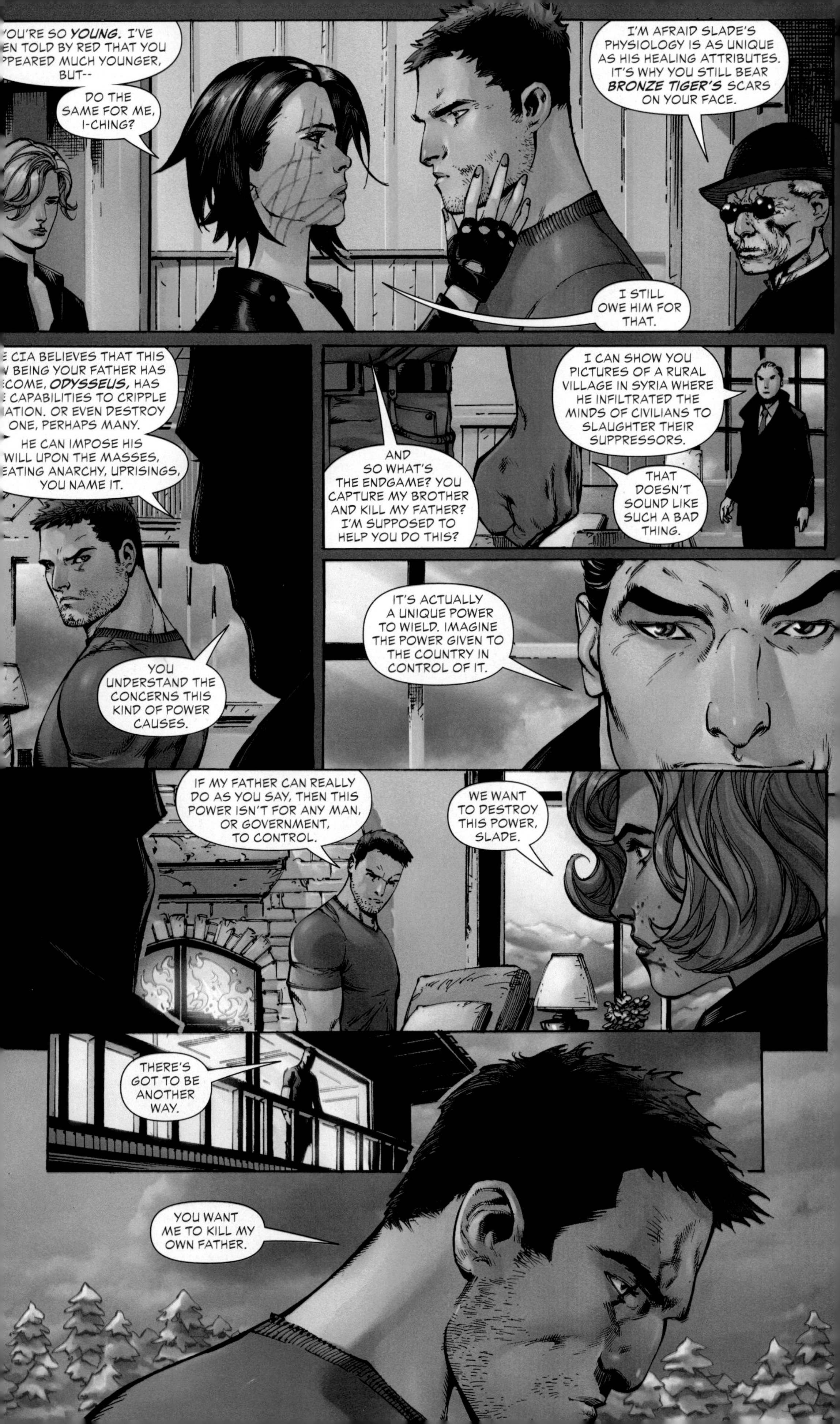

OU'RE SO YOUNG. I'VE EN TOLD BY RED THAT YOU PPEARED MUCH YOUNGER, BUT--
DO THE SAME FOR ME, I-CHING?
I'M AFRAID SLADE'S PHYSIOLOGY IS AS UNIQUE AS HIS HEALING ATTRIBUTES. IT'S WHY YOU STILL BEAR BRONZE TIGER'S SCARS ON YOUR FACE.
I STILL OWE HIM FOR THAT.
E CIA BELIEVES THAT THIS V BEING YOUR FATHER HAS ECOME, ODYSSEUS, HAS E CAPABILITIES TO CRIPPLE IATION. OR EVEN DESTROY ONE, PERHAPS MANY.
HE CAN IMPOSE HIS WILL UPON THE MASSES, EATING ANARCHY, UPRISINGS, YOU NAME IT.
YOU UNDERSTAND THE CONCERNS THIS KIND OF POWER CAUSES.
AND SO WHAT'S THE ENDGAME? YOU CAPTURE MY BROTHER AND KILL MY FATHER? I'M SUPPOSED TO HELP YOU DO THIS?
I CAN SHOW YOU PICTURES OF A RURAL VILLAGE IN SYRIA WHERE HE INFILTRATED THE MINDS OF CIVILIANS TO SLAUGHTER THEIR SUPPRESSORS.
THAT DOESN'T SOUND LIKE SUCH A BAD THING.
IT'S ACTUALLY A UNIQUE POWER TO WIELD. IMAGINE THE POWER GIVEN TO THE COUNTRY IN CONTROL OF IT.
IF MY FATHER CAN REALLY DO AS YOU SAY, THEN THIS POWER ISN'T FOR ANY MAN, OR GOVERNMENT, TO CONTROL.
WE WANT TO DESTROY THIS POWER, SLADE.
THERE'S GOT TO BE ANOTHER WAY.
YOU WANT ME TO KILL MY OWN FATHER.

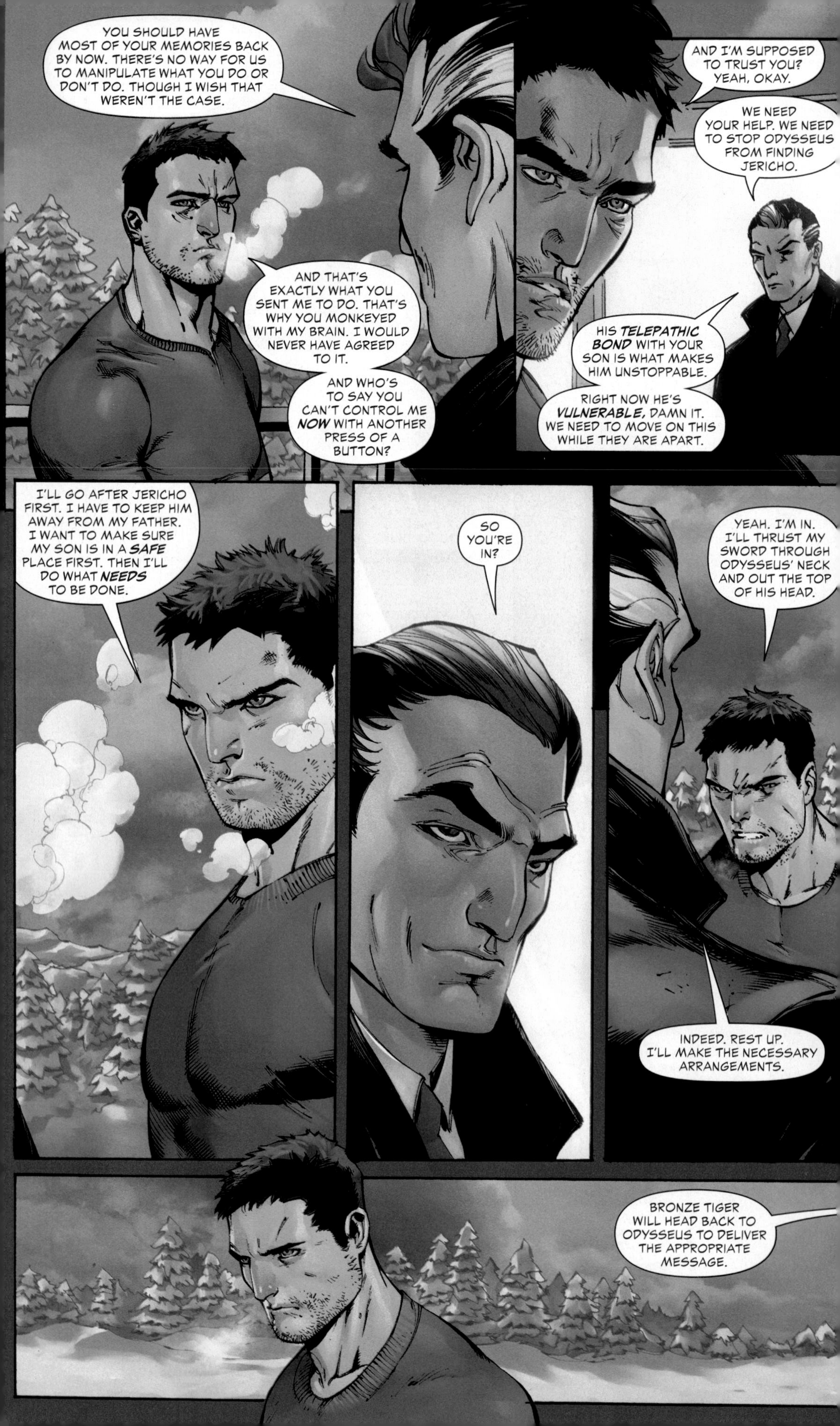
YOU SHOULD HAVE MOST OF YOUR MEMORIES BACK BY NOW. THERE'S NO WAY FOR US TO MANIPULATE WHAT YOU DO OR DON'T DO. THOUGH I WISH THAT WEREN'T THE CASE.
AND THAT'S EXACTLY WHAT YOU SENT ME TO DO. THAT'S WHY YOU MONKEYED WITH MY BRAIN. I WOULD NEVER HAVE AGREED TO IT.
AND WHO'S TO SAY YOU CAN'T CONTROL ME *NOW* WITH ANOTHER PRESS OF A BUTTON?
AND I'M SUPPOSED TO TRUST YOU? YEAH, OKAY.
WE NEED YOUR HELP. WE NEED TO STOP ODYSSEUS FROM FINDING JERICHO.
HIS *TELEPATHIC BOND* WITH YOUR SON IS WHAT MAKES HIM UNSTOPPABLE.
RIGHT NOW HE'S *VULNERABLE,* DAMN IT. WE NEED TO MOVE ON THIS WHILE THEY ARE APART.
I'LL GO AFTER JERICHO FIRST. I HAVE TO KEEP HIM AWAY FROM MY FATHER. I WANT TO MAKE SURE MY SON IS IN A *SAFE* PLACE FIRST. THEN I'LL DO WHAT *NEEDS* TO BE DONE.
SO YOU'RE IN?
YEAH. I'M IN. I'LL THRUST MY SWORD THROUGH ODYSSEUS' NECK AND OUT THE TOP OF HIS HEAD.
INDEED. REST UP. I'LL MAKE THE NECESSARY ARRANGEMENTS.
BRONZE TIGER WILL HEAD BACK TO ODYSSEUS TO DELIVER THE APPROPRIATE MESSAGE.

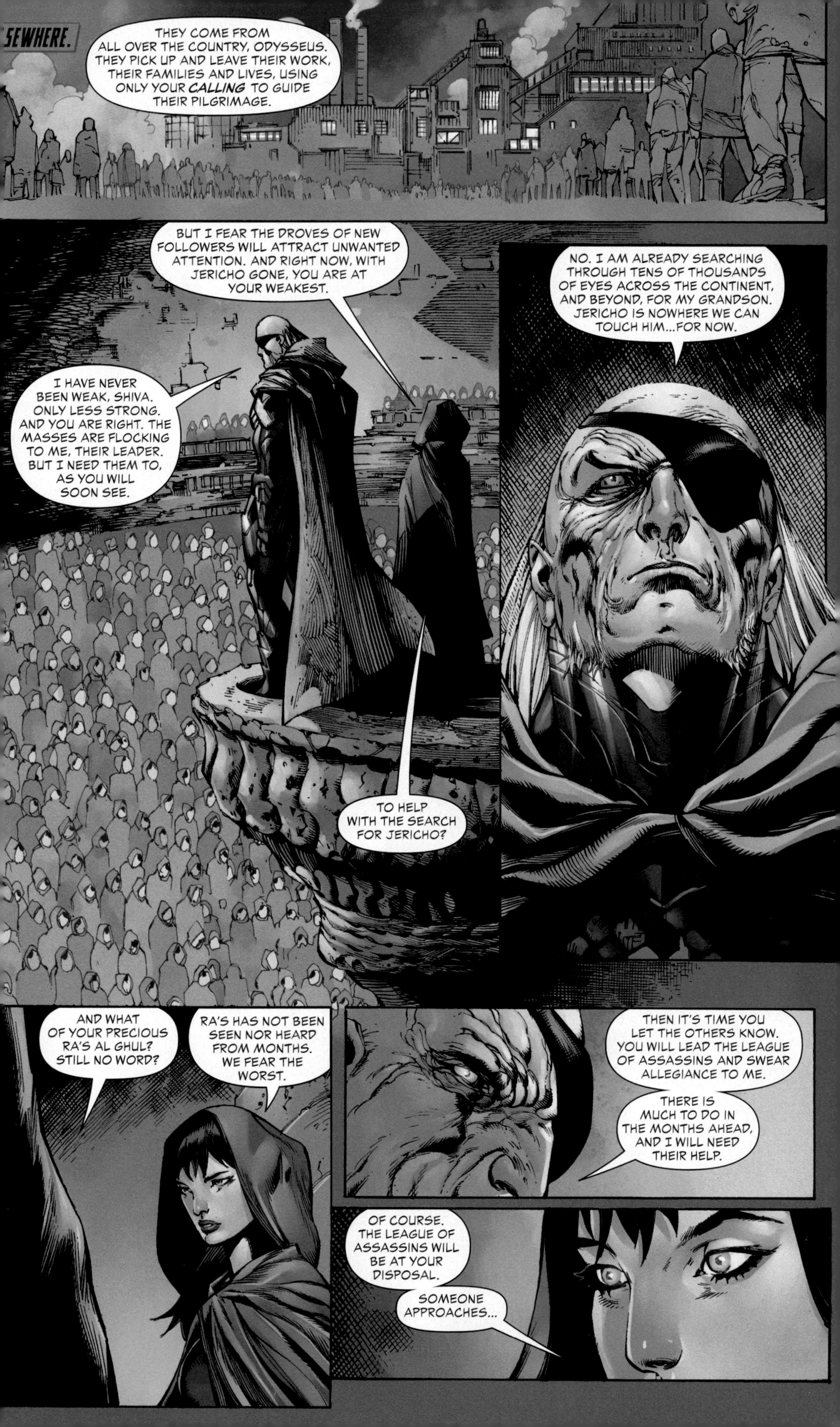
SEWHERE.
THEY COME FROM ALL OVER THE COUNTRY, ODYSSEUS. THEY PICK UP AND LEAVE THEIR WORK, THEIR FAMILIES AND LIVES, USING ONLY YOUR CALLING TO GUIDE THEIR PILGRIMAGE.
BUT I FEAR THE DROVES OF NEW FOLLOWERS WILL ATTRACT UNWANTED ATTENTION. AND RIGHT NOW, WITH JERICHO GONE, YOU ARE AT YOUR WEAKEST.
I HAVE NEVER BEEN WEAK, SHIVA. ONLY LESS STRONG. AND YOU ARE RIGHT. THE MASSES ARE FLOCKING TO ME, THEIR LEADER. BUT I NEED THEM TO, AS YOU WILL SOON SEE.
TO HELP WITH THE SEARCH FOR JERICHO?
NO. I AM ALREADY SEARCHING THROUGH TENS OF THOUSANDS OF EYES ACROSS THE CONTINENT, AND BEYOND, FOR MY GRANDSON. JERICHO IS NOWHERE WE CAN TOUCH HIM...FOR NOW.
AND WHAT OF YOUR PRECIOUS RA'S AL GHUL? STILL NO WORD?
RA'S HAS NOT BEEN SEEN NOR HEARD FROM MONTHS. WE FEAR THE WORST.
THEN IT'S TIME YOU LET THE OTHERS KNOW. YOU WILL LEAD THE LEAGUE OF ASSASSINS AND SWEAR ALLEGIANCE TO ME.
THERE IS MUCH TO DO IN THE MONTHS AHEAD, AND I WILL NEED THEIR HELP.
OF COURSE. THE LEAGUE OF ASSASSINS WILL BE AT YOUR DISPOSAL.
SOMEONE APPROACHES...

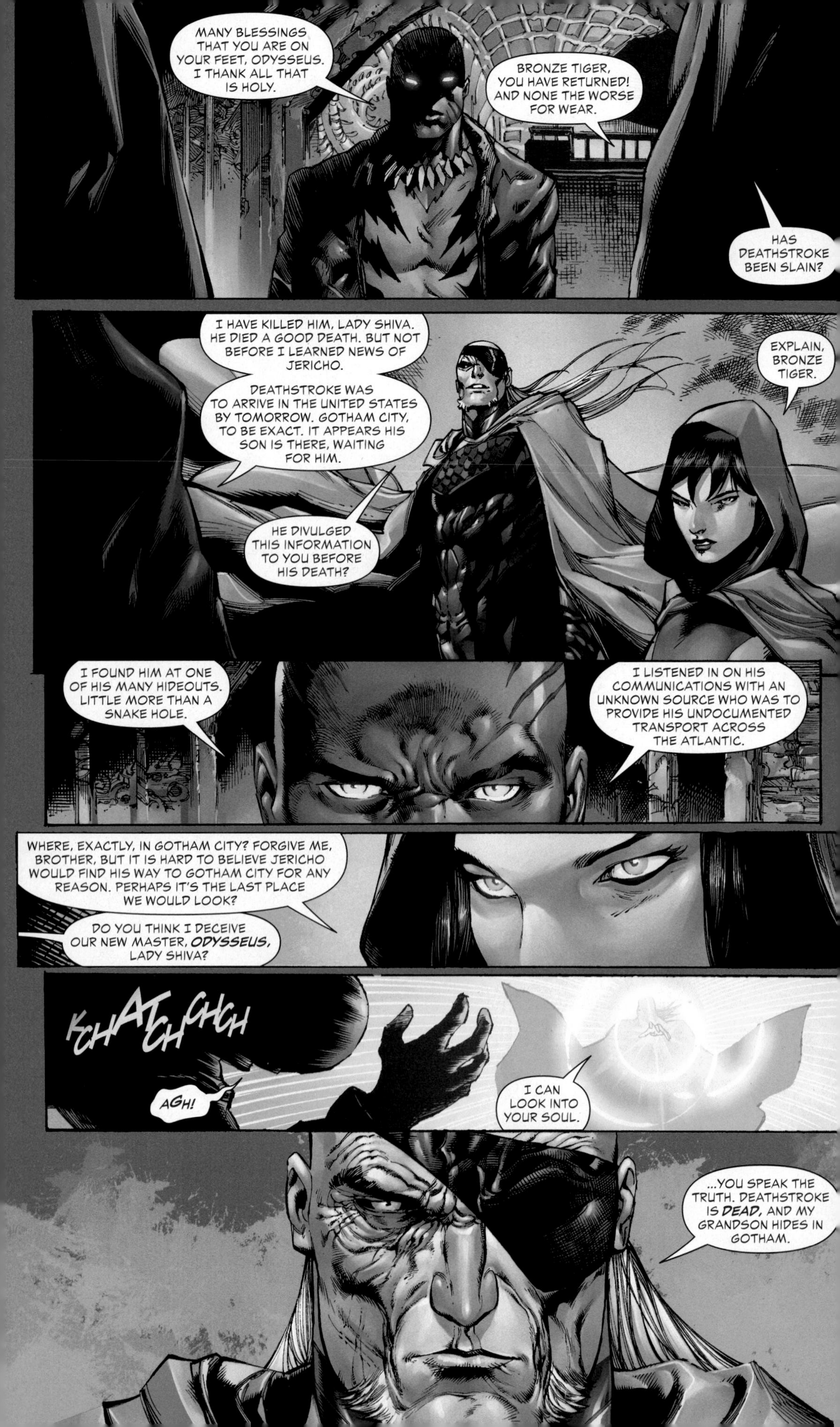
MANY BLESSINGS THAT YOU ARE ON YOUR FEET, ODYSSEUS. I THANK ALL THAT IS HOLY.
BRONZE TIGER, YOU HAVE RETURNED! AND NONE THE WORSE FOR WEAR.
HAS DEATHSTROKE BEEN SLAIN?
I HAVE KILLED HIM, LADY SHIVA. HE DIED A GOOD DEATH. BUT NOT BEFORE I LEARNED NEWS OF JERICHO.
DEATHSTROKE WAS TO ARRIVE IN THE UNITED STATES BY TOMORROW. GOTHAM CITY, TO BE EXACT. IT APPEARS HIS SON IS THERE, WAITING FOR HIM.
EXPLAIN, BRONZE TIGER.
HE DIVULGED THIS INFORMATION TO YOU BEFORE HIS DEATH?
I FOUND HIM AT ONE OF HIS MANY HIDEOUTS. LITTLE MORE THAN A SNAKE HOLE.
I LISTENED IN ON HIS COMMUNICATIONS WITH AN UNKNOWN SOURCE WHO WAS TO PROVIDE HIS UNDOCUMENTED TRANSPORT ACROSS THE ATLANTIC.
WHERE, EXACTLY, IN GOTHAM CITY? FORGIVE ME, BROTHER, BUT IT IS HARD TO BELIEVE JERICHO WOULD FIND HIS WAY TO GOTHAM CITY FOR ANY REASON. PERHAPS IT'S THE LAST PLACE WE WOULD LOOK?
DO YOU THINK I DECEIVE OUR NEW MASTER, *ODYSSEUS,* LADY SHIVA?
KCHATCHCHCH
AGH!
I CAN LOOK INTO YOUR SOUL.
...YOU SPEAK THE TRUTH. DEATHSTROKE IS *DEAD,* AND MY GRANDSON HIDES IN GOTHAM.

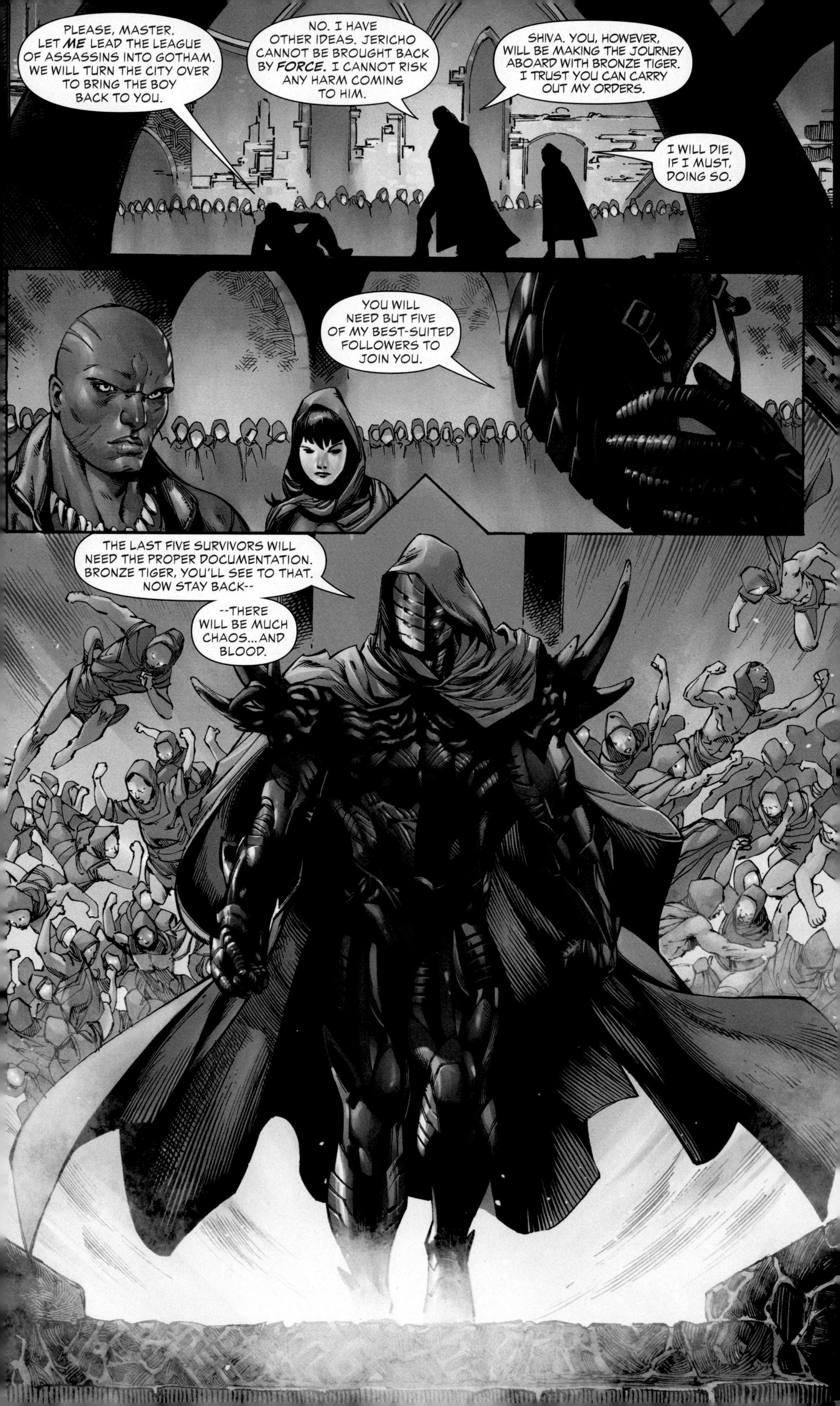
PLEASE, MASTER. LET ME LEAD THE LEAGUE OF ASSASSINS INTO GOTHAM. WE WILL TURN THE CITY OVER TO BRING THE BOY BACK TO YOU.
NO. I HAVE OTHER IDEAS. JERICHO CANNOT BE BROUGHT BACK BY FORCE. I CANNOT RISK ANY HARM COMING TO HIM.
SHIVA. YOU, HOWEVER, WILL BE MAKING THE JOURNEY ABOARD WITH BRONZE TIGER. I TRUST YOU CAN CARRY OUT MY ORDERS.
I WILL DIE, IF I MUST, DOING SO.
YOU WILL NEED BUT FIVE OF MY BEST-SUITED FOLLOWERS TO JOIN YOU.
THE LAST FIVE SURVIVORS WILL NEED THE PROPER DOCUMENTATION. BRONZE TIGER, YOU'LL SEE TO THAT. NOW STAY BACK--
--THERE WILL BE MUCH CHAOS...AND BLOOD.

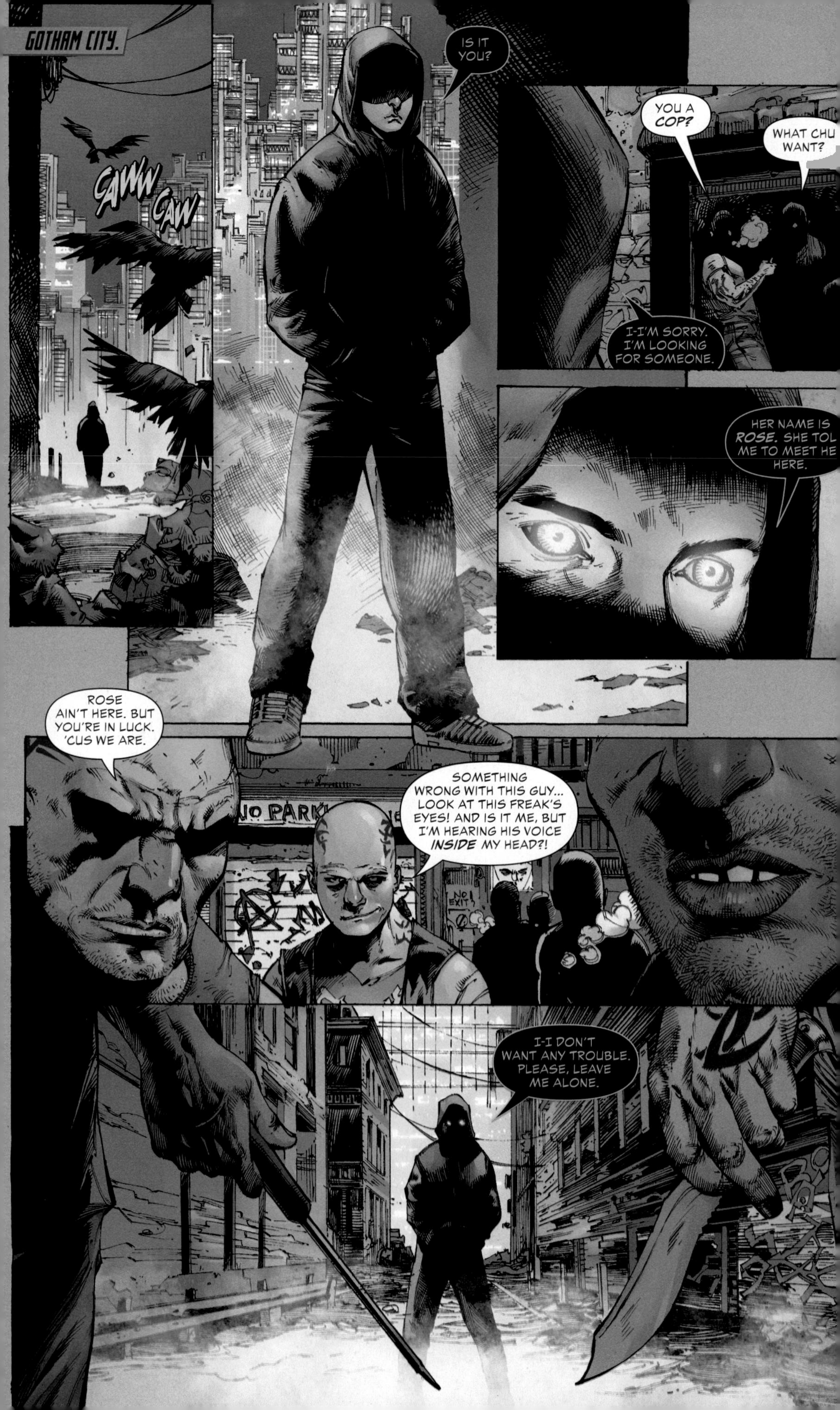
GOTHAM CITY.
CAWW CAW
IS IT YOU?
YOU A COP?
WHAT CHU WANT?
I-I'M SORRY. I'M LOOKING FOR SOMEONE.
HER NAME IS ROSE. SHE TOL ME TO MEET HE HERE.
ROSE AIN'T HERE. BUT YOU'RE IN LUCK. 'CUS WE ARE.
SOMETHING WRONG WITH THIS GUY... LOOK AT THIS FREAK'S EYES! AND IS IT ME, BUT I'M HEARING HIS VOICE INSIDE MY HEAD?!
NO PARK
NO EXIT
I-I DON'T WANT ANY TROUBLE. PLEASE, LEAVE ME ALONE.

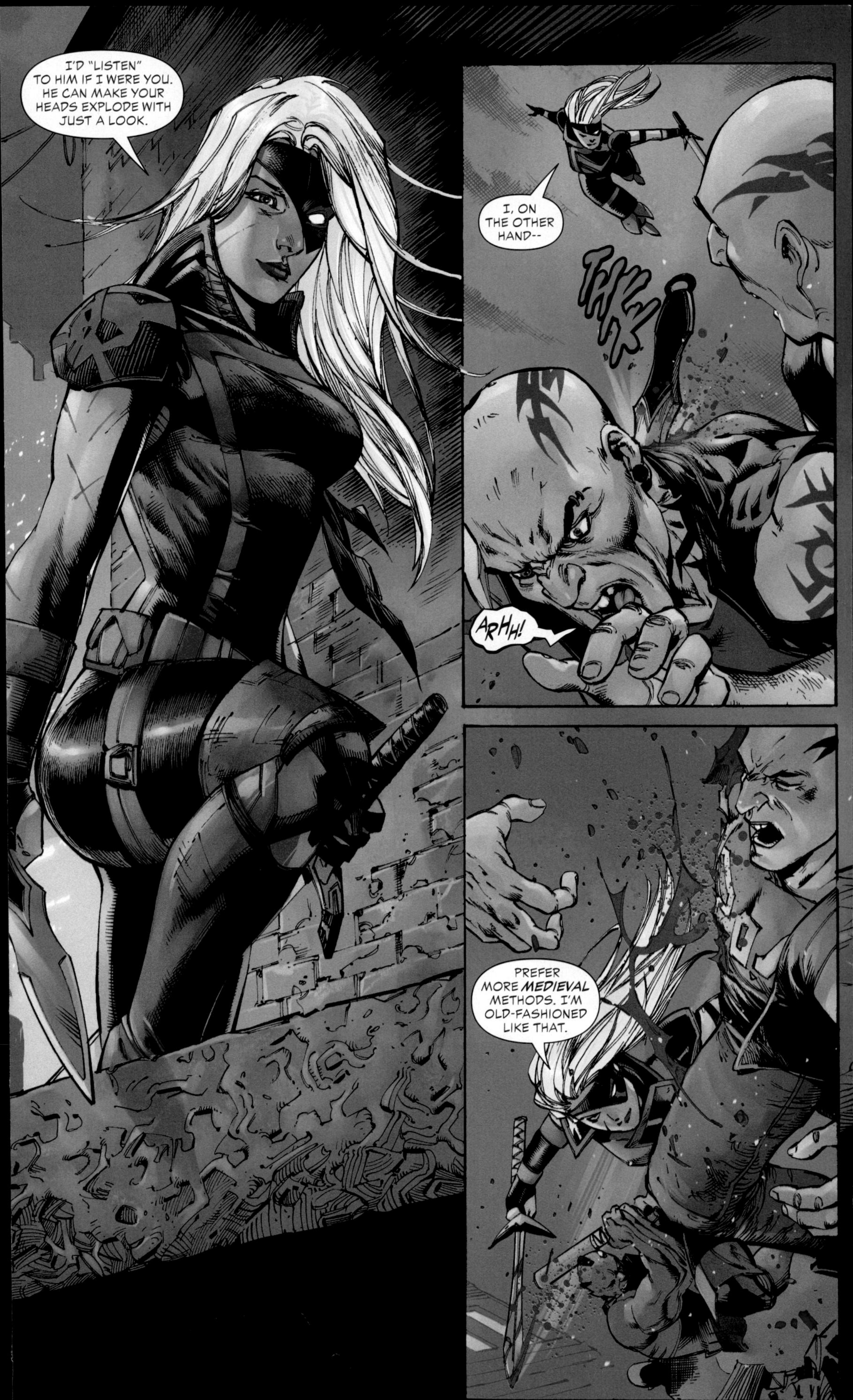
I'D "LISTEN" TO HIM IF I WERE YOU. HE CAN MAKE YOUR HEADS EXPLODE WITH JUST A LOOK.
I, ON THE OTHER HAND--
THKK
ARHH!
PREFER MORE MEDIEVAL METHODS. I'M OLD-FASHIONED LIKE THAT.

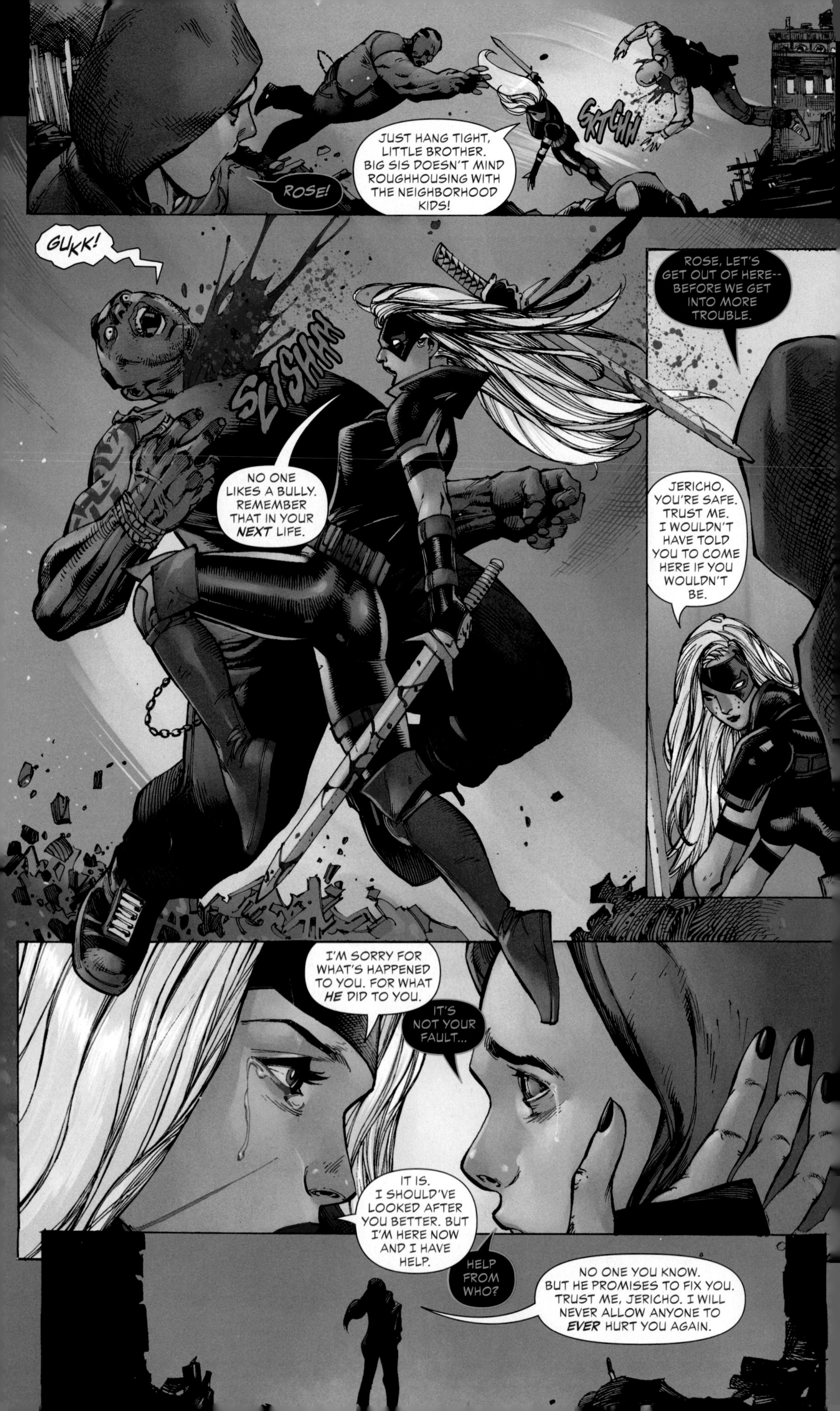

JUST HANG TIGHT, LITTLE BROTHER. BIG SIS DOESN'T MIND ROUGHHOUSING WITH THE NEIGHBORHOOD KIDS!
SKTCHH
ROSE!
GUKK!
SLISHH
NO ONE LIKES A BULLY. REMEMBER THAT IN YOUR NEXT LIFE.
ROSE, LET'S GET OUT OF HERE-- BEFORE WE GET INTO MORE TROUBLE.
JERICHO, YOU'RE SAFE. TRUST ME. I WOULDN'T HAVE TOLD YOU TO COME HERE IF YOU WOULDN'T BE.
I'M SORRY FOR WHAT'S HAPPENED TO YOU. FOR WHAT HE DID TO YOU.
IT'S NOT YOUR FAULT...
IT IS. I SHOULD'VE LOOKED AFTER YOU BETTER. BUT I'M HERE NOW AND I HAVE HELP.
HELP FROM WHO?
NO ONE YOU KNOW. BUT HE PROMISES TO FIX YOU. TRUST ME, JERICHO. I WILL NEVER ALLOW ANYONE TO EVER HURT YOU AGAIN.

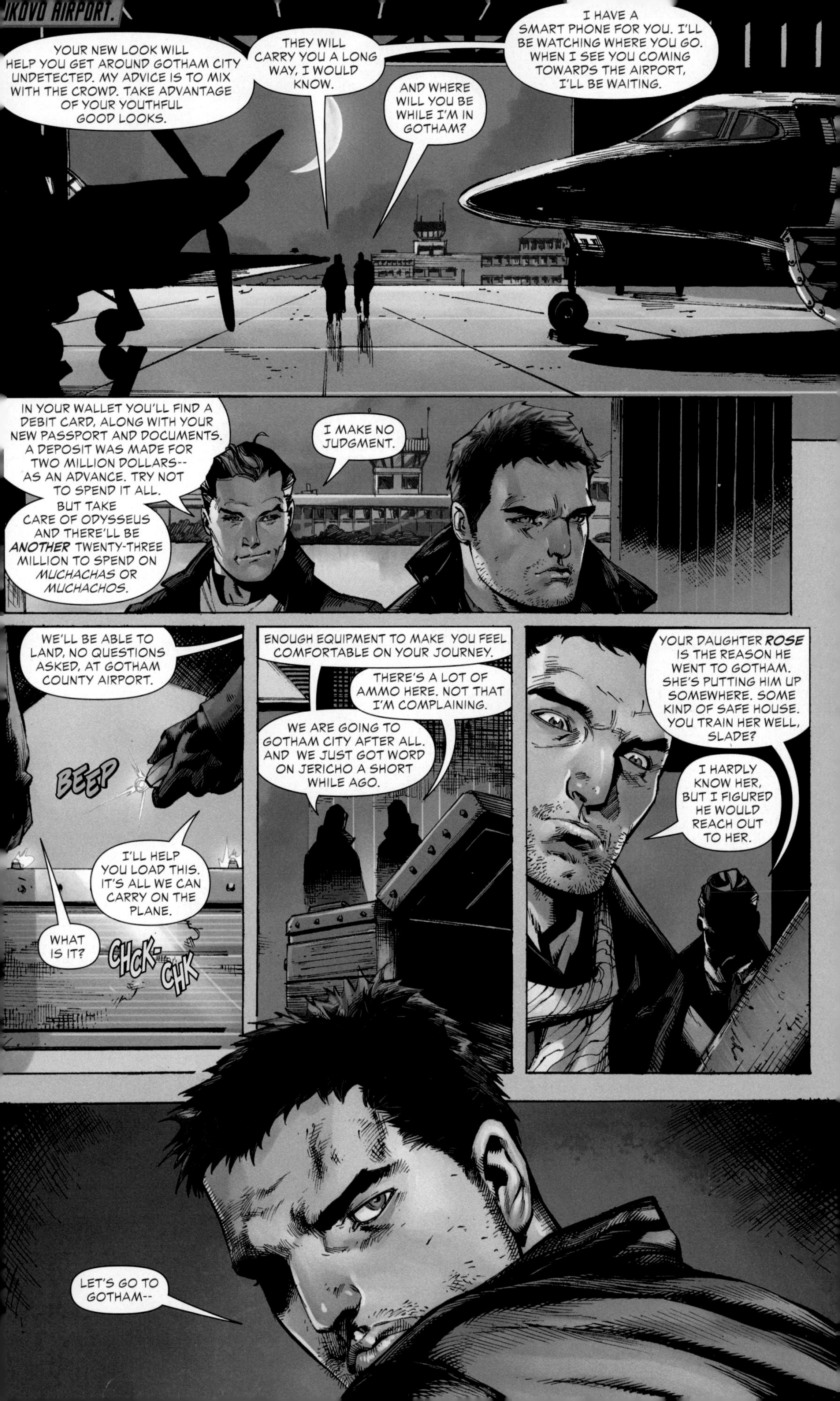

...IKOVO AIRPORT.
YOUR NEW LOOK WILL HELP YOU GET AROUND GOTHAM CITY UNDETECTED. MY ADVICE IS TO MIX WITH THE CROWD. TAKE ADVANTAGE OF YOUR YOUTHFUL GOOD LOOKS.
THEY WILL CARRY YOU A LONG WAY, I WOULD KNOW.
AND WHERE WILL YOU BE WHILE I'M IN GOTHAM?
I HAVE A SMART PHONE FOR YOU. I'LL BE WATCHING WHERE YOU GO. WHEN I SEE YOU COMING TOWARDS THE AIRPORT, I'LL BE WAITING.
IN YOUR WALLET YOU'LL FIND A DEBIT CARD, ALONG WITH YOUR NEW PASSPORT AND DOCUMENTS. A DEPOSIT WAS MADE FOR TWO MILLION DOLLARS-- AS AN ADVANCE. TRY NOT TO SPEND IT ALL.
BUT TAKE CARE OF ODYSSEUS AND THERE'LL BE ***ANOTHER*** TWENTY-THREE MILLION TO SPEND ON *MUCHACHAS* OR *MUCHACHOS*.
I MAKE NO JUDGMENT.
WE'LL BE ABLE TO LAND, NO QUESTIONS ASKED, AT GOTHAM COUNTY AIRPORT.
BEEP
WHAT IS IT?
I'LL HELP YOU LOAD THIS. IT'S ALL WE CAN CARRY ON THE PLANE.
CHCK-CHK
ENOUGH EQUIPMENT TO MAKE YOU FEEL COMFORTABLE ON YOUR JOURNEY.
THERE'S A LOT OF AMMO HERE. NOT THAT I'M COMPLAINING.
WE ARE GOING TO GOTHAM CITY AFTER ALL. AND WE JUST GOT WORD ON JERICHO A SHORT WHILE AGO.
YOUR DAUGHTER ***ROSE*** IS THE REASON HE WENT TO GOTHAM. SHE'S PUTTING HIM UP SOMEWHERE. SOME KIND OF SAFE HOUSE. YOU TRAIN HER WELL, SLADE?
I HARDLY KNOW HER, BUT I FIGURED HE WOULD REACH OUT TO HER.
LET'S GO TO GOTHAM--

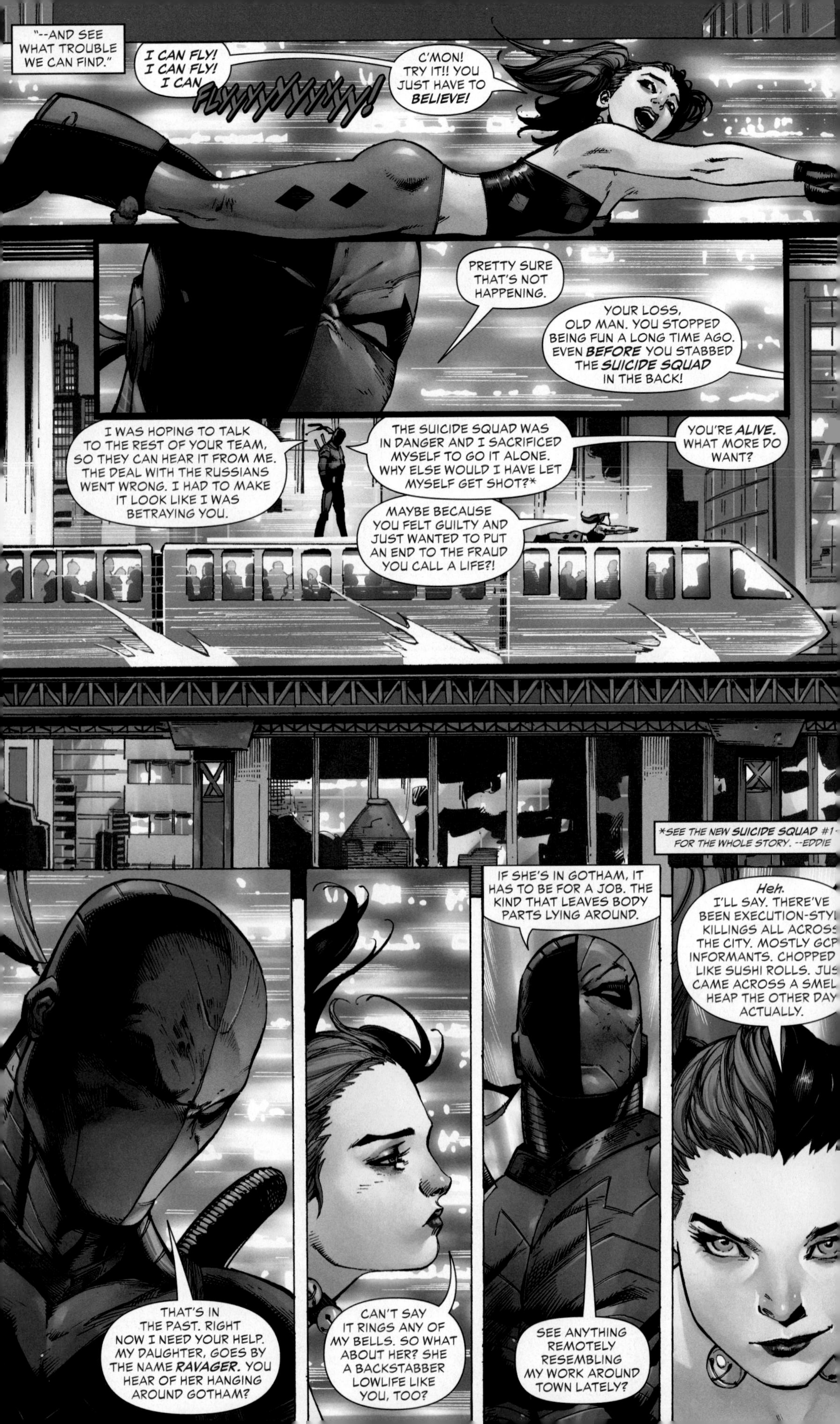
"--AND SEE WHAT TROUBLE WE CAN FIND."
I CAN FLY! I CAN FLY! I CAN FLYYYYYYYYYYY!
C'MON! TRY IT!! YOU JUST HAVE TO BELIEVE!
PRETTY SURE THAT'S NOT HAPPENING.
YOUR LOSS, OLD MAN. YOU STOPPED BEING FUN A LONG TIME AGO. EVEN BEFORE YOU STABBED THE SUICIDE SQUAD IN THE BACK!
I WAS HOPING TO TALK TO THE REST OF YOUR TEAM, SO THEY CAN HEAR IT FROM ME. THE DEAL WITH THE RUSSIANS WENT WRONG. I HAD TO MAKE IT LOOK LIKE I WAS BETRAYING YOU.
THE SUICIDE SQUAD WAS IN DANGER AND I SACRIFICED MYSELF TO GO IT ALONE. WHY ELSE WOULD I HAVE LET MYSELF GET SHOT?*
YOU'RE ALIVE. WHAT MORE DO WANT?
MAYBE BECAUSE YOU FELT GUILTY AND JUST WANTED TO PUT AN END TO THE FRAUD YOU CALL A LIFE?!
*SEE THE NEW SUICIDE SQUAD #1 FOR THE WHOLE STORY. --EDDIE
THAT'S IN THE PAST. RIGHT NOW I NEED YOUR HELP. MY DAUGHTER, GOES BY THE NAME RAVAGER. YOU HEAR OF HER HANGING AROUND GOTHAM?
CAN'T SAY IT RINGS ANY OF MY BELLS. SO WHAT ABOUT HER? SHE A BACKSTABBER LOWLIFE LIKE YOU, TOO?
IF SHE'S IN GOTHAM, IT HAS TO BE FOR A JOB. THE KIND THAT LEAVES BODY PARTS LYING AROUND.
SEE ANYTHING REMOTELY RESEMBLING MY WORK AROUND TOWN LATELY?
Heh. I'LL SAY. THERE'VE BEEN EXECUTION-STYL KILLINGS ALL ACROSS THE CITY. MOSTLY GCP INFORMANTS. CHOPPED LIKE SUSHI ROLLS. JUS CAME ACROSS A SMEL HEAP THE OTHER DAY ACTUALLY.

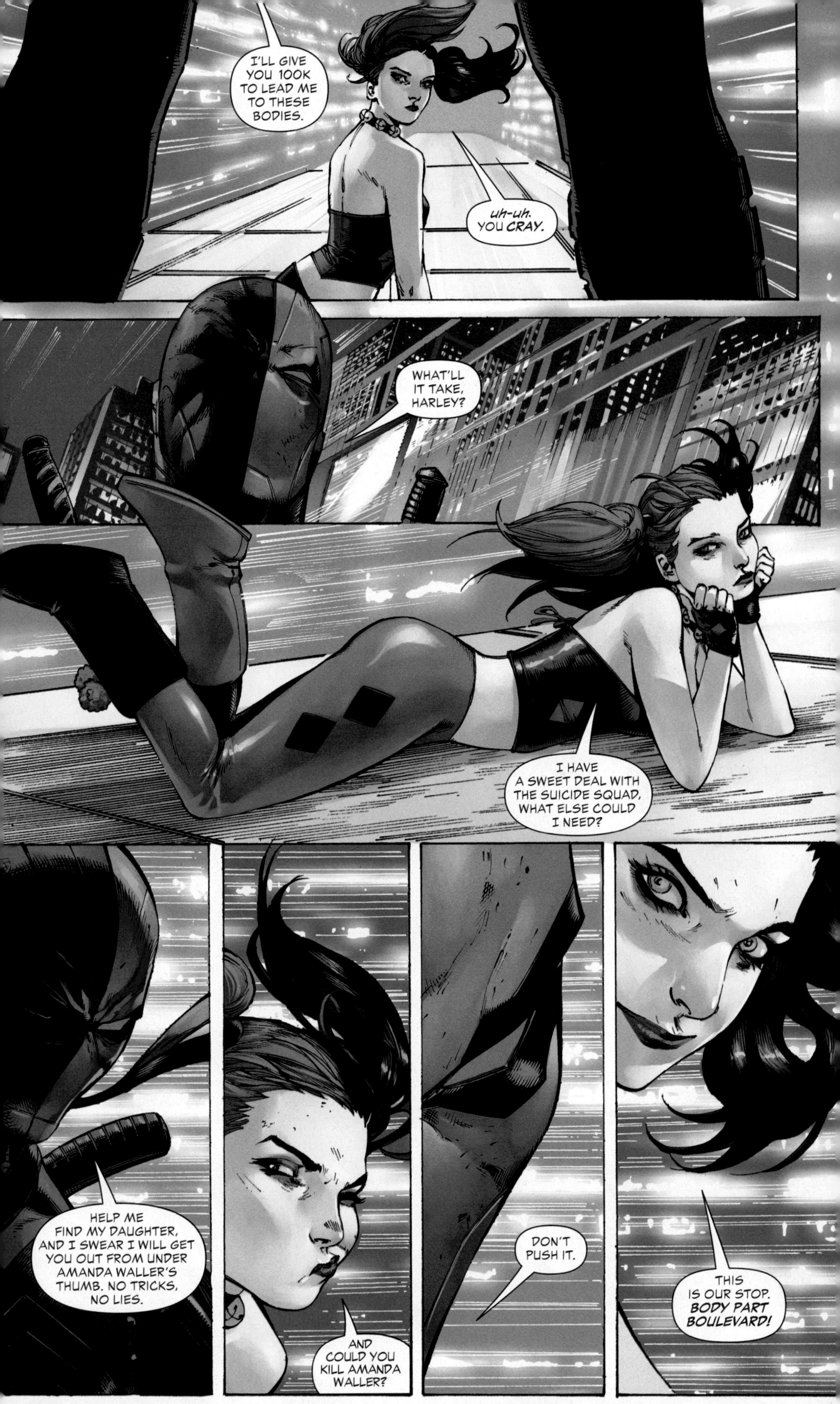
I'LL GIVE YOU 100K TO LEAD ME TO THESE BODIES.
uh-uh. YOU ***CRAY.***
WHAT'LL IT TAKE, HARLEY?
I HAVE A SWEET DEAL WITH THE SUICIDE SQUAD, WHAT ELSE COULD I NEED?
HELP ME FIND MY DAUGHTER, AND I SWEAR I WILL GET YOU OUT FROM UNDER AMANDA WALLER'S THUMB. NO TRICKS, NO LIES.
AND COULD YOU KILL AMANDA WALLER?
DON'T PUSH IT.
THIS IS OUR STOP. ***BODY PART BOULEVARD!***

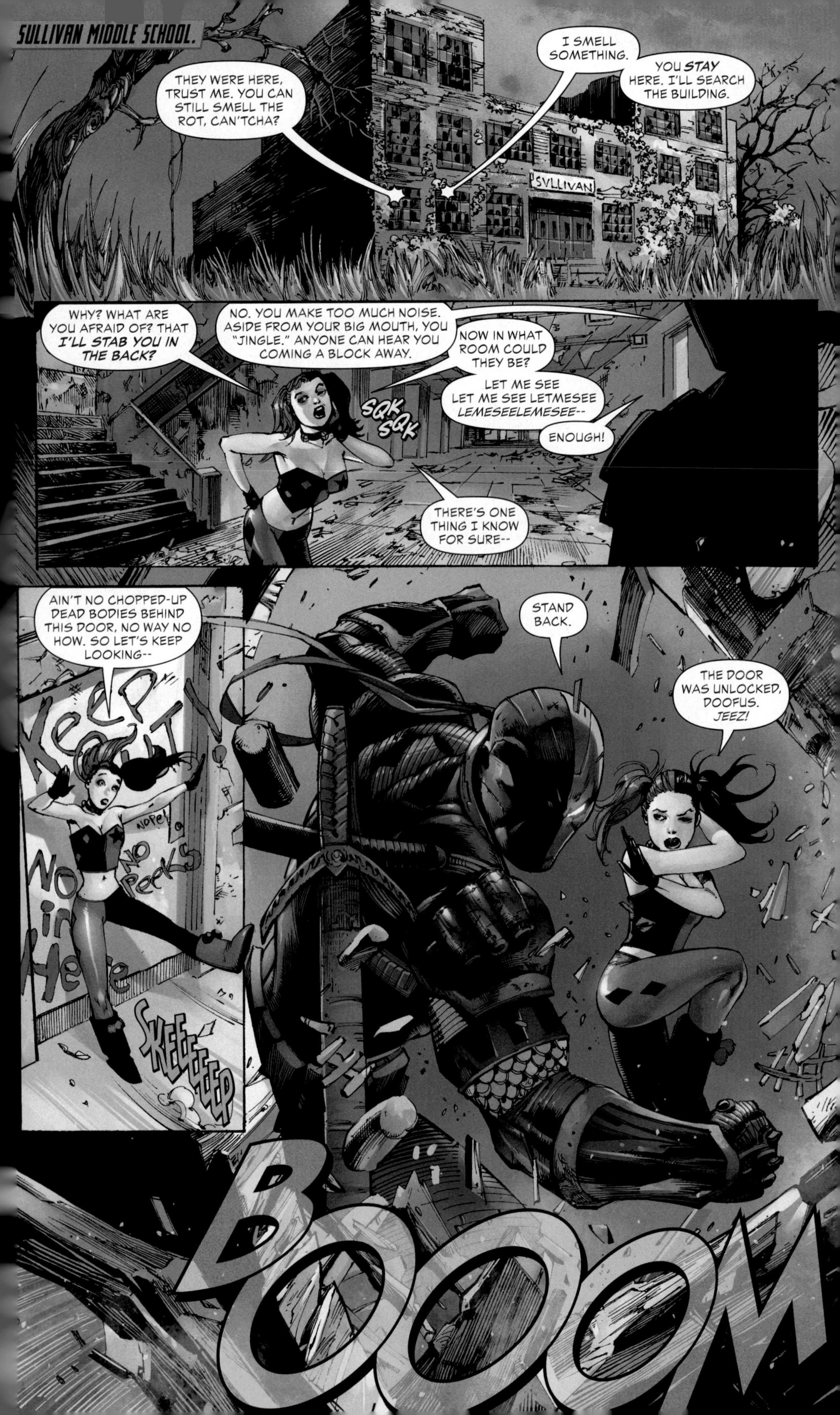
SULLIVAN MIDDLE SCHOOL.
THEY WERE HERE, TRUST ME. YOU CAN STILL SMELL THE ROT, CAN'TCHA?
I SMELL SOMETHING.
YOU STAY HERE. I'LL SEARCH THE BUILDING.
SVLLIVAN
WHY? WHAT ARE YOU AFRAID OF? THAT I'LL STAB YOU IN THE BACK?
NO. YOU MAKE TOO MUCH NOISE. ASIDE FROM YOUR BIG MOUTH, YOU "JINGLE." ANYONE CAN HEAR YOU COMING A BLOCK AWAY.
NOW IN WHAT ROOM COULD THEY BE?
LET ME SEE LET ME SEE LETMESEE LEMESEELEMESEE--
SQK SQK
ENOUGH!
THERE'S ONE THING I KNOW FOR SURE--
AIN'T NO CHOPPED-UP DEAD BODIES BEHIND THIS DOOR, NO WAY NO HOW. SO LET'S KEEP LOOKING--
KEEP OUT
NOPE!
NO PEEKS
NO ... in Here
SKEEEEEEP
STAND BACK.
THE DOOR WAS UNLOCKED, DOOFUS. JEEZ!
BOOOOM

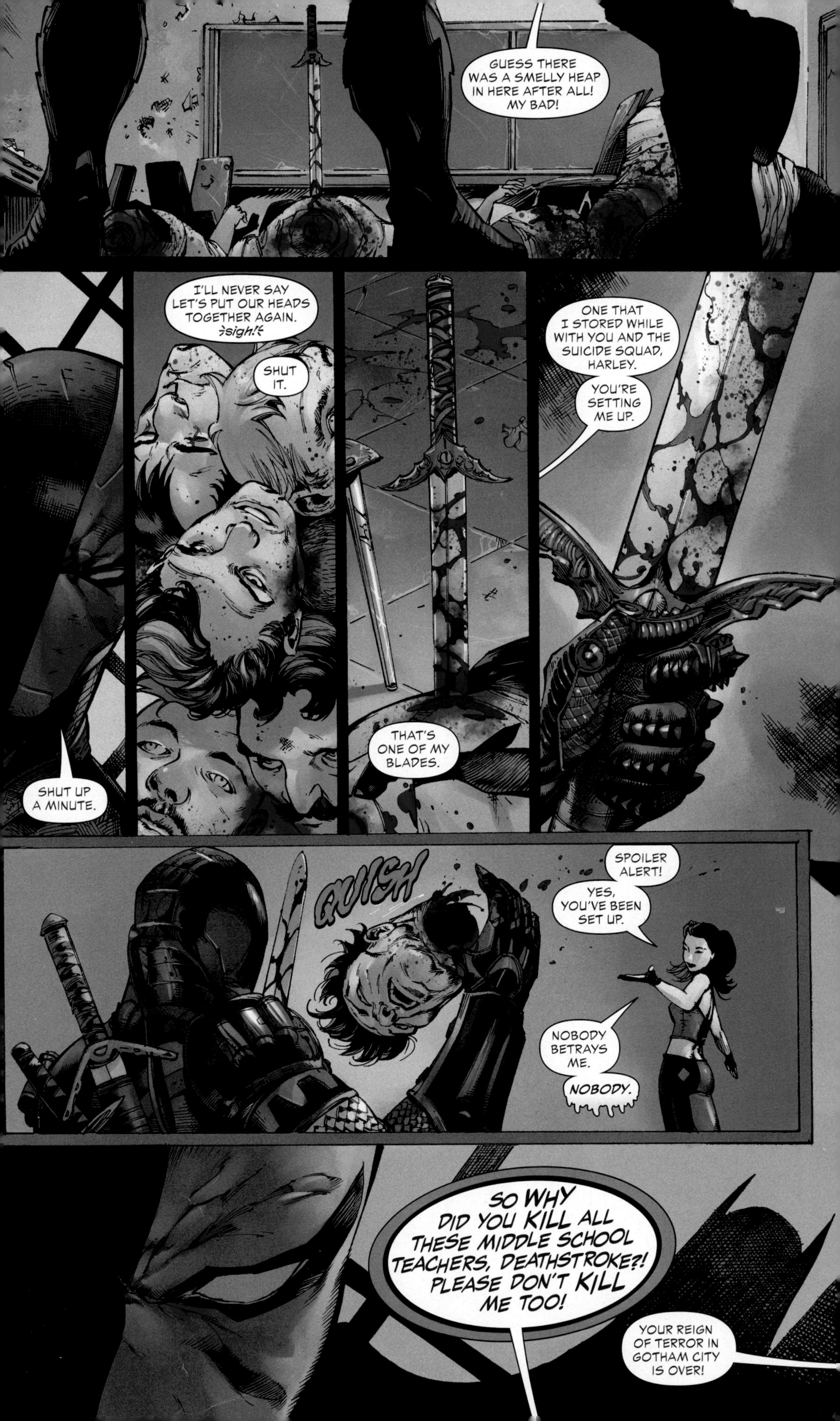

GUESS THERE WAS A SMELLY HEAP IN HERE AFTER ALL! MY BAD!
I'LL NEVER SAY LET'S PUT OUR HEADS TOGETHER AGAIN. *sigh!*
SHUT IT.
SHUT UP A MINUTE.
THAT'S ONE OF MY BLADES.
ONE THAT I STORED WHILE WITH YOU AND THE SUICIDE SQUAD, HARLEY.
YOU'RE SETTING ME UP.
QUISH
SPOILER ALERT!
YES, YOU'VE BEEN SET UP.
NOBODY BETRAYS ME.
NOBODY.
SO WHY DID YOU KILL ALL THESE MIDDLE SCHOOL TEACHERS, DEATHSTROKE?! PLEASE DON'T KILL ME TOO!
YOUR REIGN OF TERROR IN GOTHAM CITY IS OVER!

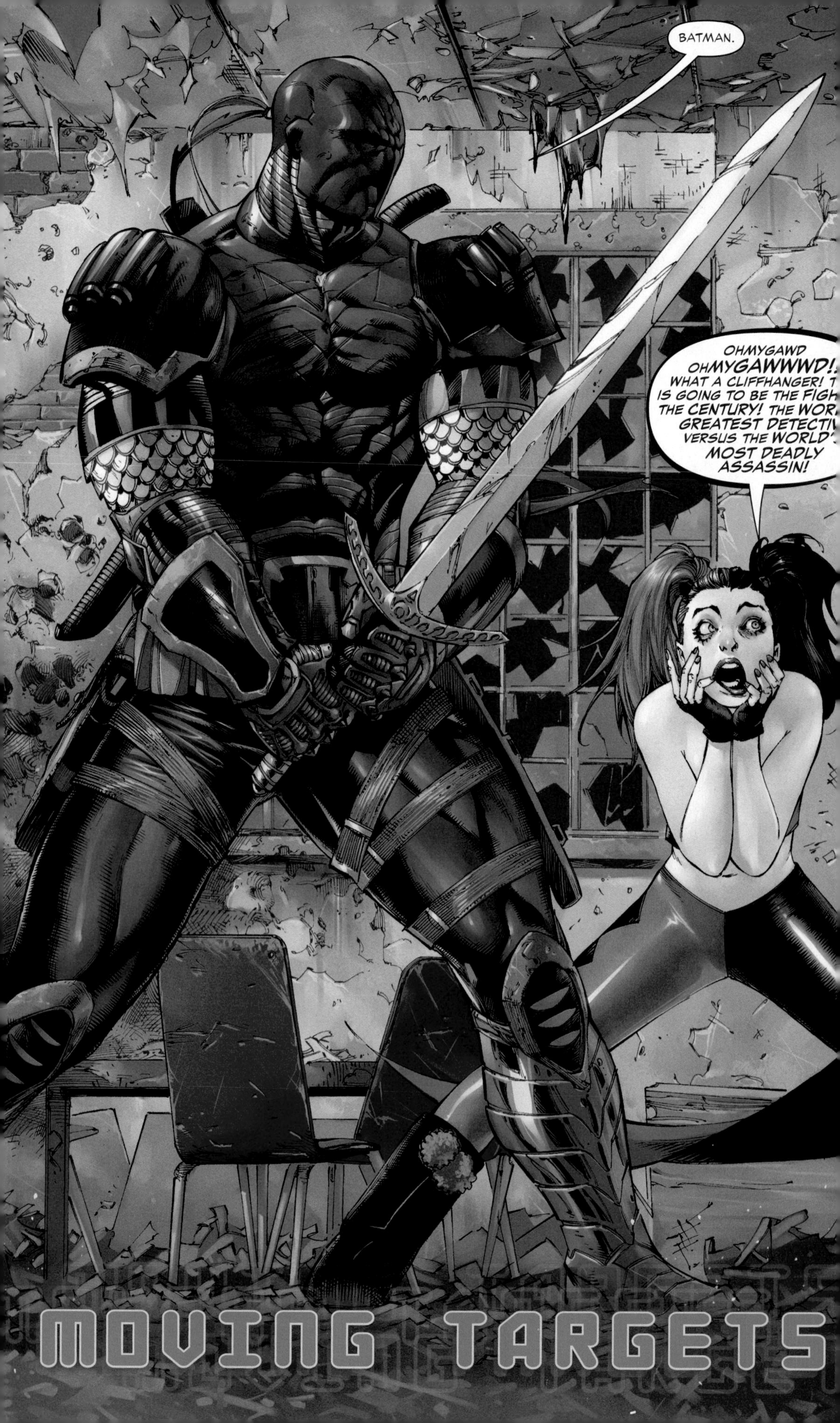
BATMAN.
OHMYGAWD OHMYGAWWWD!. WHAT A CLIFFHANGER! T IS GOING TO BE THE FIGH THE CENTURY! THE WOR GREATEST DETECTI VERSUS THE WORLD' MOST DEADLY ASSASSIN!
MOVING TARGETS

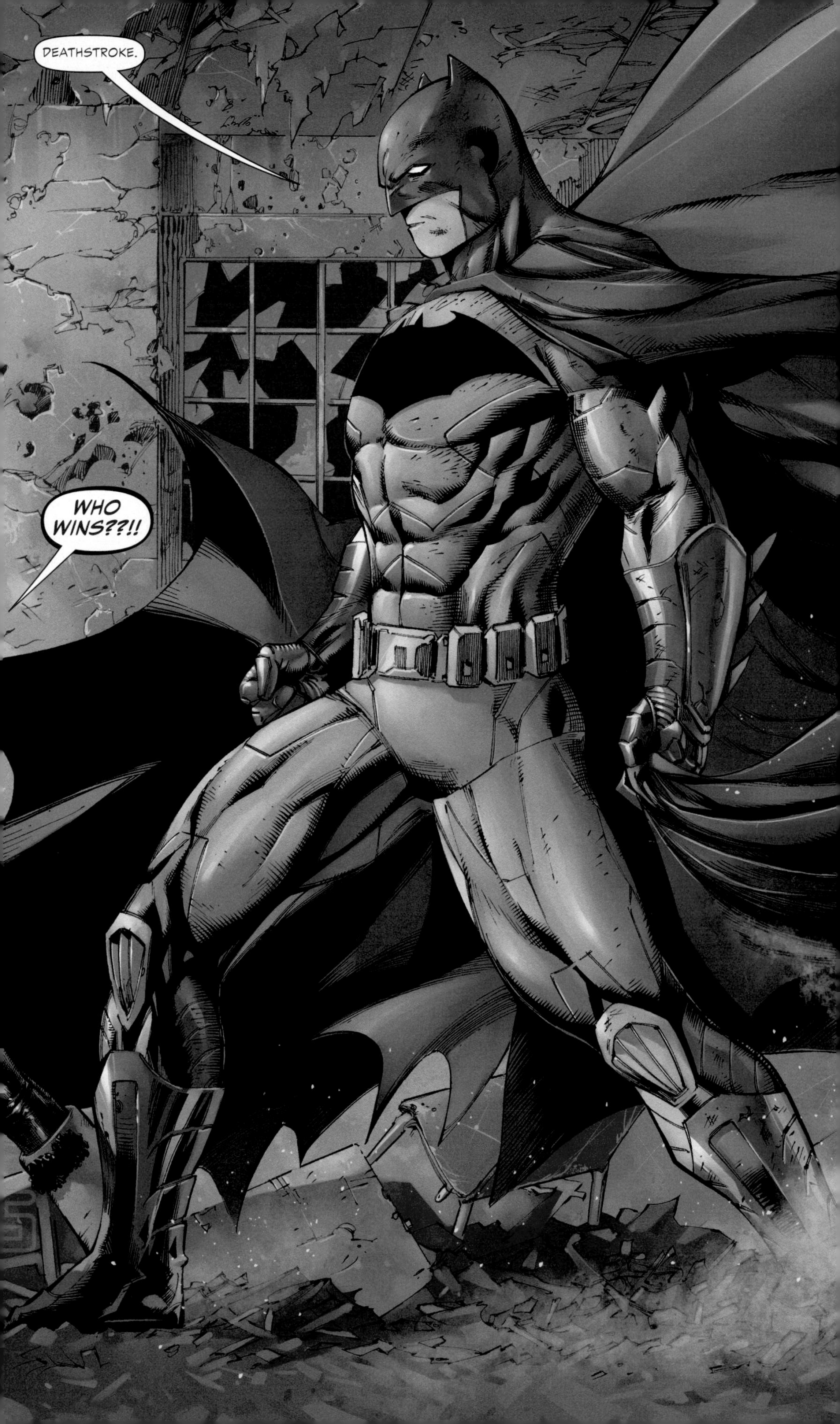
DEATHSTROKE.
WHO WINS??!!

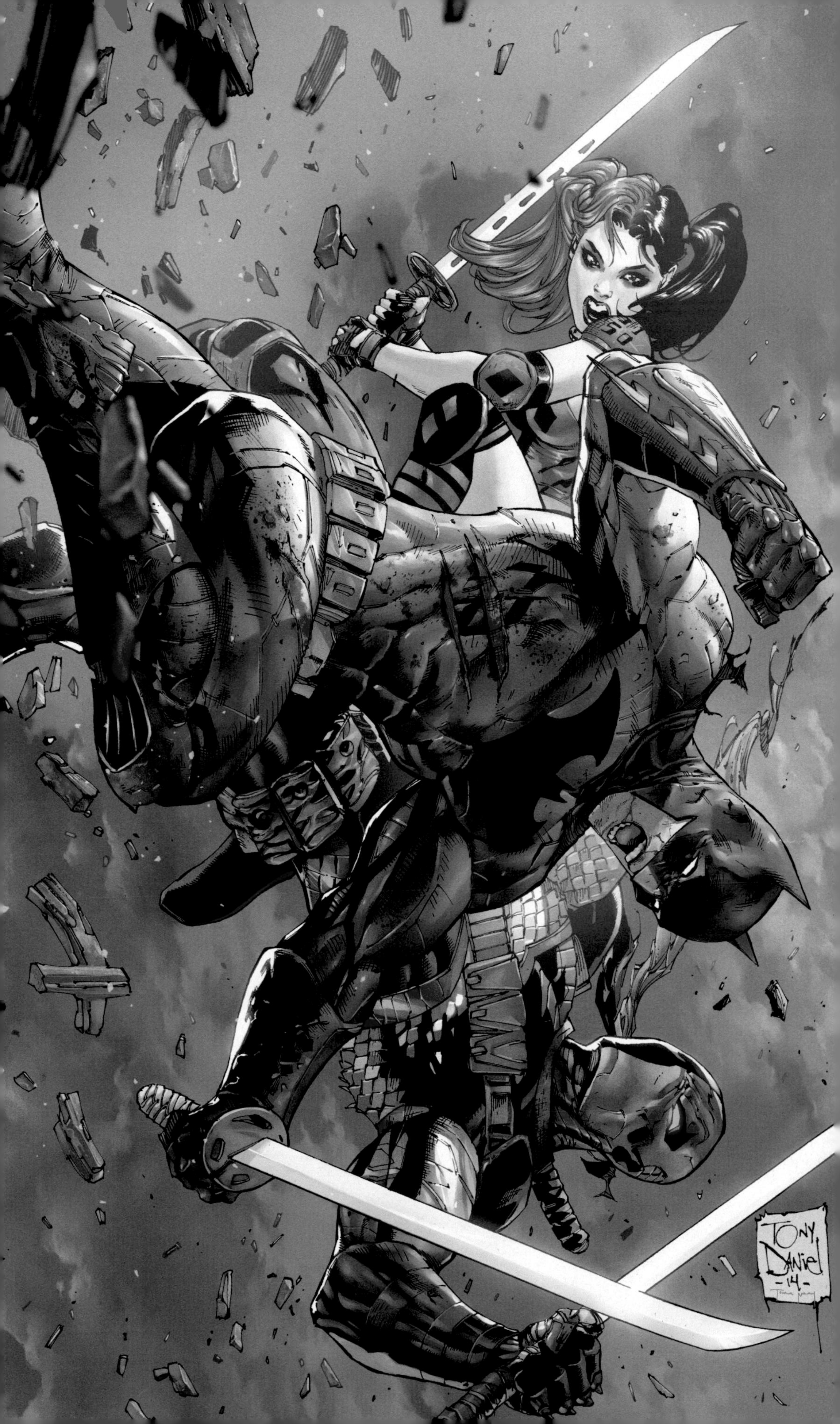
TONY DANIEL
-14-

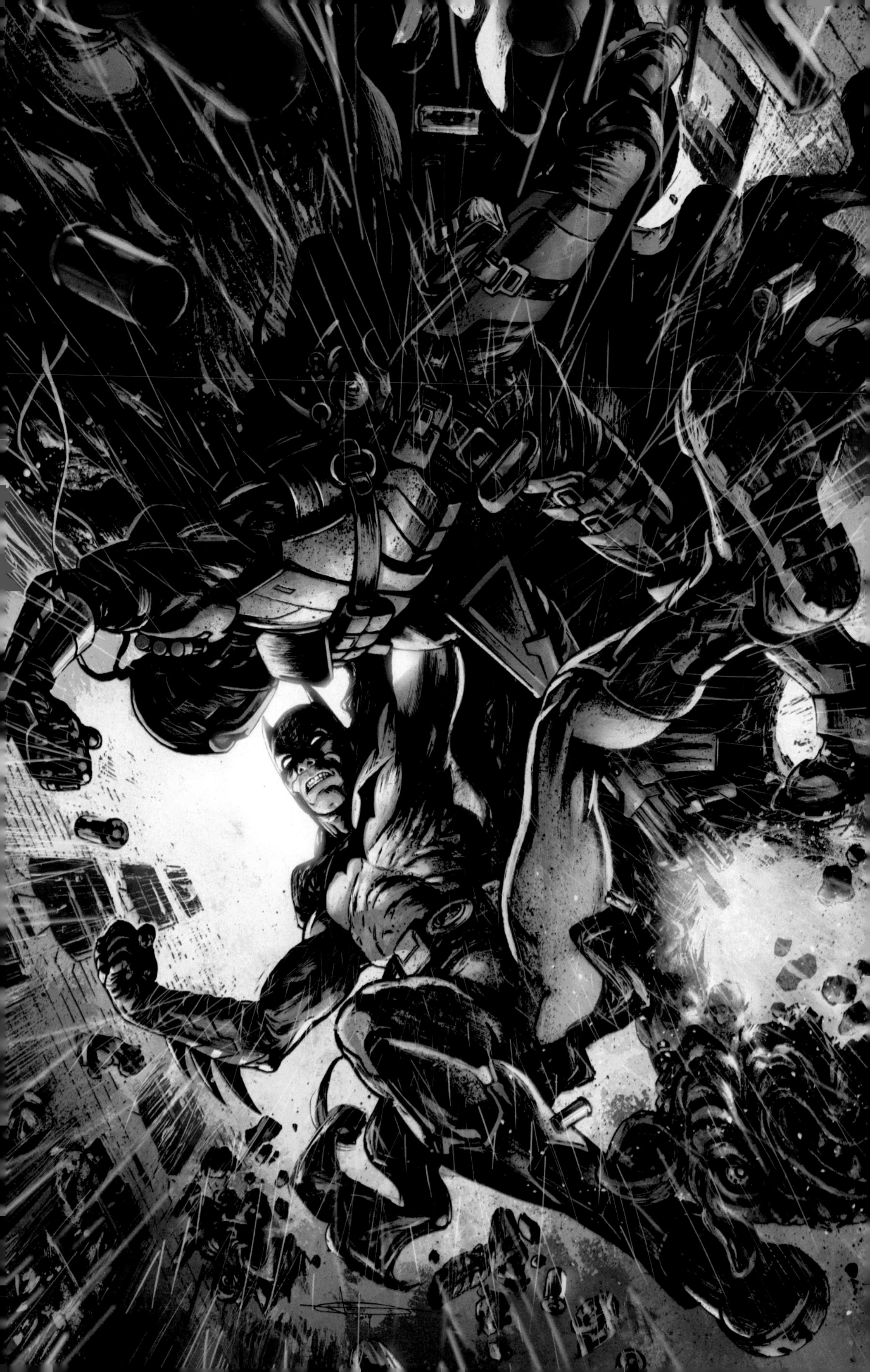

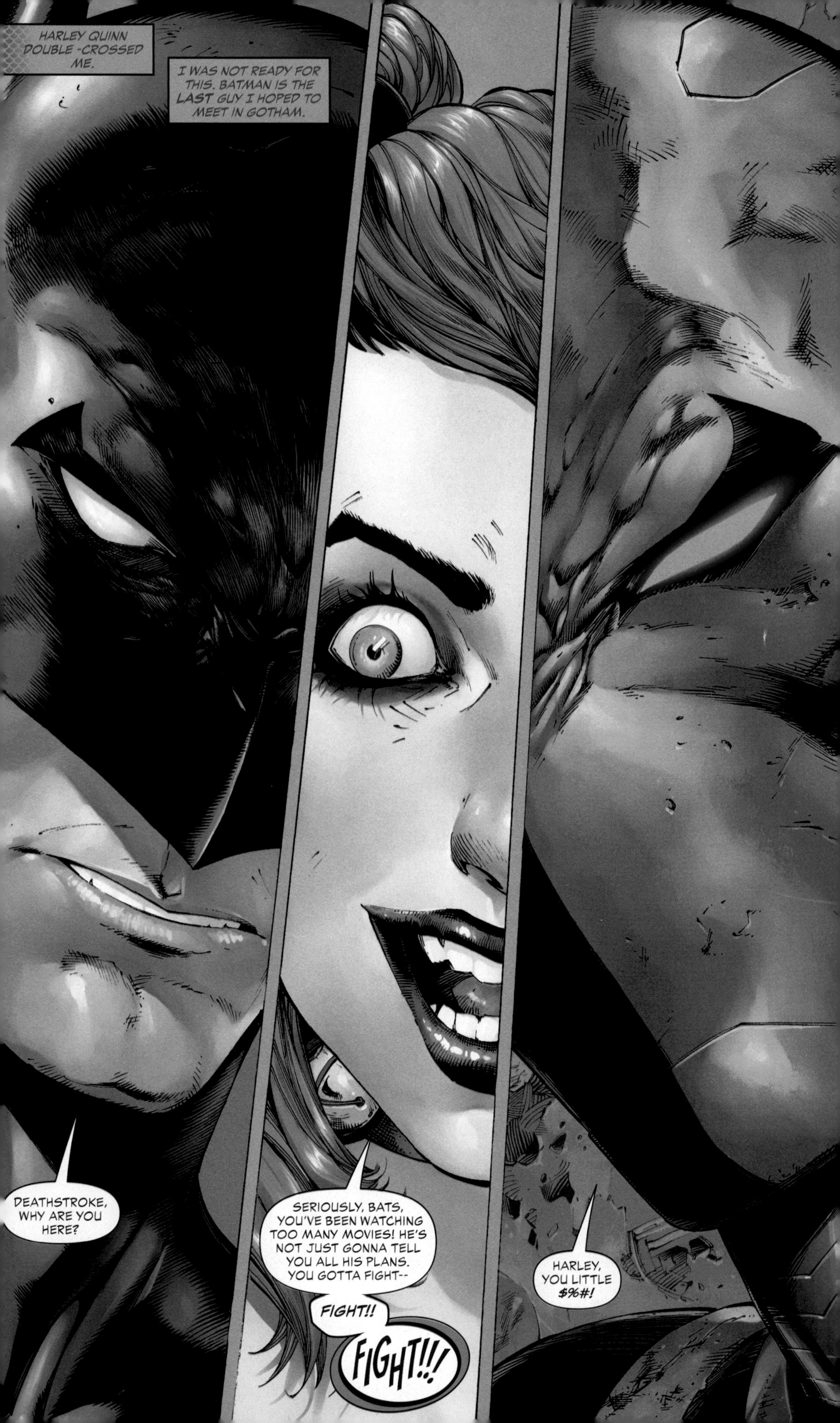
HARLEY QUINN DOUBLE-CROSSED ME.
I WAS NOT READY FOR THIS. BATMAN IS THE LAST GUY I HOPED TO MEET IN GOTHAM.
DEATHSTROKE, WHY ARE YOU HERE?
SERIOUSLY, BATS, YOU'VE BEEN WATCHING TOO MANY MOVIES! HE'S NOT JUST GONNA TELL YOU ALL HIS PLANS. YOU GOTTA FIGHT--
FIGHT!!
FIGHT!!!
HARLEY, YOU LITTLE $%#!

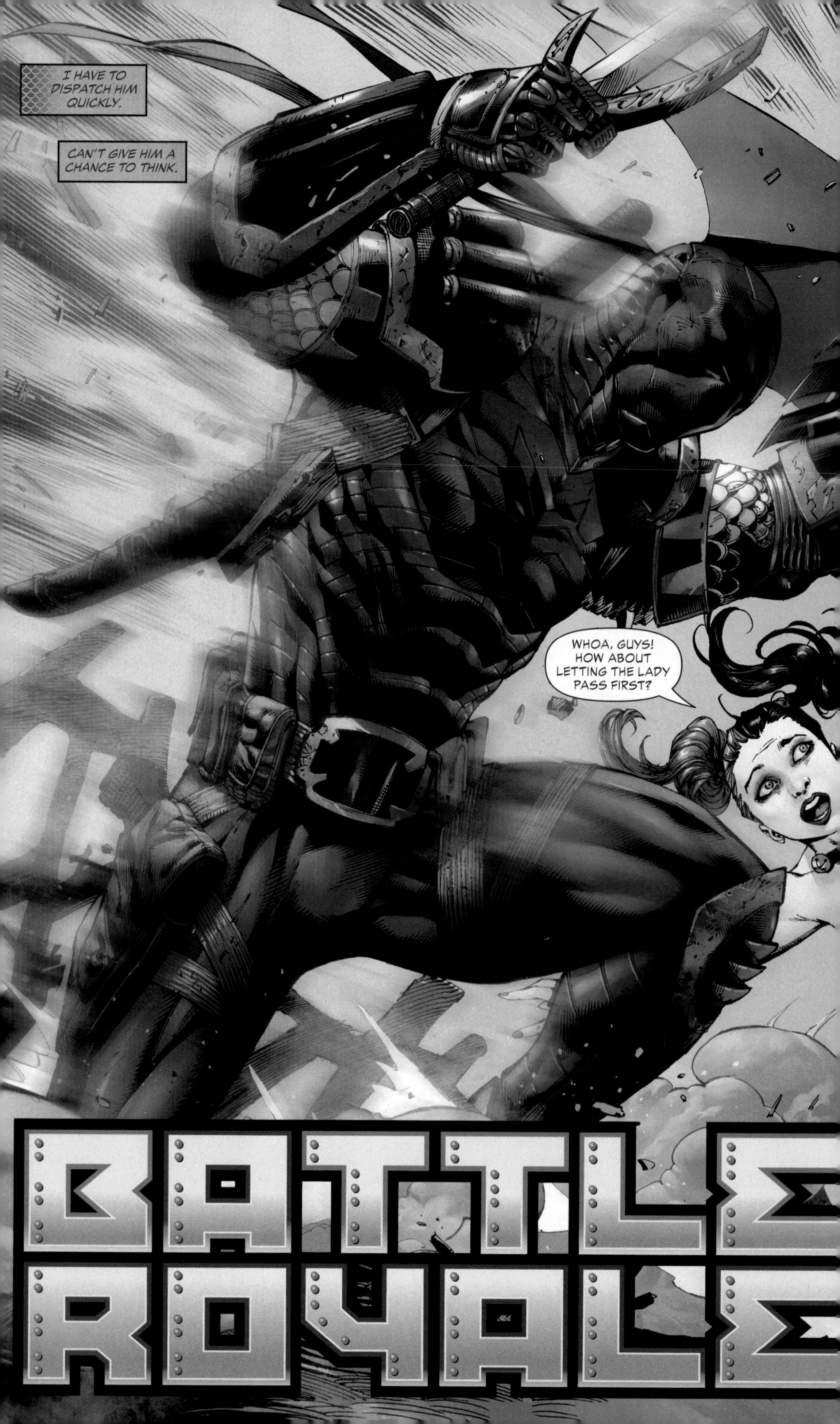
I HAVE TO DISPATCH HIM QUICKLY.
CAN'T GIVE HIM A CHANCE TO THINK.
WHOA, GUYS! HOW ABOUT LETTING THE LADY PASS FIRST?
BATTLE ROYALE

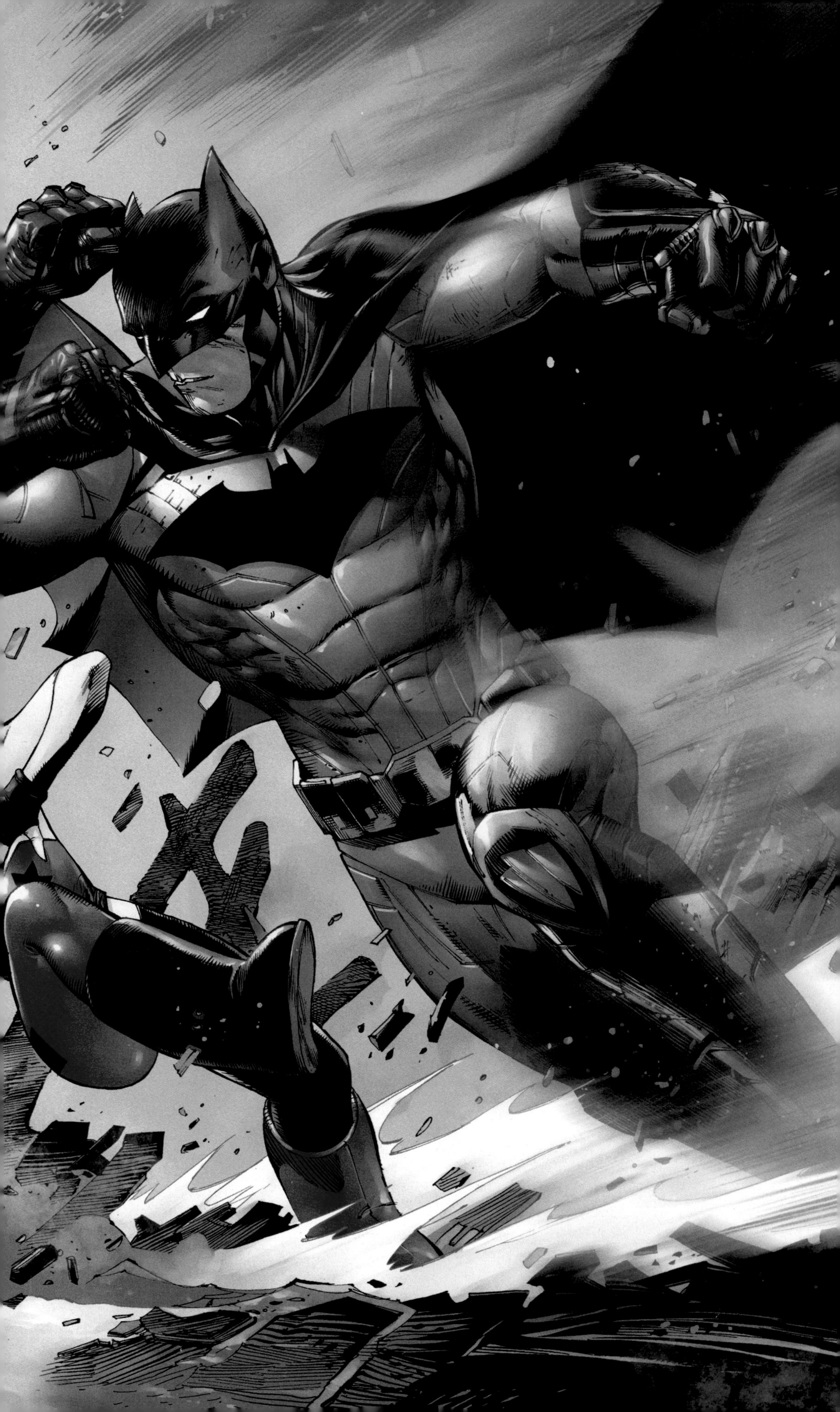

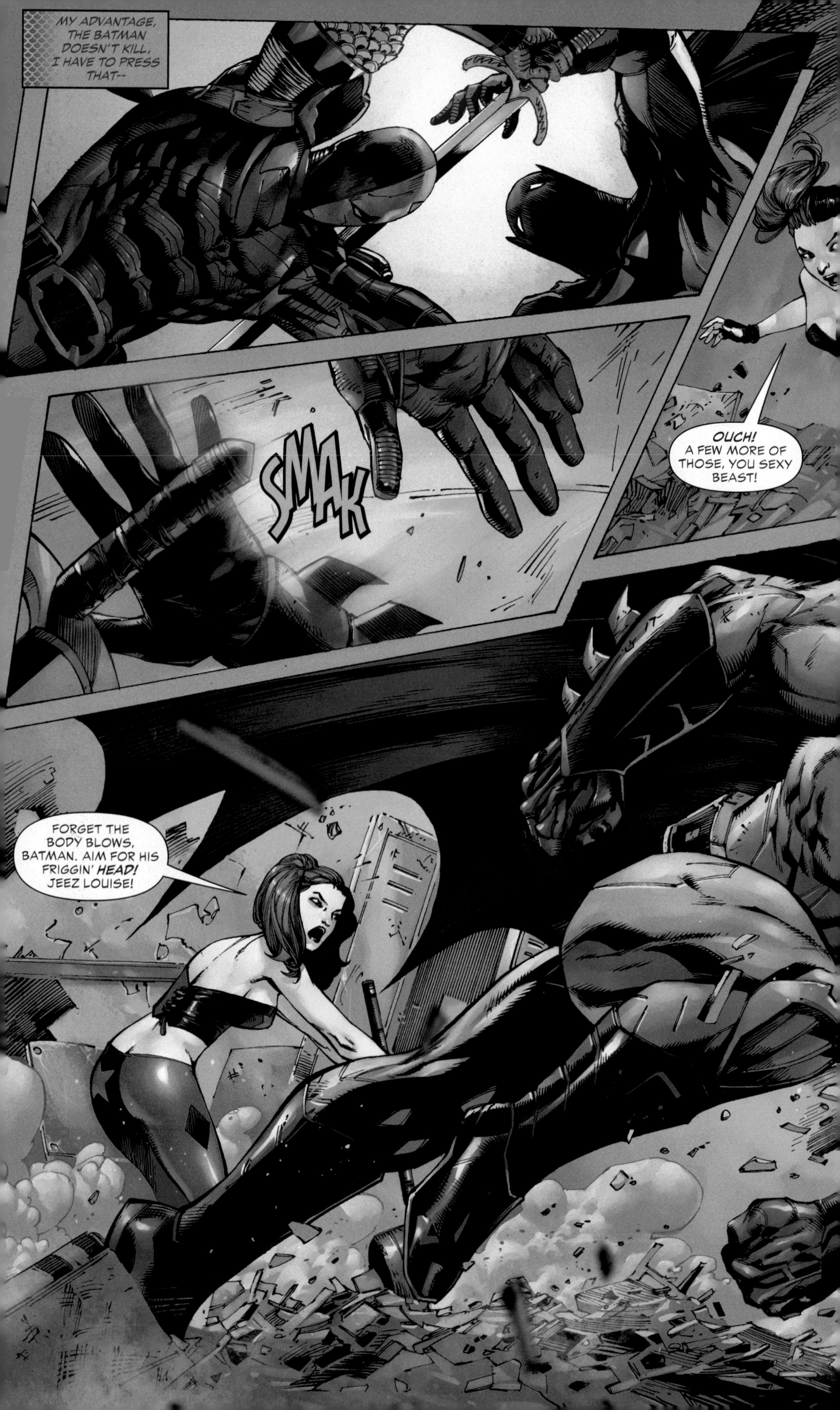
MY ADVANTAGE, THE BATMAN DOESN'T KILL, I HAVE TO PRESS THAT--
SMAK
OUCH! A FEW MORE OF THOSE, YOU SEXY BEAST!
FORGET THE BODY BLOWS, BATMAN. AIM FOR HIS FRIGGIN' HEAD! JEEZ LOUISE!

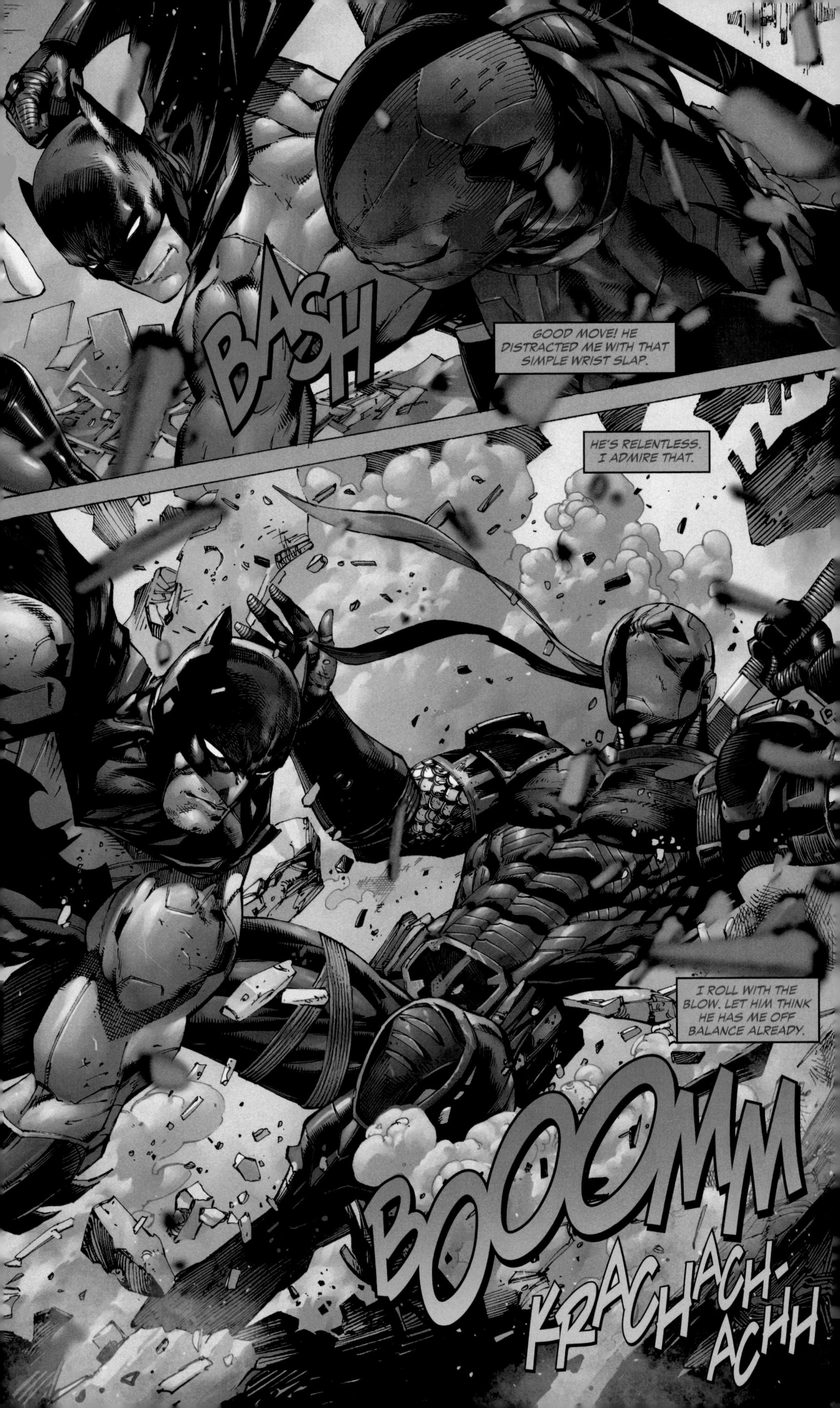
BASH
GOOD MOVE! HE DISTRACTED ME WITH THAT SIMPLE WRIST SLAP.
HE'S RELENTLESS. I ADMIRE THAT.
I ROLL WITH THE BLOW. LET HIM THINK HE HAS ME OFF BALANCE ALREADY.
BOOOMM
KRACHACH-ACHH

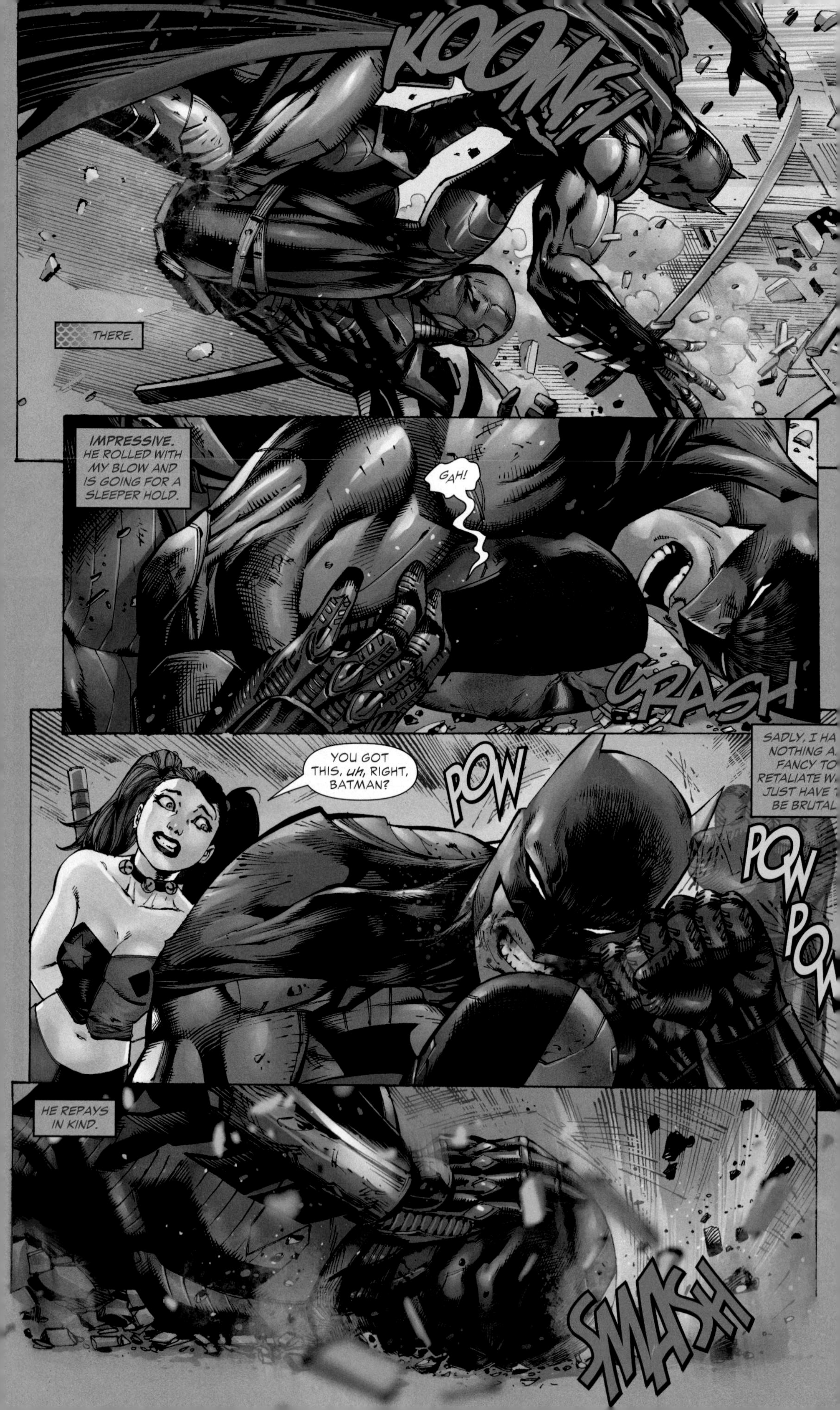
KOOMM
THERE.
IMPRESSIVE. HE ROLLED WITH MY BLOW AND IS GOING FOR A SLEEPER HOLD.
GAH!
CRASH
YOU GOT THIS, uh, RIGHT, BATMAN?
POW
POW
POW
HE REPAYS IN KIND.
SMASH

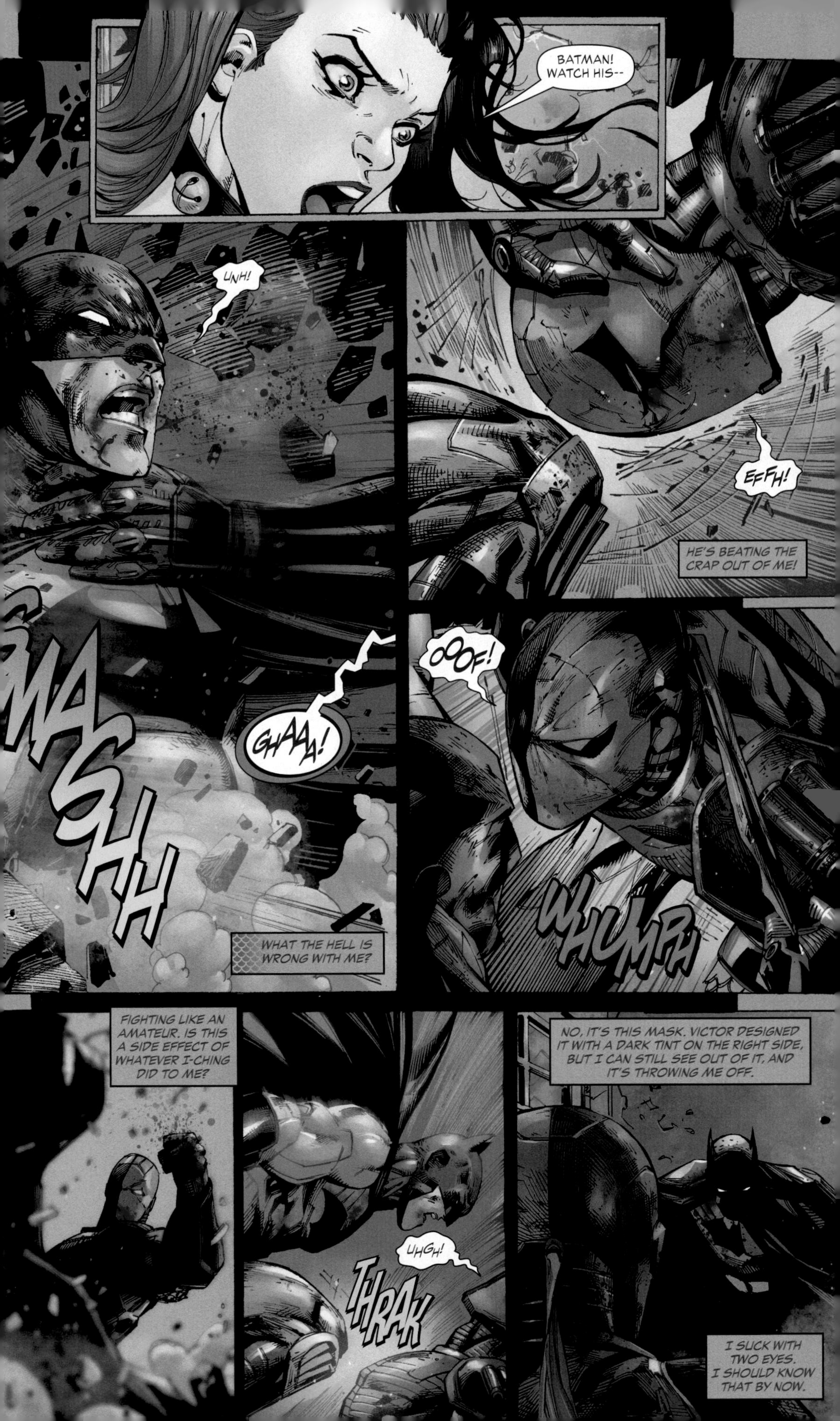

BATMAN! WATCH HIS--
UNH!
EFFH!
HE'S BEATING THE CRAP OUT OF ME!
MASHH
GHAAA!
WHAT THE HELL IS WRONG WITH ME?
OOOF!
WHUMPH
FIGHTING LIKE AN AMATEUR. IS THIS A SIDE EFFECT OF WHATEVER I-CHING DID TO ME?
UHGH!
THRAK
NO, IT'S THIS MASK. VICTOR DESIGNED IT WITH A DARK TINT ON THE RIGHT SIDE, BUT I CAN STILL SEE OUT OF IT, AND IT'S THROWING ME OFF.
I SUCK WITH TWO EYES. I SHOULD KNOW THAT BY NOW.

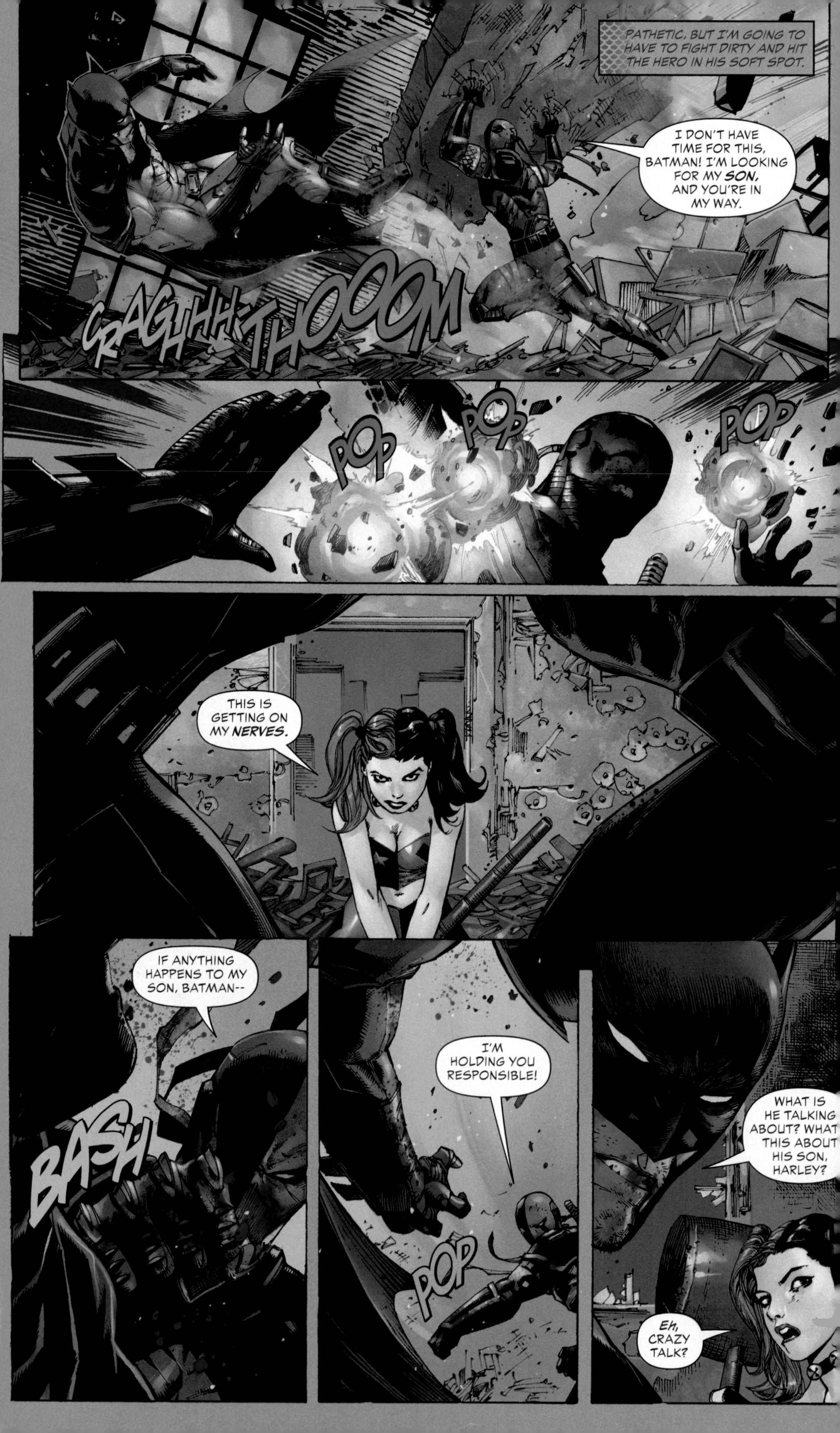
PATHETIC, BUT I'M GOING TO HAVE TO FIGHT DIRTY AND HIT THE HERO IN HIS SOFT SPOT.
I DON'T HAVE TIME FOR THIS, BATMAN! I'M LOOKING FOR MY SON, AND YOU'RE IN MY WAY.
CRAGHHH THOOOM
POP
POP
POP
THIS IS GETTING ON MY NERVES.
IF ANYTHING HAPPENS TO MY SON, BATMAN--
BASH
I'M HOLDING YOU RESPONSIBLE!
POP
WHAT IS HE TALKING ABOUT? WHAT THIS ABOUT HIS SON, HARLEY?
Eh, CRAZY TALK?

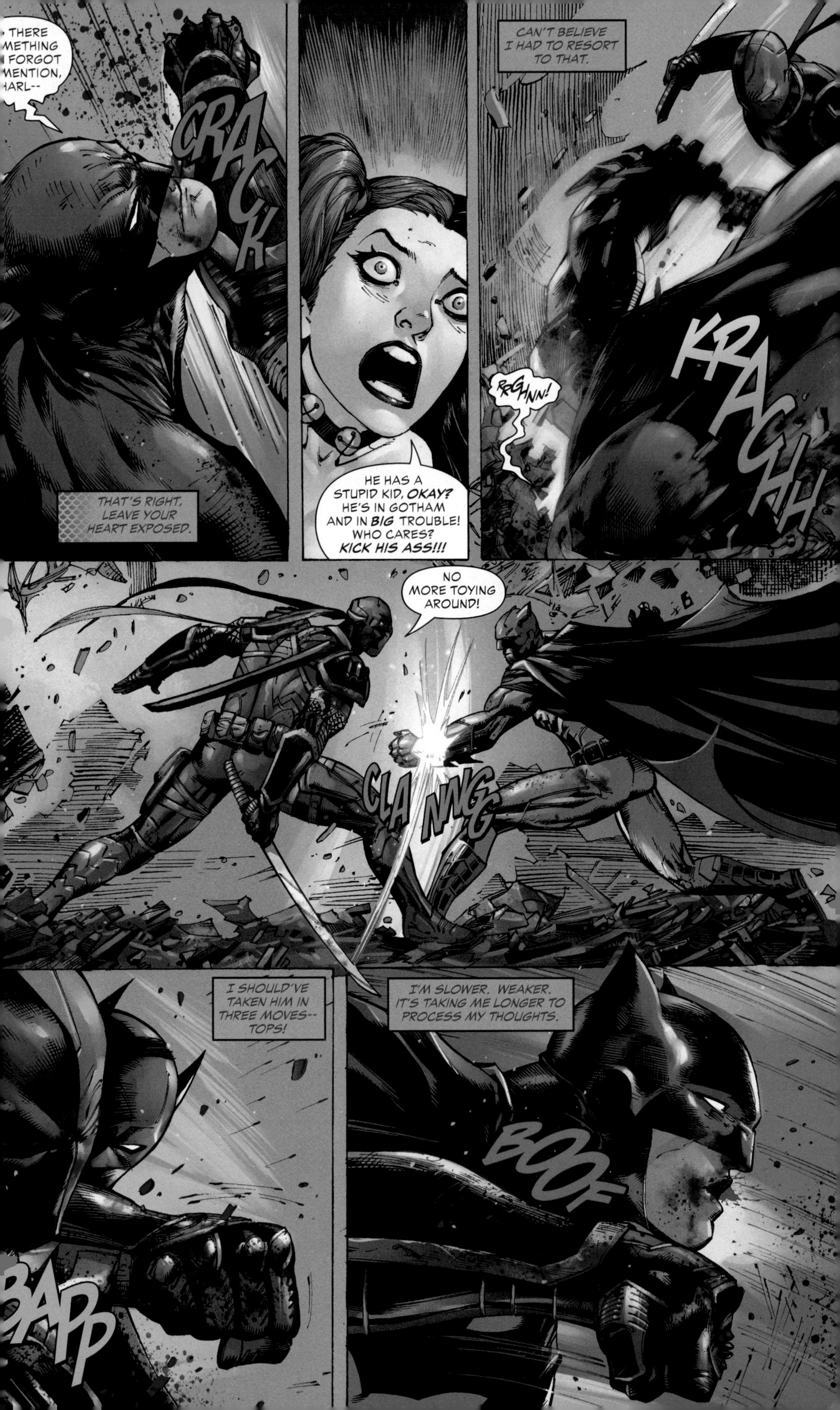

THERE
METHING
FORGOT
MENTION,
HARL--
CRACK
THAT'S RIGHT, LEAVE YOUR HEART EXPOSED.
HE HAS A STUPID KID, OKAY? HE'S IN GOTHAM AND IN BIG TROUBLE! WHO CARES? KICK HIS ASS!!!
CAN'T BELIEVE I HAD TO RESORT TO THAT.
RRGHNN!
KRACHH
NO MORE TOYING AROUND!
CLANNGG
I SHOULD'VE TAKEN HIM IN THREE MOVES--TOPS!
BAPP
I'M SLOWER. WEAKER. IT'S TAKING ME LONGER TO PROCESS MY THOUGHTS.
BOOF

KA-CRAMM

AND IN BATTLE AGAINST SOMEONE LIKE BATMAN, BEING A MILLISECOND OFF IS THE DIFFERENCE BETWEEN VICTORY OR DEFEAT.

I'M BEING OUTSMARTED. OUTFOUGHT.

BAMM

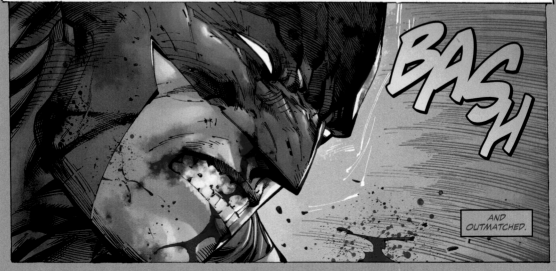

BASH

AND OUTMATCHED.

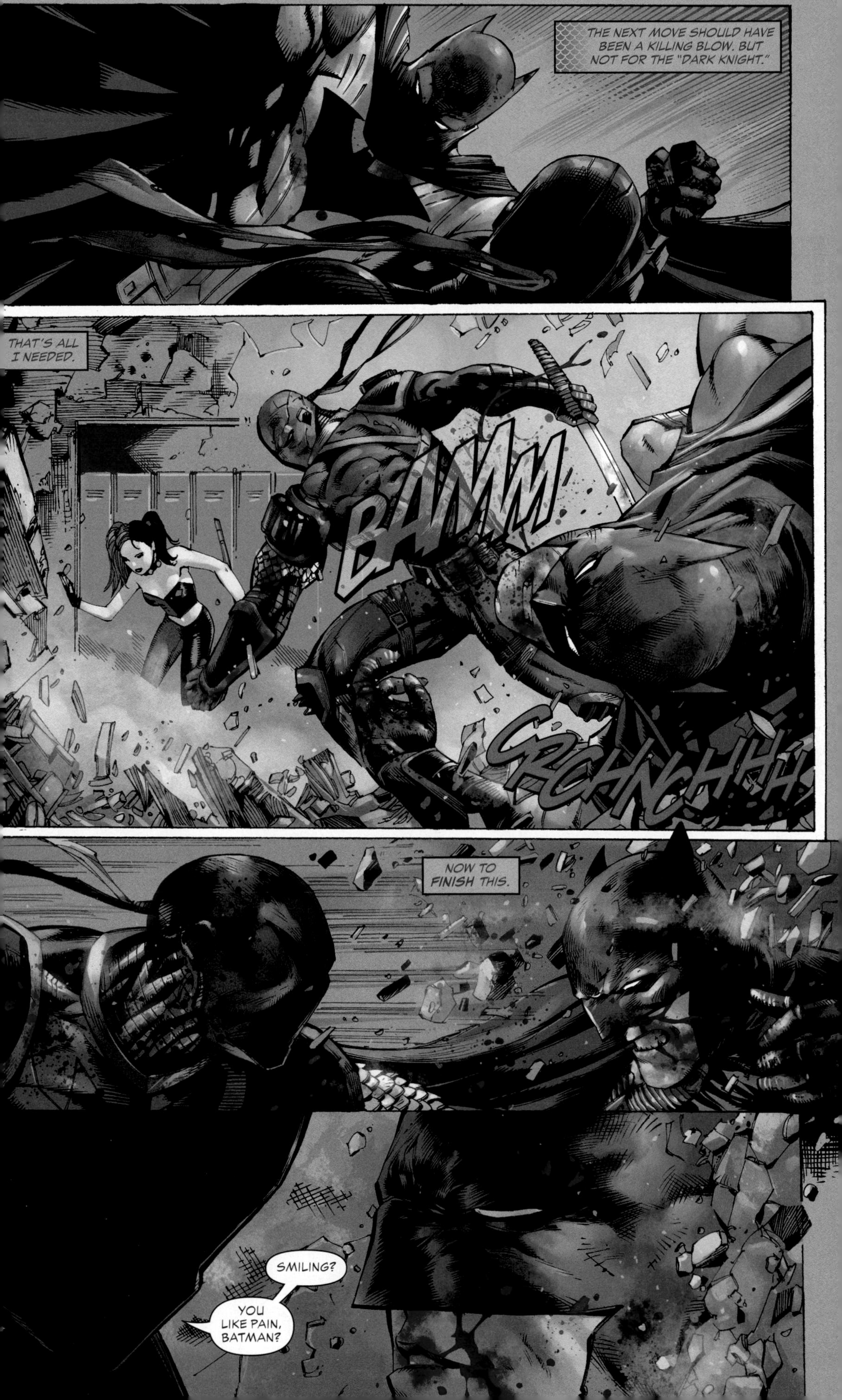
THE NEXT MOVE SHOULD HAVE BEEN A KILLING BLOW. BUT NOT FOR THE "DARK KNIGHT."
THAT'S ALL I NEEDED.
BAMM
GRCHNCHHH
NOW TO FINISH THIS.
SMILING?
YOU LIKE PAIN, BATMAN?

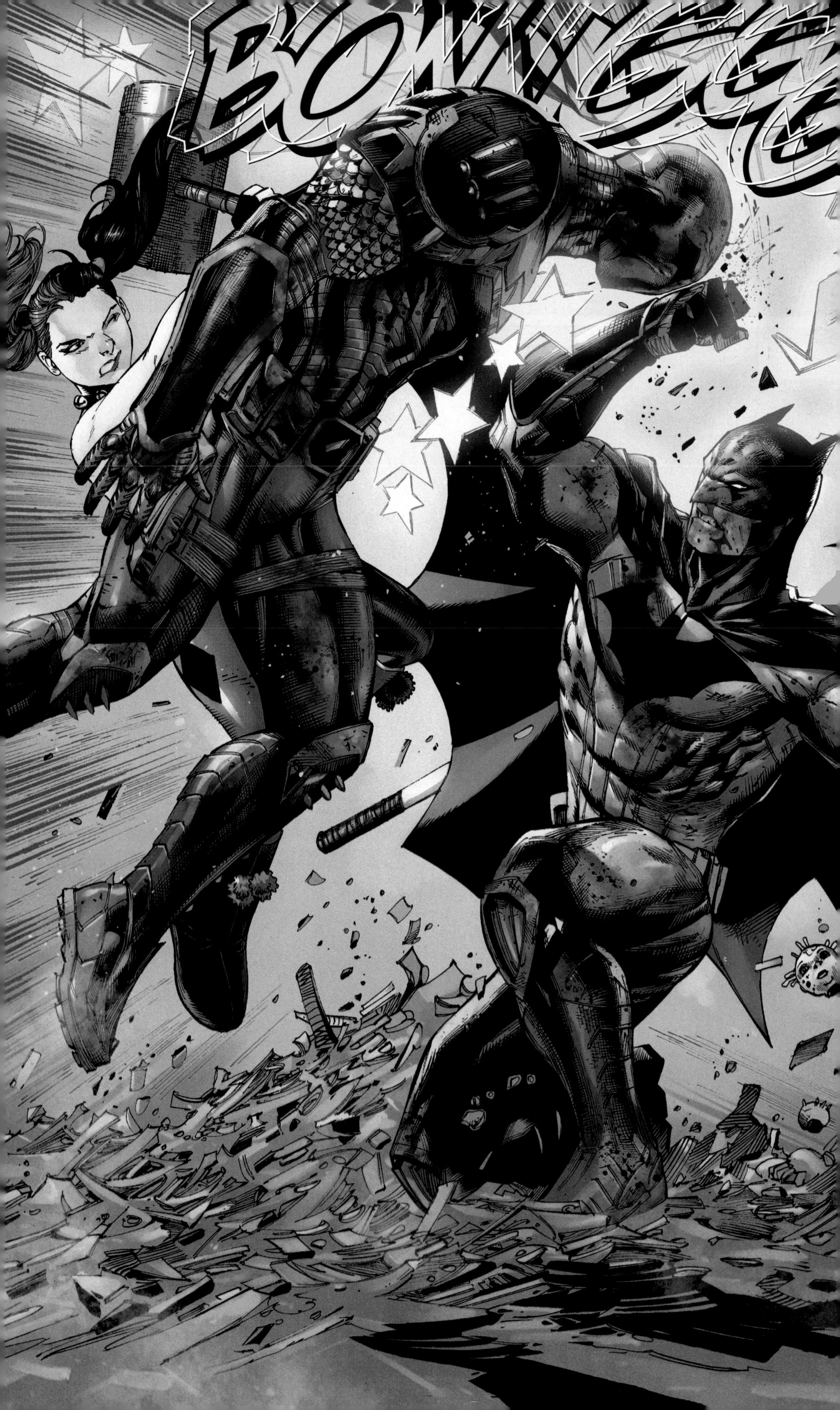

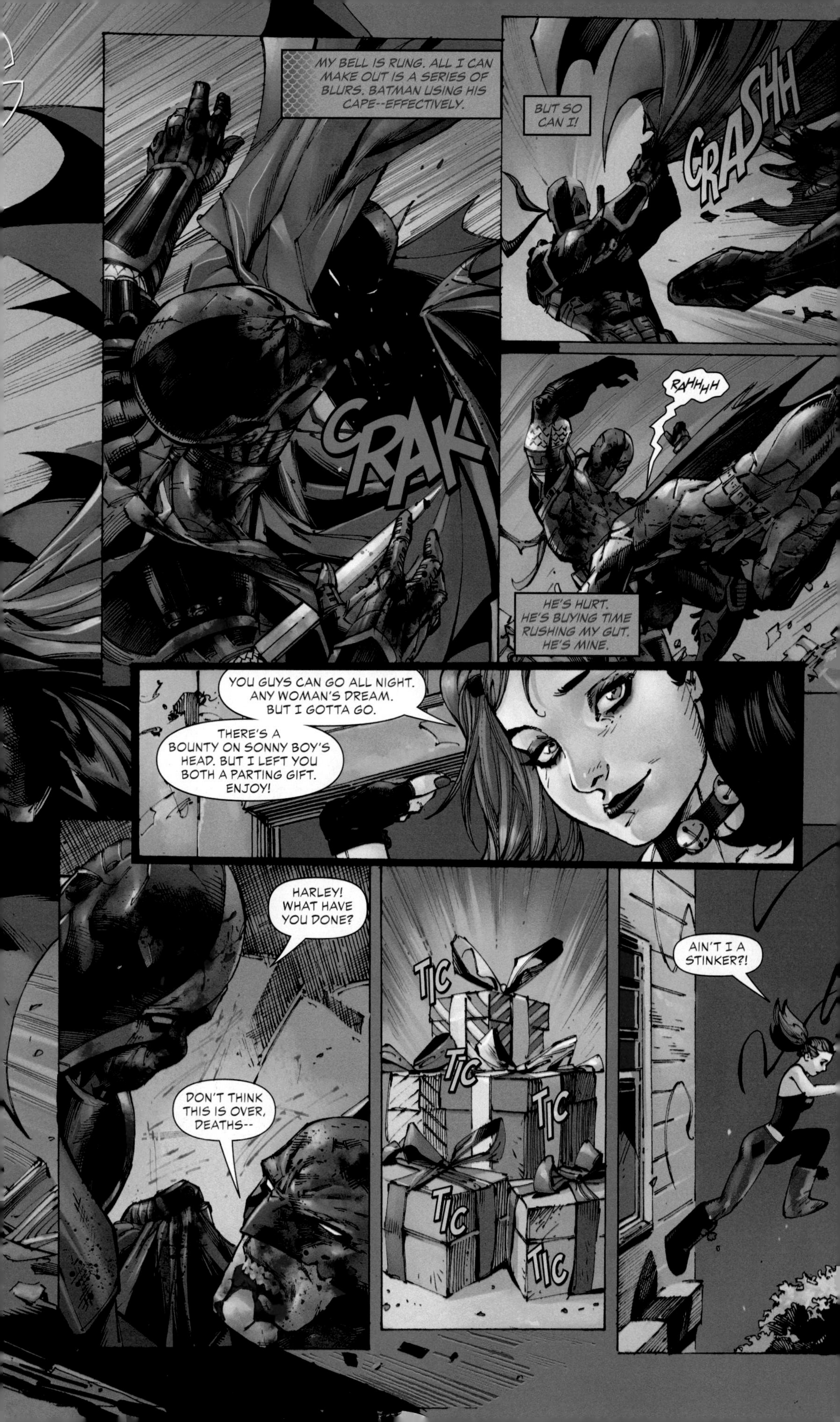
MY BELL IS RUNG. ALL I CAN MAKE OUT IS A SERIES OF BLURS. BATMAN USING HIS CAPE--EFFECTIVELY.
CRAK
BUT SO CAN I!
CRASHH
RAHHHH
HE'S HURT. HE'S BUYING TIME RUSHING MY GUT. HE'S MINE.
YOU GUYS CAN GO ALL NIGHT. ANY WOMAN'S DREAM. BUT I GOTTA GO.
THERE'S A BOUNTY ON SONNY BOY'S HEAD. BUT I LEFT YOU BOTH A PARTING GIFT. ENJOY!
HARLEY! WHAT HAVE YOU DONE?
DON'T THINK THIS IS OVER, DEATHS--
TIC
TIC
TIC
TIC
TIC
AIN'T I A STINKER?!

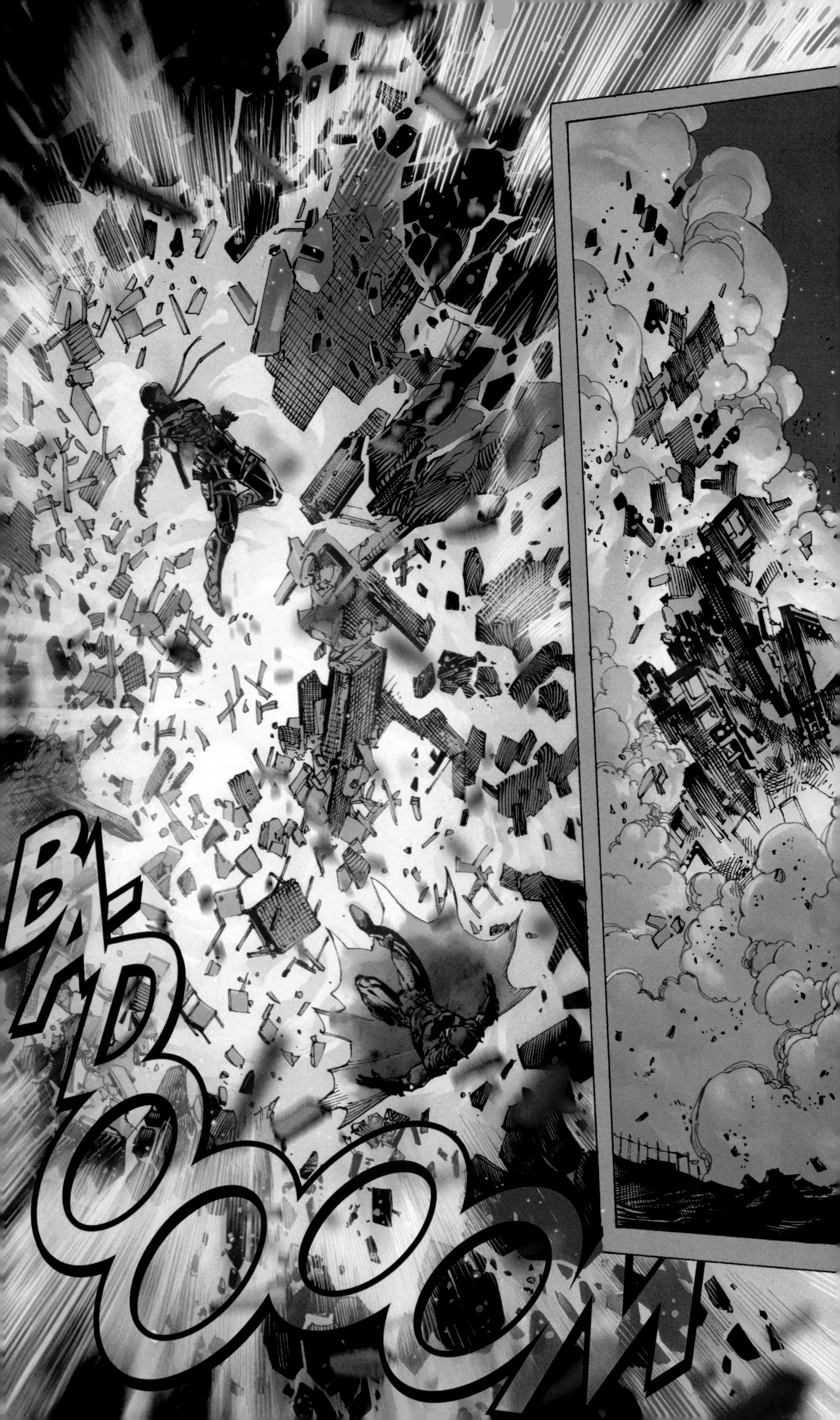
BADOOOOOM

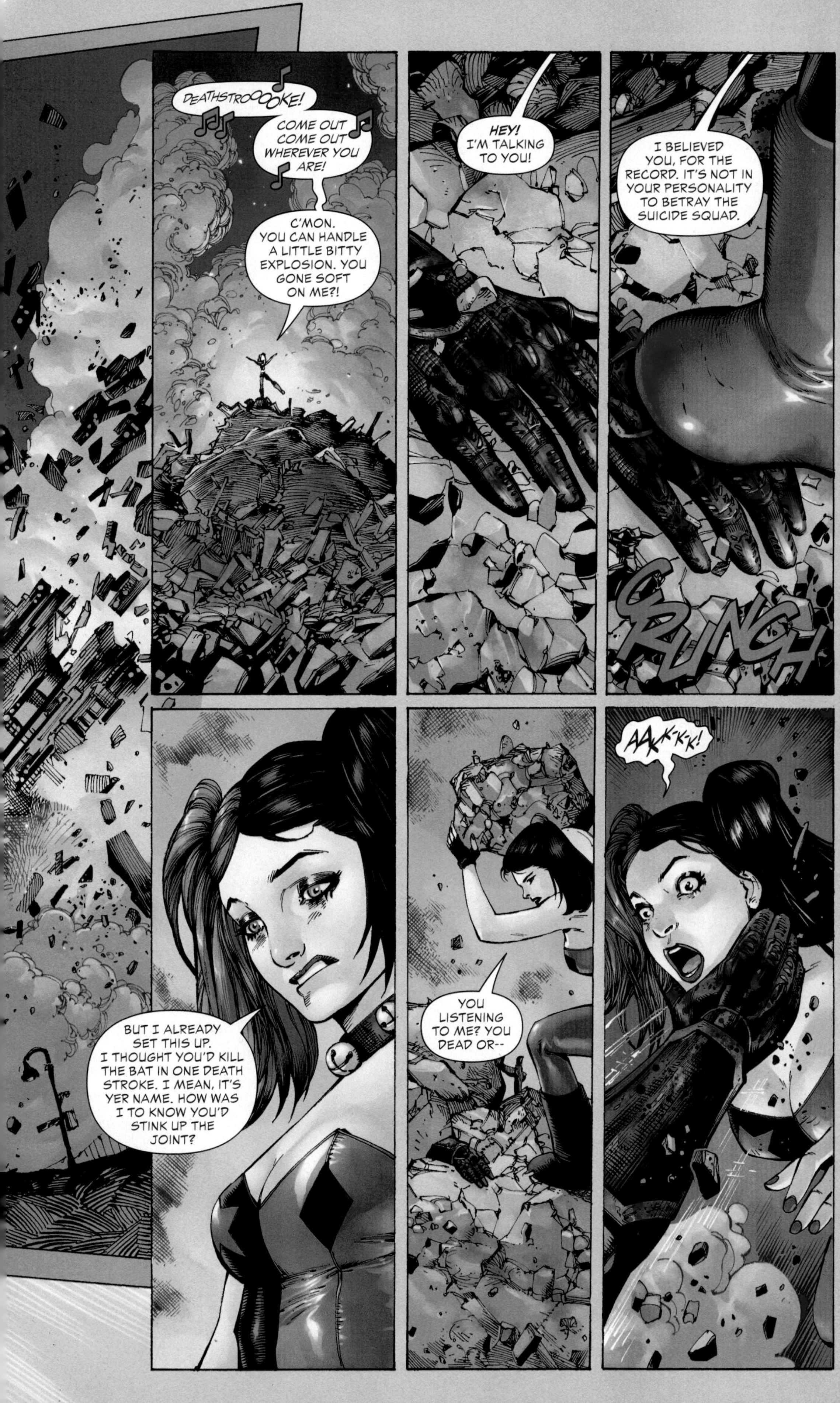
DEATHSTROOOOOKE!
COME OUT COME OUT WHEREVER YOU ARE!
C'MON. YOU CAN HANDLE A LITTLE BITTY EXPLOSION. YOU GONE SOFT ON ME?!
HEY! I'M TALKING TO YOU!
I BELIEVED YOU, FOR THE RECORD. IT'S NOT IN YOUR PERSONALITY TO BETRAY THE SUICIDE SQUAD.
CRUNCH
BUT I ALREADY SET THIS UP. I THOUGHT YOU'D KILL THE BAT IN ONE DEATH STROKE. I MEAN, IT'S YER NAME. HOW WAS I TO KNOW YOU'D STINK UP THE JOINT?
YOU LISTENING TO ME? YOU DEAD OR--
AAKK-K-K!

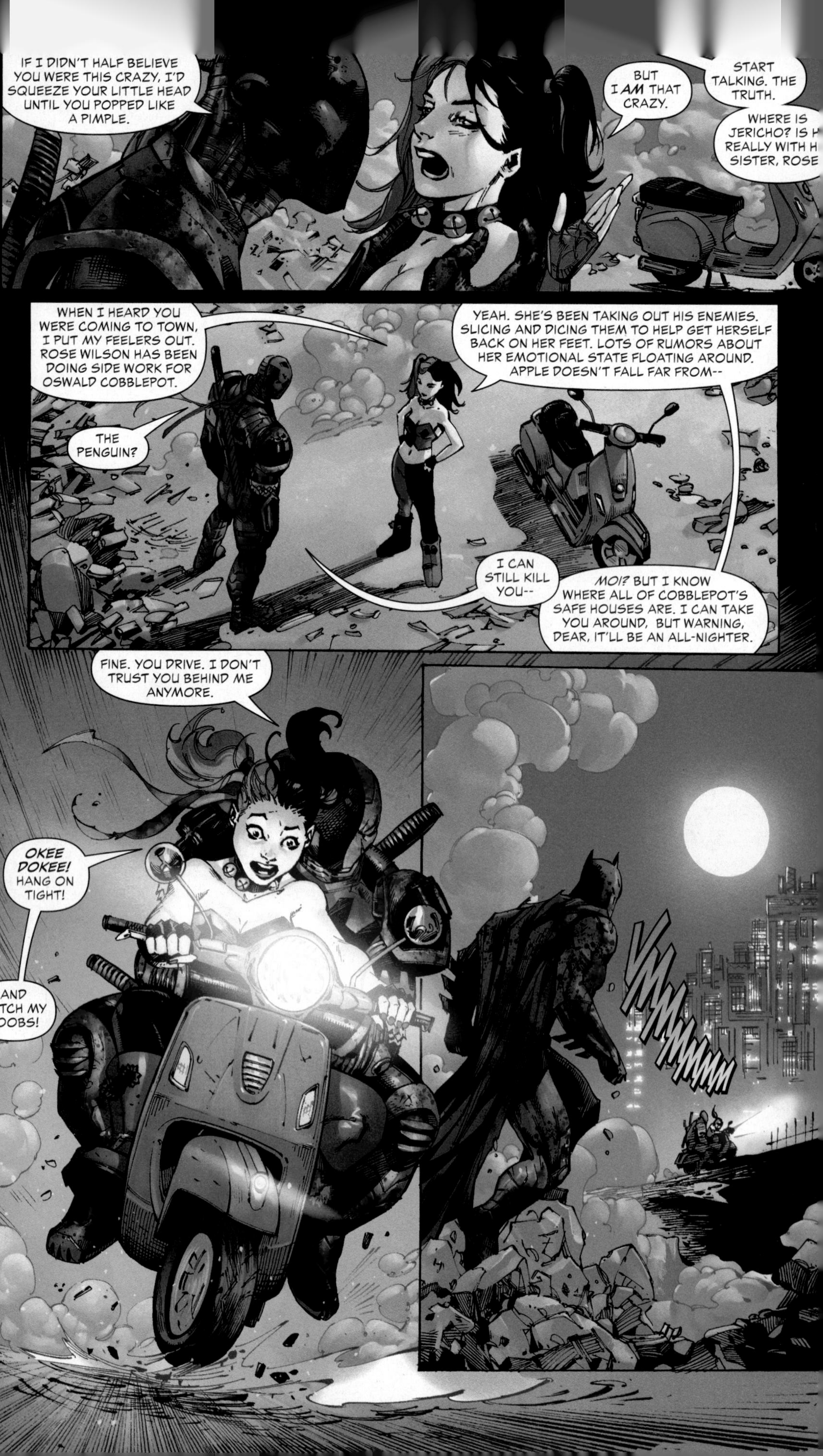
IF I DIDN'T HALF BELIEVE YOU WERE THIS CRAZY, I'D SQUEEZE YOUR LITTLE HEAD UNTIL YOU POPPED LIKE A PIMPLE.
BUT I AM THAT CRAZY.
START TALKING. THE TRUTH.
WHERE IS JERICHO? IS H REALLY WITH H SISTER, ROSE
WHEN I HEARD YOU WERE COMING TO TOWN, I PUT MY FEELERS OUT. ROSE WILSON HAS BEEN DOING SIDE WORK FOR OSWALD COBBLEPOT.
THE PENGUIN?
YEAH. SHE'S BEEN TAKING OUT HIS ENEMIES. SLICING AND DICING THEM TO HELP GET HERSELF BACK ON HER FEET. LOTS OF RUMORS ABOUT HER EMOTIONAL STATE FLOATING AROUND. APPLE DOESN'T FALL FAR FROM--
I CAN STILL KILL YOU--
MOI? BUT I KNOW WHERE ALL OF COBBLEPOT'S SAFE HOUSES ARE. I CAN TAKE YOU AROUND, BUT WARNING, DEAR, IT'LL BE AN ALL-NIGHTER.
FINE. YOU DRIVE. I DON'T TRUST YOU BEHIND ME ANYMORE.
OKEE DOKEE! HANG ON TIGHT!
AND WATCH MY BOOBS!
VMMMMMMMM

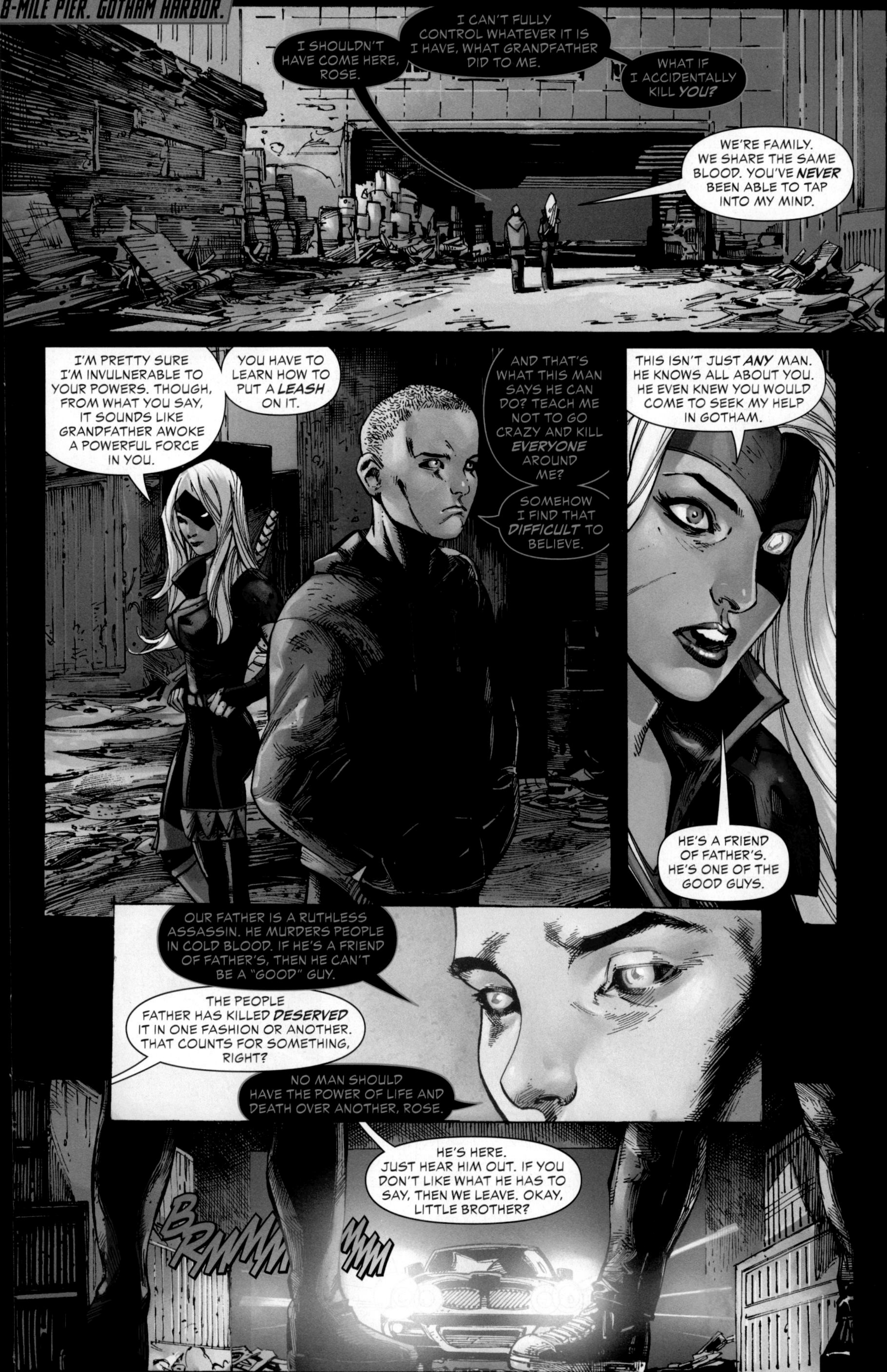
8-MILE PIER. GOTHAM HARBOR.
I SHOULDN'T HAVE COME HERE, ROSE.
I CAN'T FULLY CONTROL WHATEVER IT IS I HAVE, WHAT GRANDFATHER DID TO ME.
WHAT IF I ACCIDENTALLY KILL YOU?
WE'RE FAMILY. WE SHARE THE SAME BLOOD. YOU'VE NEVER BEEN ABLE TO TAP INTO MY MIND.
I'M PRETTY SURE I'M INVULNERABLE TO YOUR POWERS. THOUGH, FROM WHAT YOU SAY, IT SOUNDS LIKE GRANDFATHER AWOKE A POWERFUL FORCE IN YOU.
YOU HAVE TO LEARN HOW TO PUT A LEASH ON IT.
AND THAT'S WHAT THIS MAN SAYS HE CAN DO? TEACH ME NOT TO GO CRAZY AND KILL EVERYONE AROUND ME?
SOMEHOW I FIND THAT DIFFICULT TO BELIEVE.
THIS ISN'T JUST ANY MAN. HE KNOWS ALL ABOUT YOU. HE EVEN KNEW YOU WOULD COME TO SEEK MY HELP IN GOTHAM.
HE'S A FRIEND OF FATHER'S. HE'S ONE OF THE GOOD GUYS.
OUR FATHER IS A RUTHLESS ASSASSIN. HE MURDERS PEOPLE IN COLD BLOOD. IF HE'S A FRIEND OF FATHER'S, THEN HE CAN'T BE A "GOOD" GUY.
THE PEOPLE FATHER HAS KILLED DESERVED IT IN ONE FASHION OR ANOTHER. THAT COUNTS FOR SOMETHING, RIGHT?
NO MAN SHOULD HAVE THE POWER OF LIFE AND DEATH OVER ANOTHER, ROSE.
HE'S HERE. JUST HEAR HIM OUT. IF YOU DON'T LIKE WHAT HE HAS TO SAY, THEN WE LEAVE. OKAY, LITTLE BROTHER?
BRMMMMMMMM

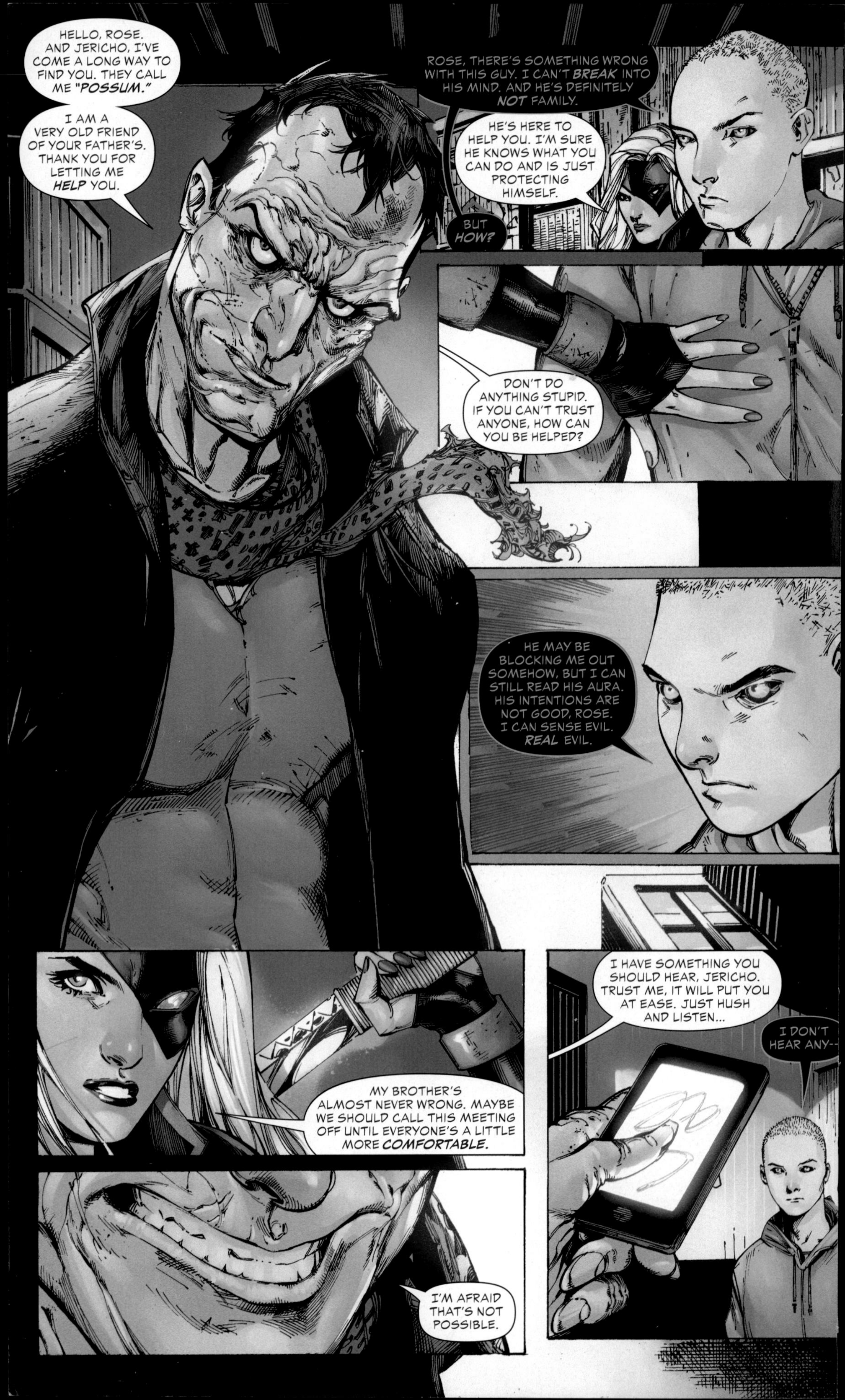
HELLO, ROSE. AND JERICHO, I'VE COME A LONG WAY TO FIND YOU. THEY CALL ME "POSSUM."
I AM A VERY OLD FRIEND OF YOUR FATHER'S. THANK YOU FOR LETTING ME HELP YOU.
ROSE, THERE'S SOMETHING WRONG WITH THIS GUY. I CAN'T BREAK INTO HIS MIND. AND HE'S DEFINITELY NOT FAMILY.
HE'S HERE TO HELP YOU. I'M SURE HE KNOWS WHAT YOU CAN DO AND IS JUST PROTECTING HIMSELF.
BUT HOW?
DON'T DO ANYTHING STUPID. IF YOU CAN'T TRUST ANYONE, HOW CAN YOU BE HELPED?
HE MAY BE BLOCKING ME OUT SOMEHOW, BUT I CAN STILL READ HIS AURA. HIS INTENTIONS ARE NOT GOOD, ROSE. I CAN SENSE EVIL. REAL EVIL.
MY BROTHER'S ALMOST NEVER WRONG. MAYBE WE SHOULD CALL THIS MEETING OFF UNTIL EVERYONE'S A LITTLE MORE COMFORTABLE.
I'M AFRAID THAT'S NOT POSSIBLE.
I HAVE SOMETHING YOU SHOULD HEAR, JERICHO. TRUST ME, IT WILL PUT YOU AT EASE. JUST HUSH AND LISTEN...
I DON'T HEAR ANY--

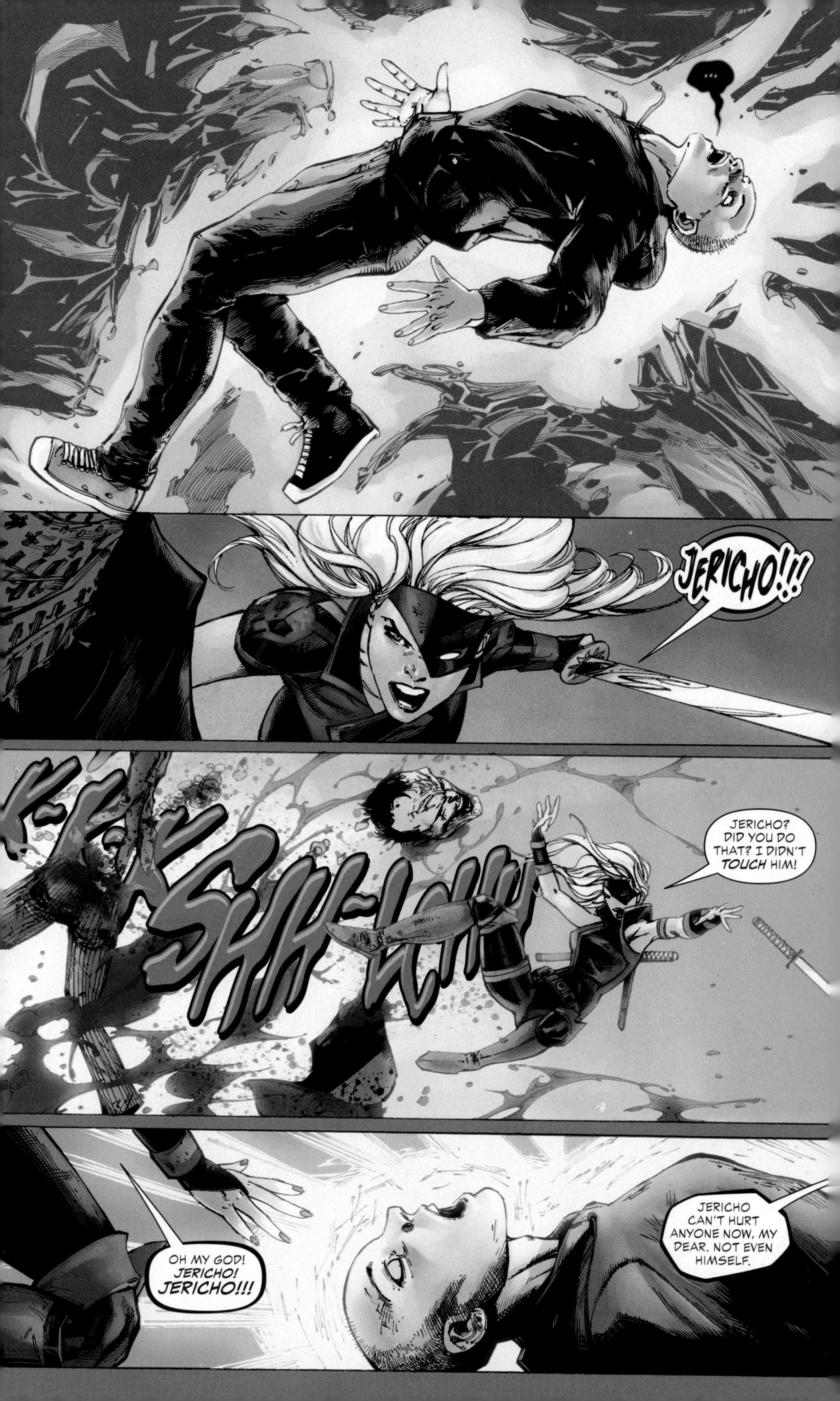
...
JERICHO!!!
K-K-K-SHH-LCHH
JERICHO? DID YOU DO THAT? I DIDN'T *TOUCH* HIM!
OH MY GOD! JERICHO! **JERICHO!!!**
JERICHO CAN'T HURT ANYONE NOW, MY DEAR. NOT EVEN HIMSELF.

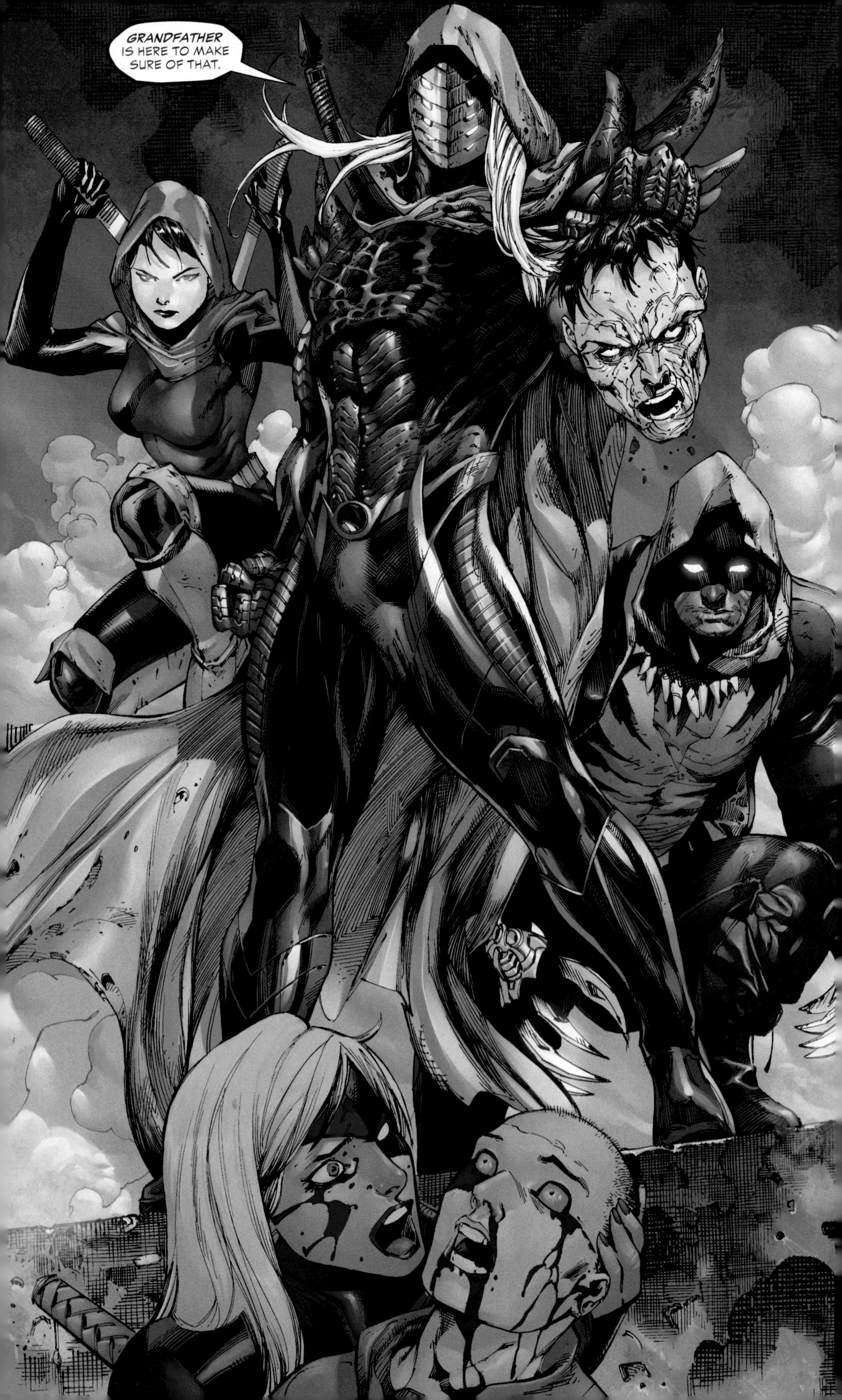
GRANDFATHER IS HERE TO MAKE SURE OF THAT.

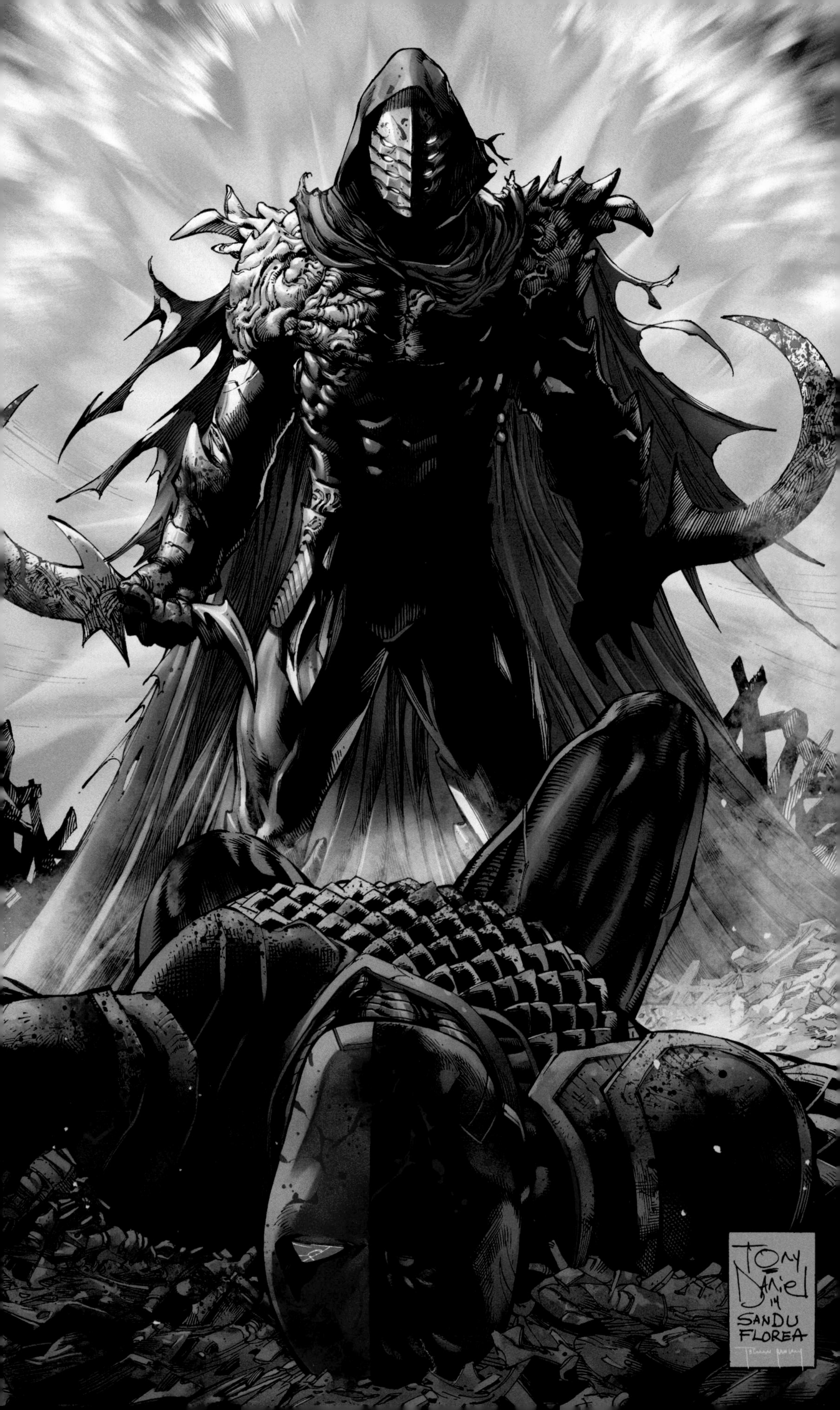
TONY DANIEL '14
SANDU FLOREA

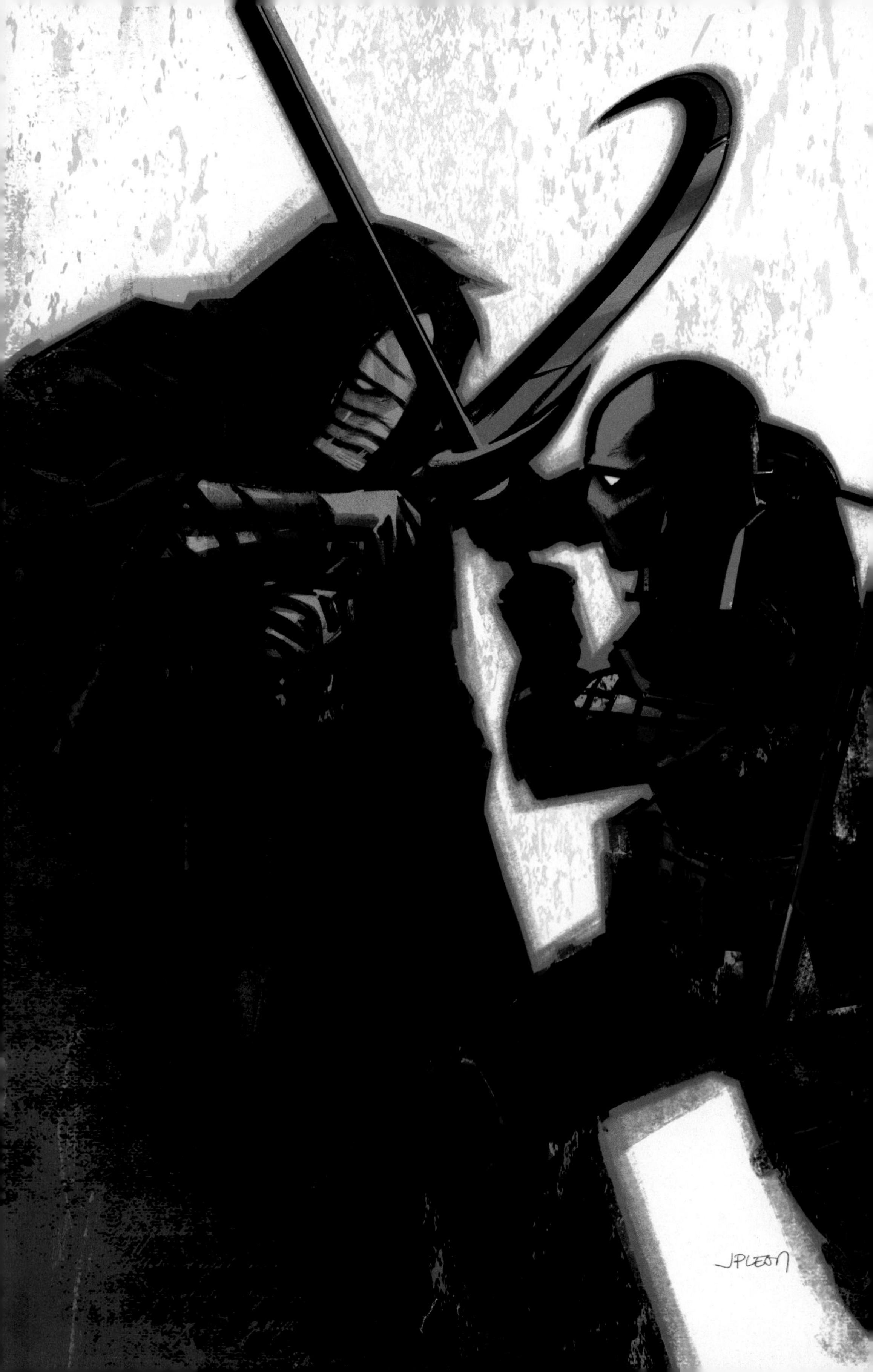

JPLEON

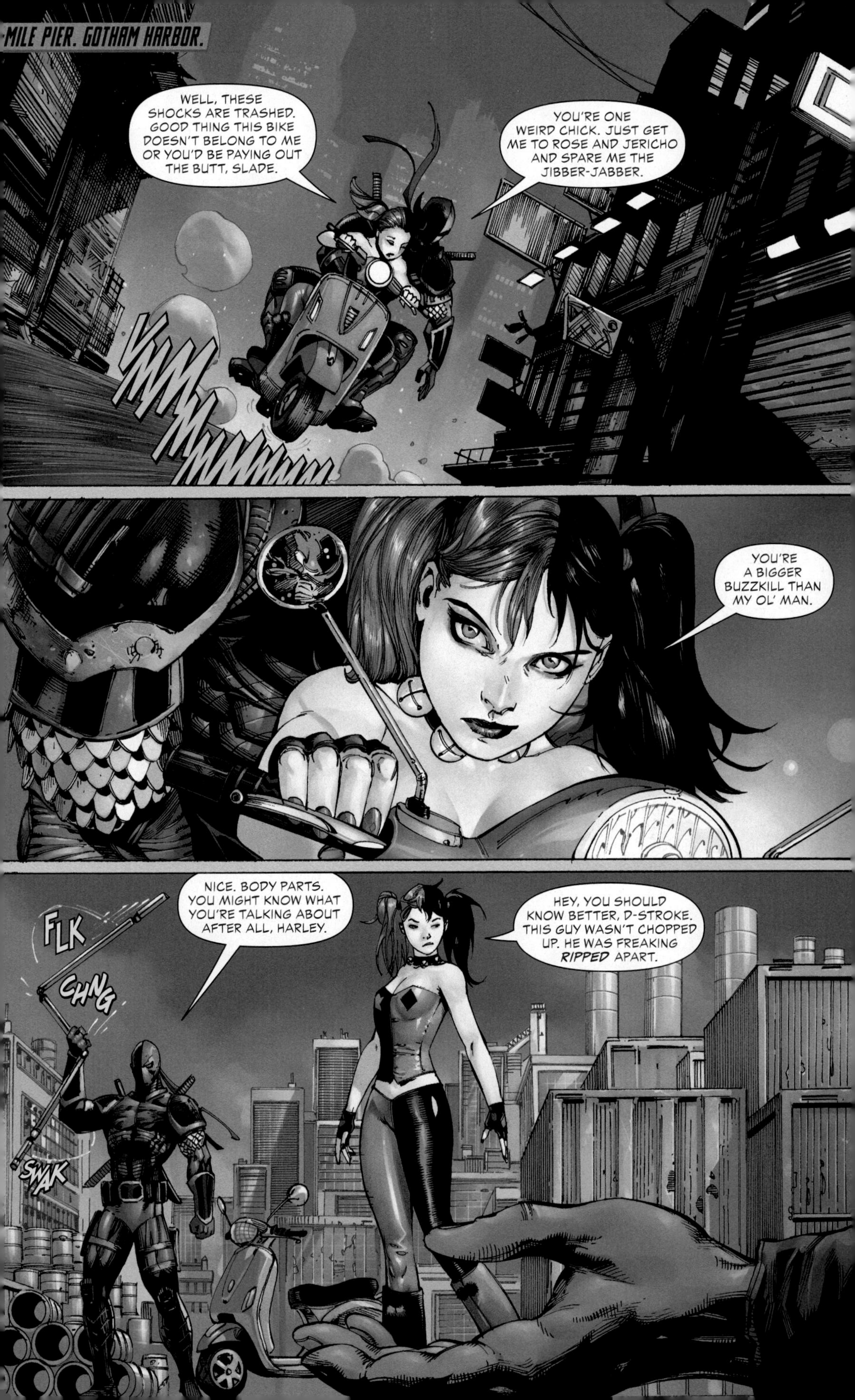
MILE PIER. GOTHAM HARBOR.
WELL, THESE SHOCKS ARE TRASHED. GOOD THING THIS BIKE DOESN'T BELONG TO ME OR YOU'D BE PAYING OUT THE BUTT, SLADE.
YOU'RE ONE WEIRD CHICK. JUST GET ME TO ROSE AND JERICHO AND SPARE ME THE JIBBER-JABBER.
VMMMMMMMMMMM
YOU'RE A BIGGER BUZZKILL THAN MY OL' MAN.
FLK
CHNG
SWAK
NICE. BODY PARTS. YOU MIGHT KNOW WHAT YOU'RE TALKING ABOUT AFTER ALL, HARLEY.
HEY, YOU SHOULD KNOW BETTER, D-STROKE. THIS GUY WASN'T CHOPPED UP. HE WAS FREAKING *RIPPED* APART.

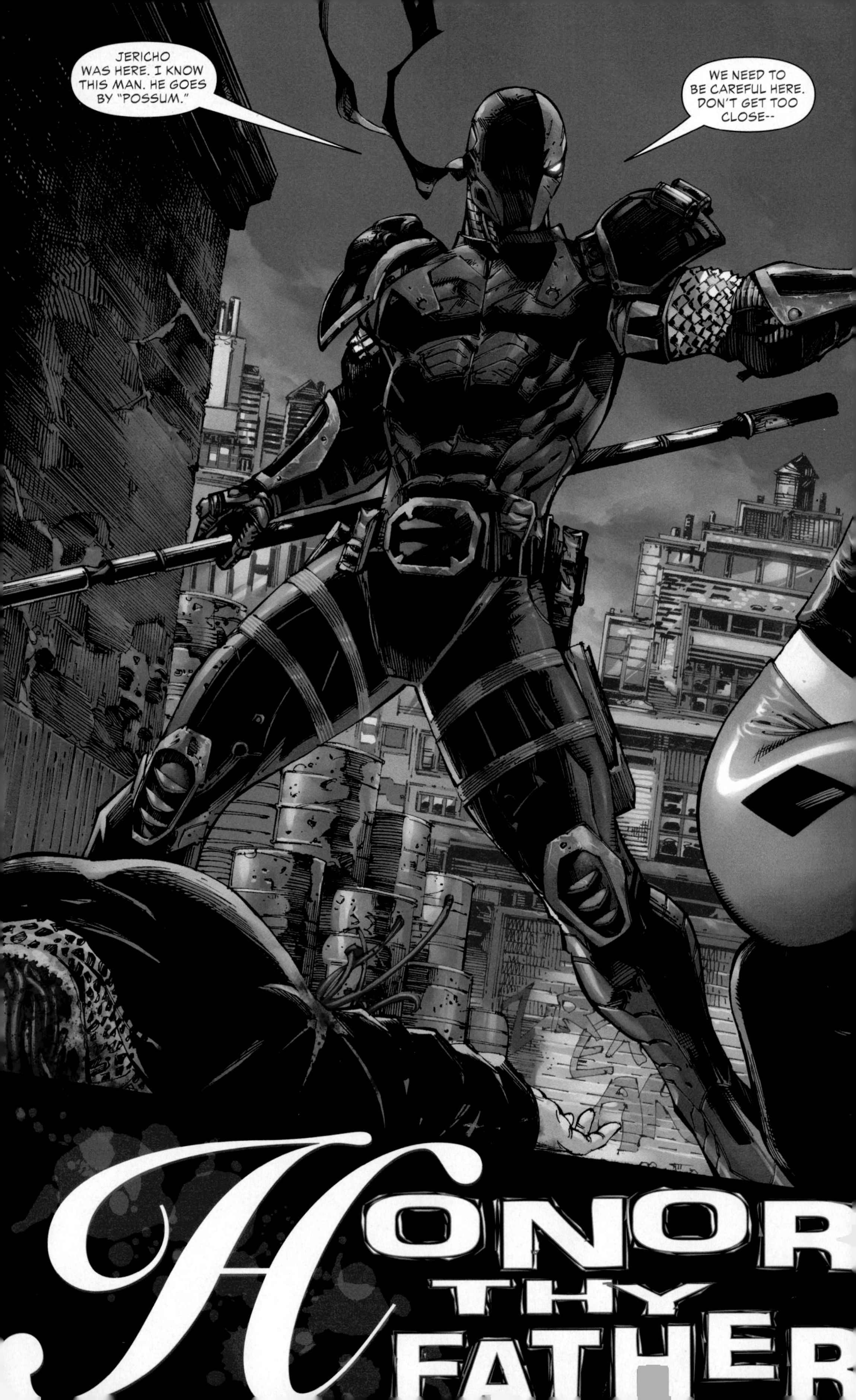
JERICHO WAS HERE. I KNOW THIS MAN. HE GOES BY "POSSUM."
WE NEED TO BE CAREFUL HERE. DON'T GET TOO CLOSE--
HONOR THY FATHER

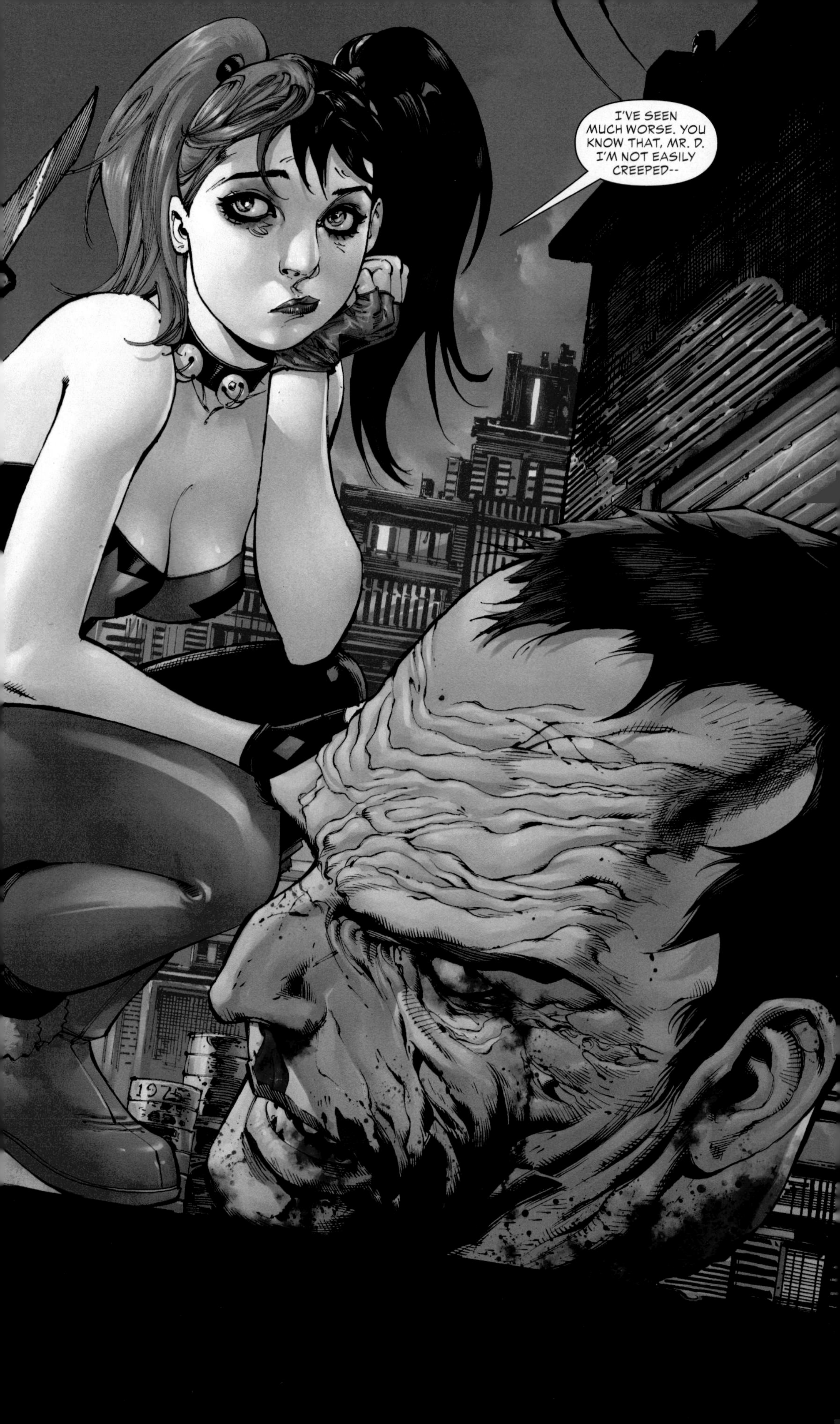
I'VE SEEN MUCH WORSE. YOU KNOW THAT, MR. D. I'M NOT EASILY CREEPED--

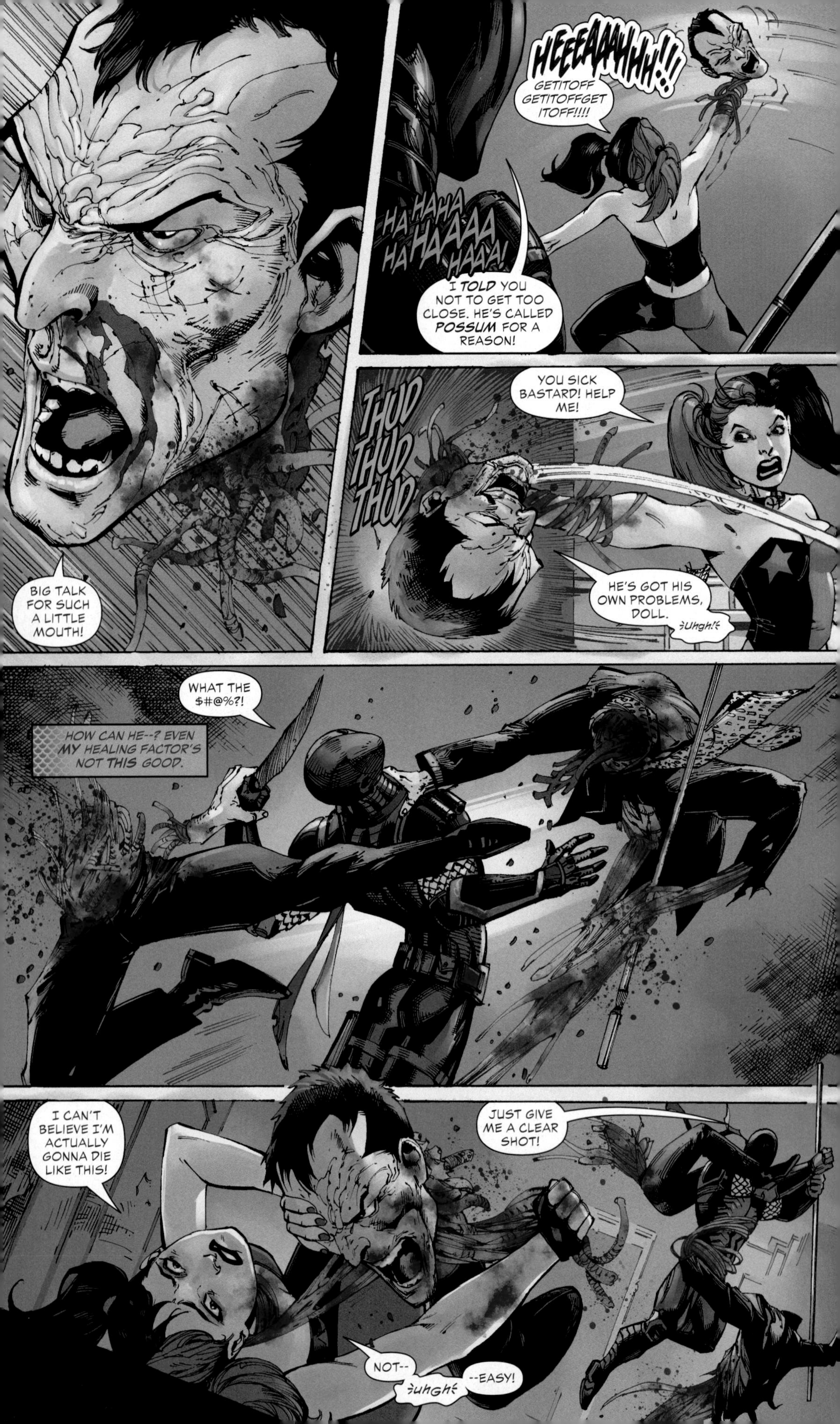
BIG TALK FOR SUCH A LITTLE MOUTH!
HEEEAAAHHH!!!
GETITOFF GETITOFFGET ITOFF!!!!
HA HAHA HA HAAAA HAAA!
I TOLD YOU NOT TO GET TOO CLOSE. HE'S CALLED POSSUM FOR A REASON!
THUD THUD THUD
YOU SICK BASTARD! HELP ME!
HE'S GOT HIS OWN PROBLEMS, DOLL.
uhgh!
WHAT THE $#@%?!
HOW CAN HE--? EVEN MY HEALING FACTOR'S NOT THIS GOOD.
I CAN'T BELIEVE I'M ACTUALLY GONNA DIE LIKE THIS!
JUST GIVE ME A CLEAR SHOT!
NOT--
uhgh
--EASY!

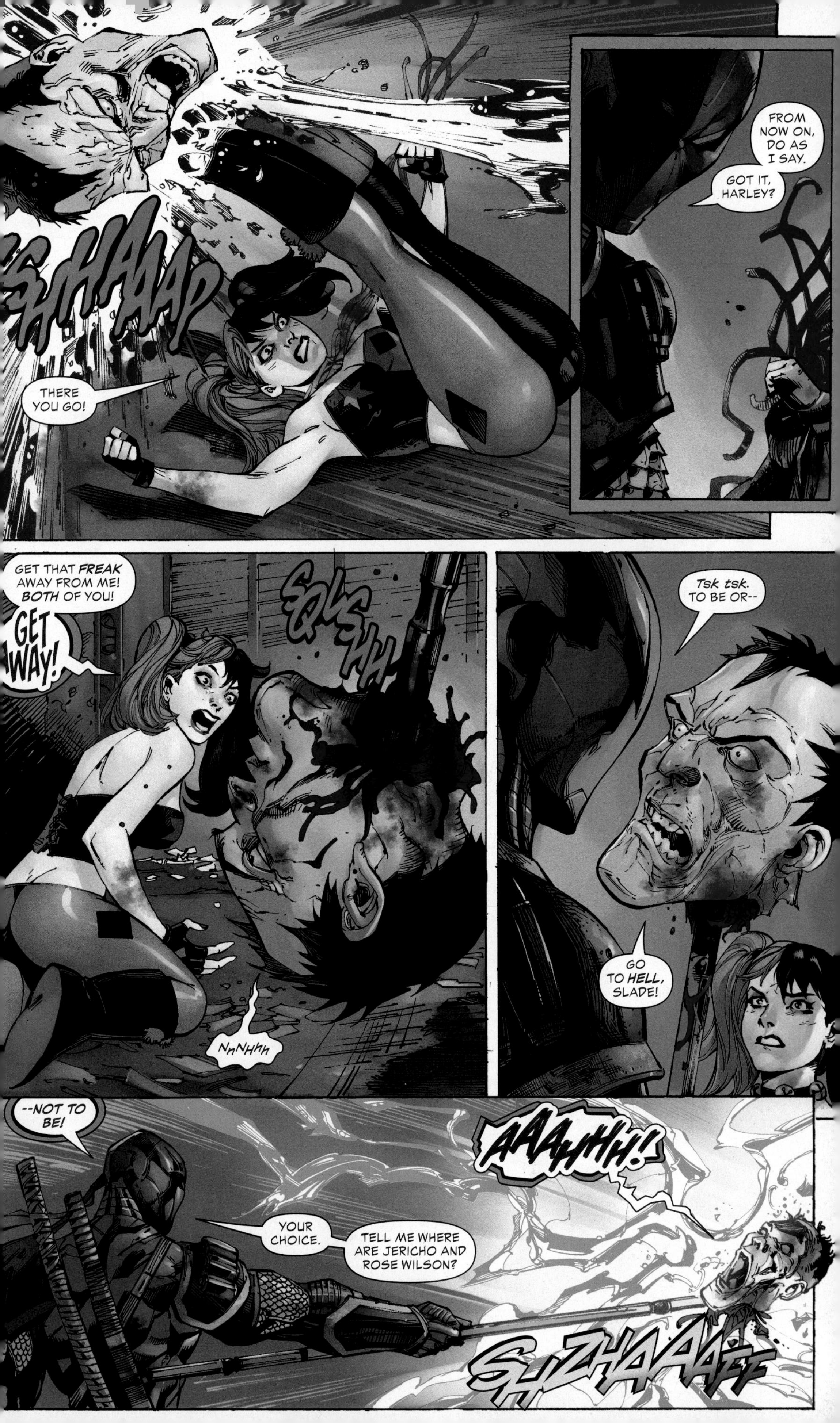
SHHAAAP
THERE YOU GO!
FROM NOW ON, DO AS I SAY.
GOT IT, HARLEY?
GET THAT FREAK AWAY FROM ME! BOTH OF YOU!
GET AWAY!
SQUSHH
NnNhhh
Tsk tsk. TO BE OR--
GO TO HELL, SLADE!
--NOT TO BE!
AAAHHH!
YOUR CHOICE.
TELL ME WHERE ARE JERICHO AND ROSE WILSON?
SHZHAAAFF

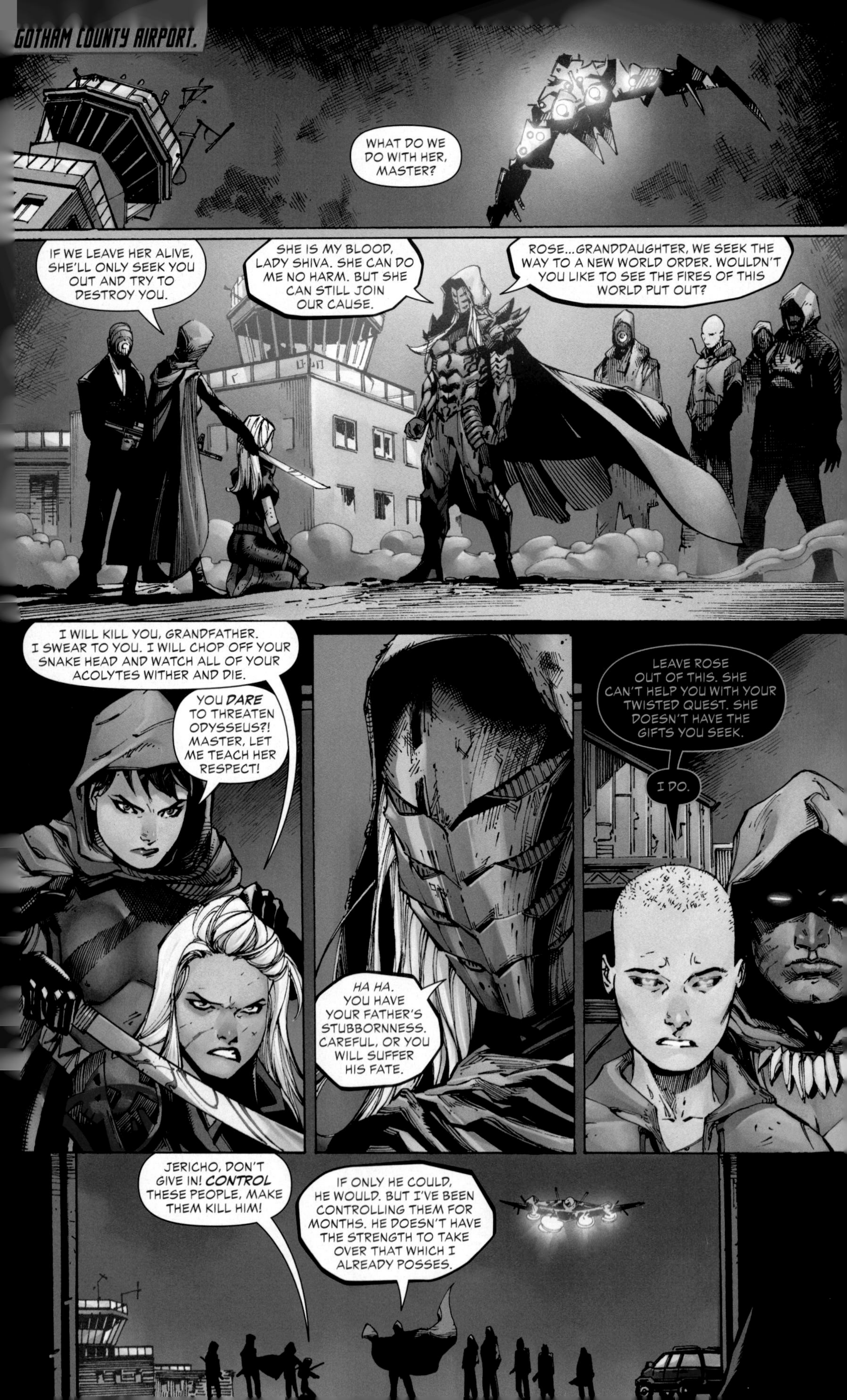

GOTHAM COUNTY AIRPORT.
WHAT DO WE DO WITH HER, MASTER?
IF WE LEAVE HER ALIVE, SHE'LL ONLY SEEK YOU OUT AND TRY TO DESTROY YOU.
SHE IS MY BLOOD, LADY SHIVA. SHE CAN DO ME NO HARM. BUT SHE CAN STILL JOIN OUR CAUSE.
ROSE...GRANDDAUGHTER, WE SEEK THE WAY TO A NEW WORLD ORDER. WOULDN'T YOU LIKE TO SEE THE FIRES OF THIS WORLD PUT OUT?
I WILL KILL YOU, GRANDFATHER. I SWEAR TO YOU. I WILL CHOP OFF YOUR SNAKE HEAD AND WATCH ALL OF YOUR ACOLYTES WITHER AND DIE.
YOU DARE TO THREATEN ODYSSEUS?! MASTER, LET ME TEACH HER RESPECT!
HA HA. YOU HAVE YOUR FATHER'S STUBBORNNESS. CAREFUL, OR YOU WILL SUFFER HIS FATE.
LEAVE ROSE OUT OF THIS. SHE CAN'T HELP YOU WITH YOUR TWISTED QUEST. SHE DOESN'T HAVE THE GIFTS YOU SEEK.
I DO.
JERICHO, DON'T GIVE IN! CONTROL THESE PEOPLE, MAKE THEM KILL HIM!
IF ONLY HE COULD, HE WOULD. BUT I'VE BEEN CONTROLLING THEM FOR MONTHS. HE DOESN'T HAVE THE STRENGTH TO TAKE OVER THAT WHICH I ALREADY POSSES.

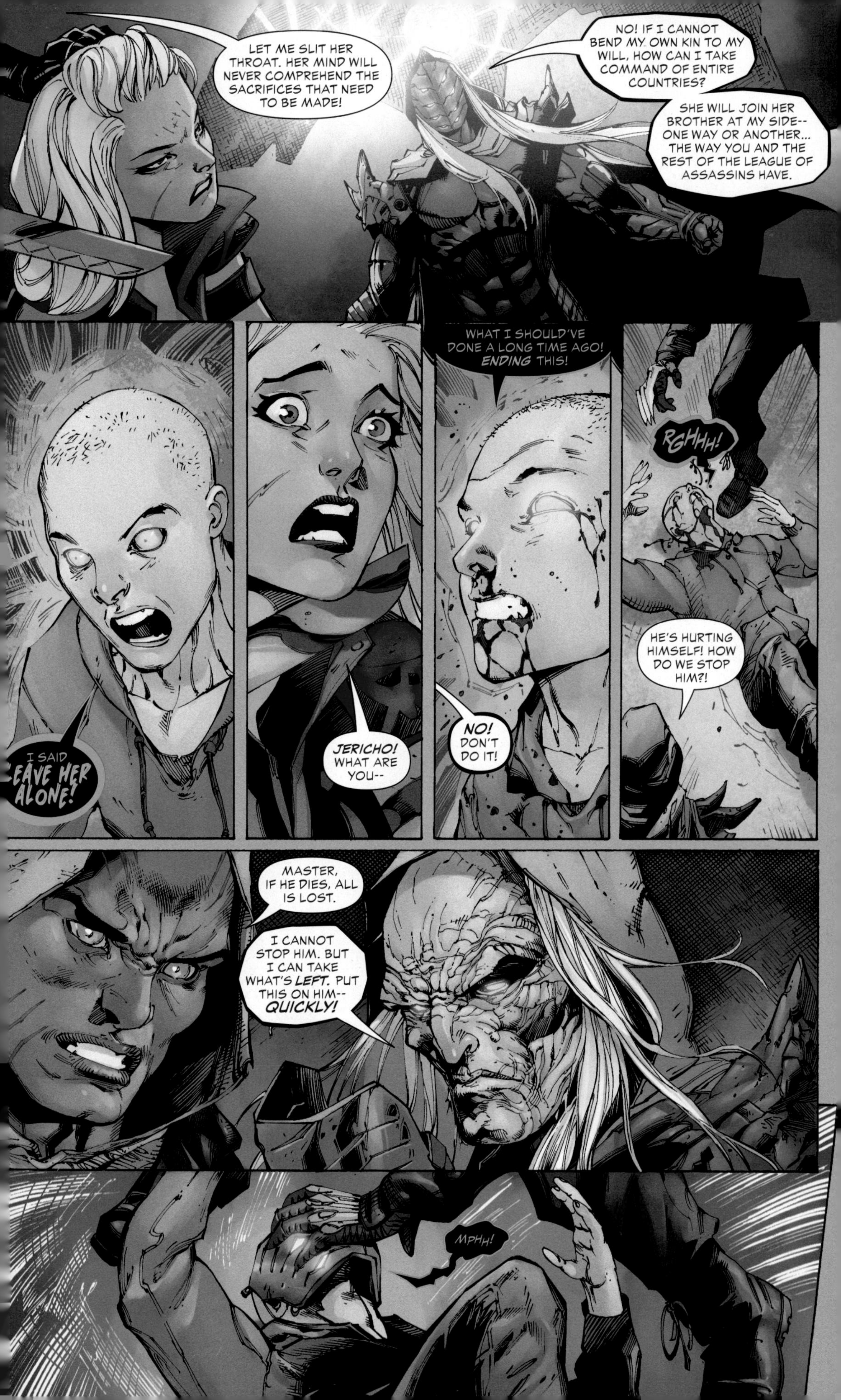
LET ME SLIT HER THROAT. HER MIND WILL NEVER COMPREHEND THE SACRIFICES THAT NEED TO BE MADE!
NO! IF I CANNOT BEND MY OWN KIN TO MY WILL, HOW CAN I TAKE COMMAND OF ENTIRE COUNTRIES?
SHE WILL JOIN HER BROTHER AT MY SIDE-- ONE WAY OR ANOTHER... THE WAY YOU AND THE REST OF THE LEAGUE OF ASSASSINS HAVE.
I SAID LEAVE HER ALONE!
JERICHO! WHAT ARE YOU--
WHAT I SHOULD'VE DONE A LONG TIME AGO! ENDING THIS!
NO! DON'T DO IT!
RGHHH!
HE'S HURTING HIMSELF! HOW DO WE STOP HIM?!
MASTER, IF HE DIES, ALL IS LOST.
I CANNOT STOP HIM. BUT I CAN TAKE WHAT'S LEFT. PUT THIS ON HIM-- QUICKLY!
MPHH!

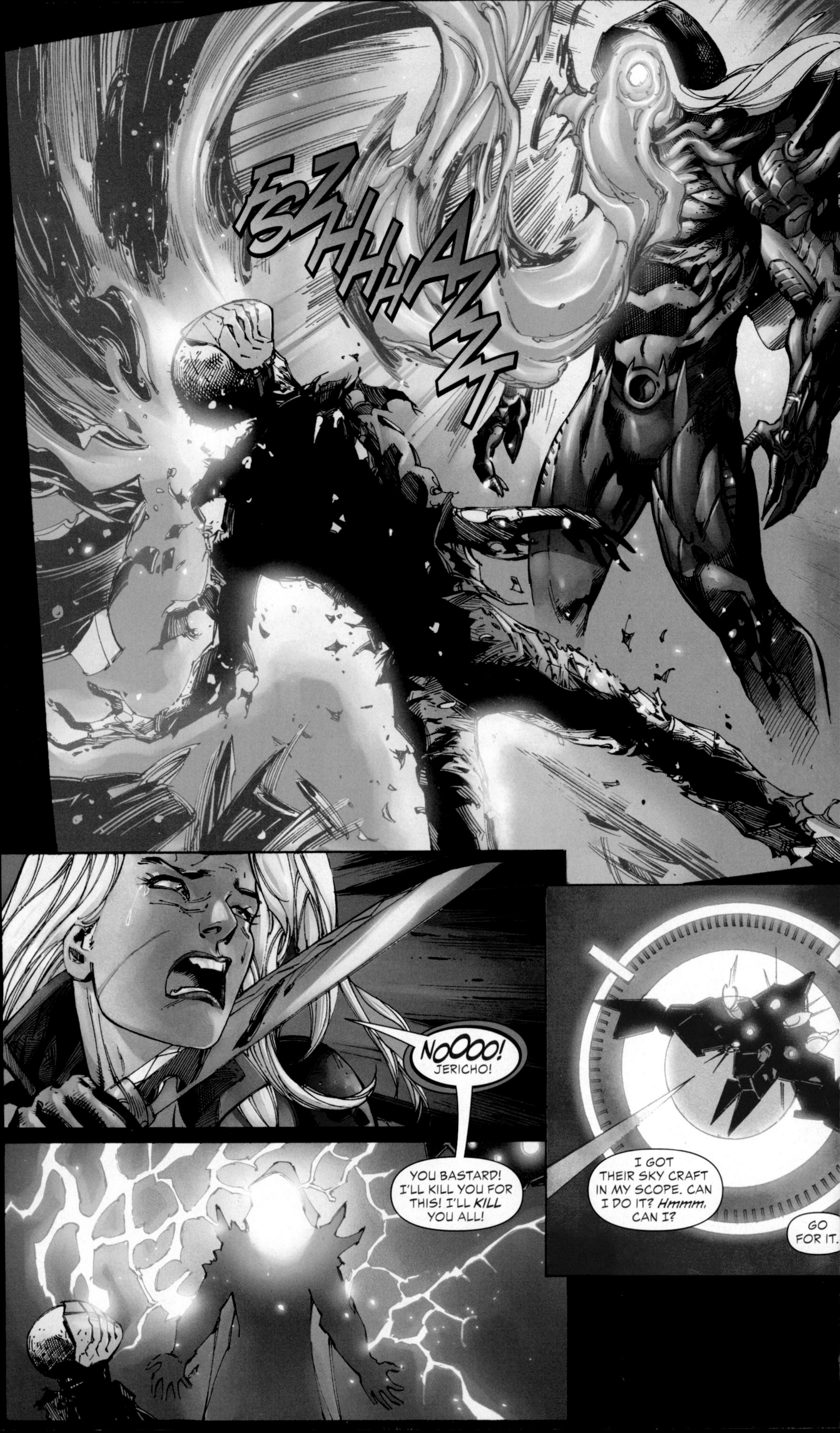
FSZHHHAZZM
NOOOO! JERICHO!
YOU BASTARD! I'LL KILL YOU FOR THIS! I'LL KILL YOU ALL!
I GOT THEIR SKY CRAFT IN MY SCOPE. CAN I DO IT? Hmmm. CAN I?
GO FOR IT.

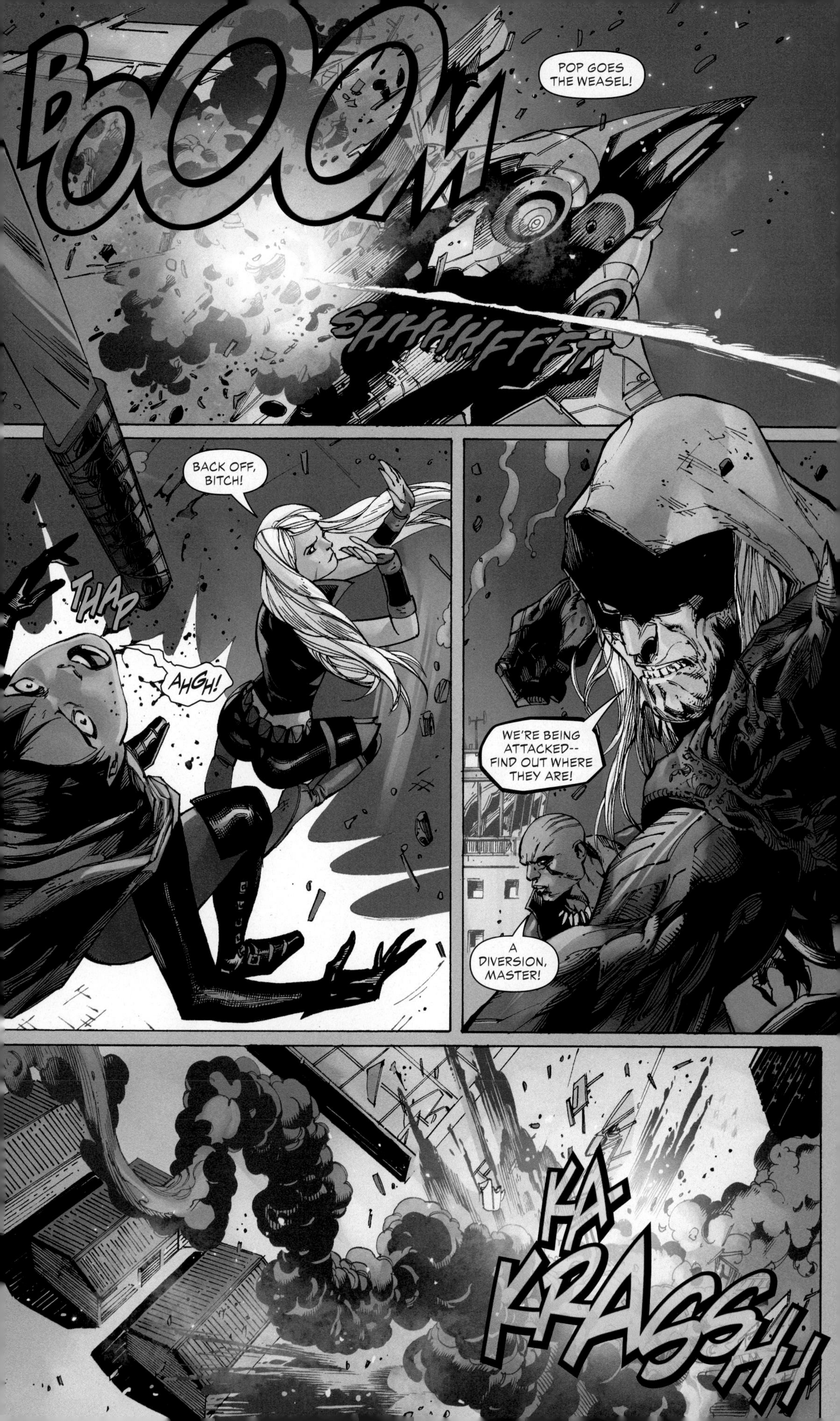
BOOM
POP GOES THE WEASEL!
SHHHHFFFT
BACK OFF, BITCH!
THAP
AHGH!
WE'RE BEING ATTACKED-- FIND OUT WHERE THEY ARE!
A DIVERSION, MASTER!
KA-KRASSH

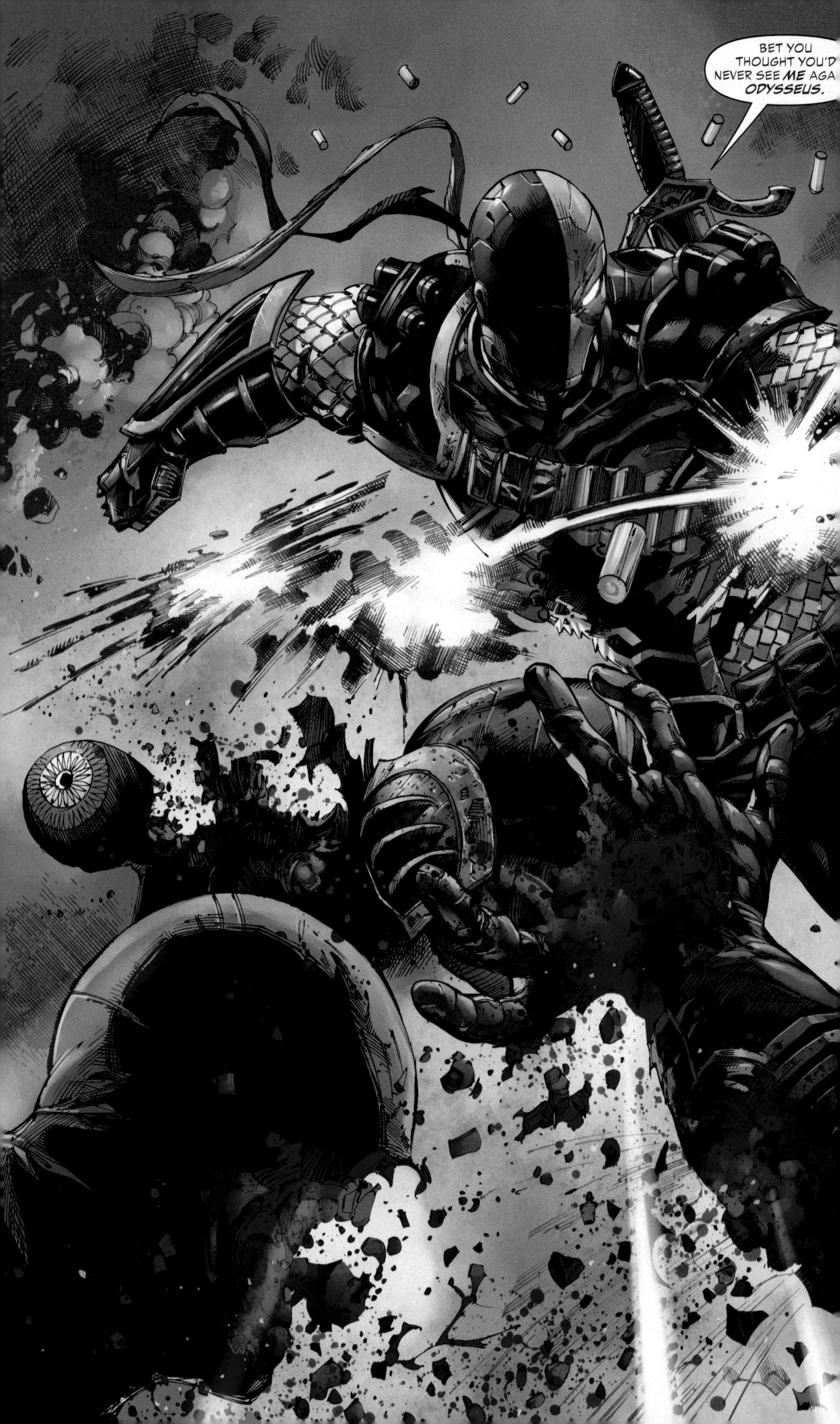
BET YOU THOUGHT YOU'D NEVER SEE ***ME*** AGA ***ODYSSEUS.***

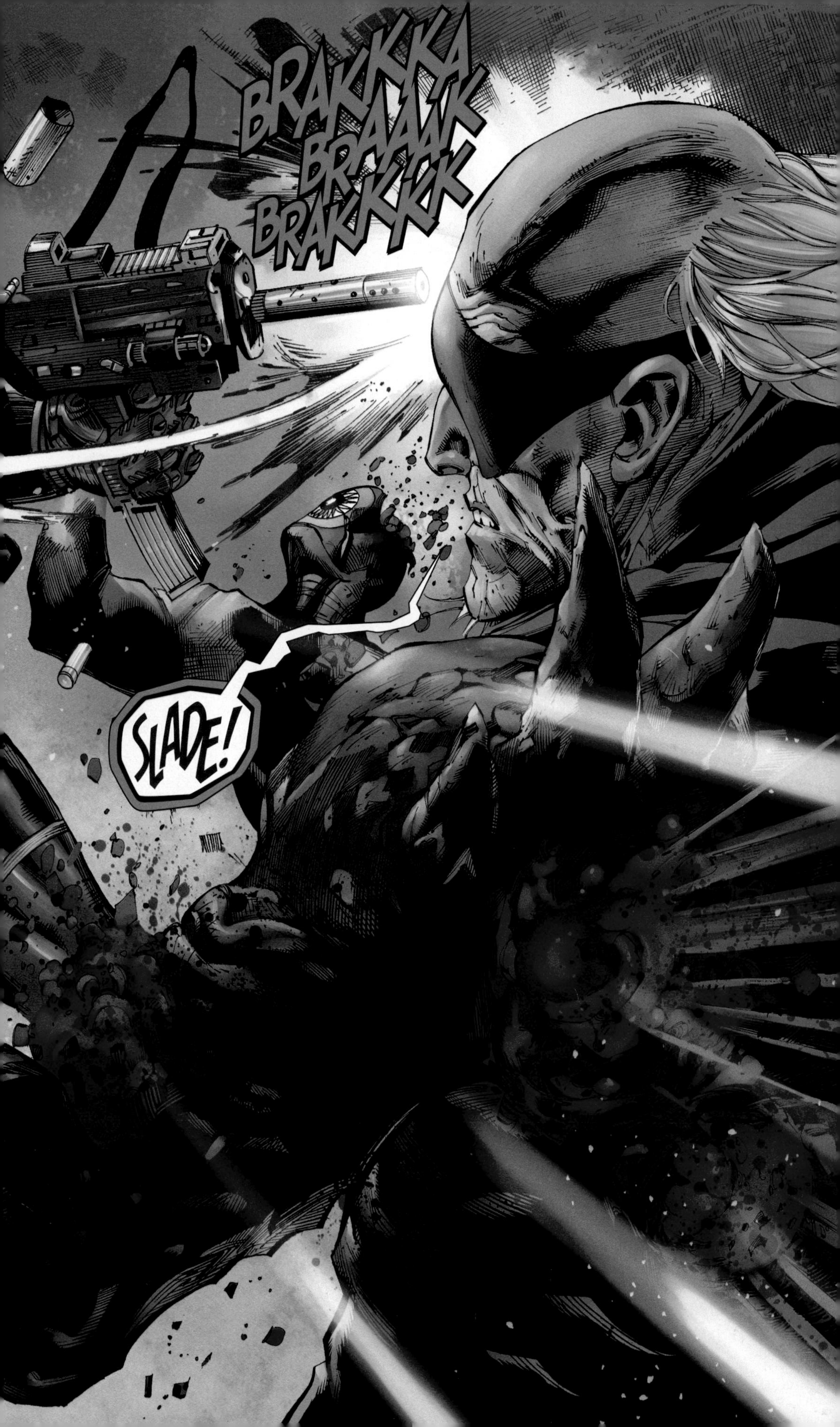
BRAKKKA
BRAAAAK
BRAKKKK
SLADE!

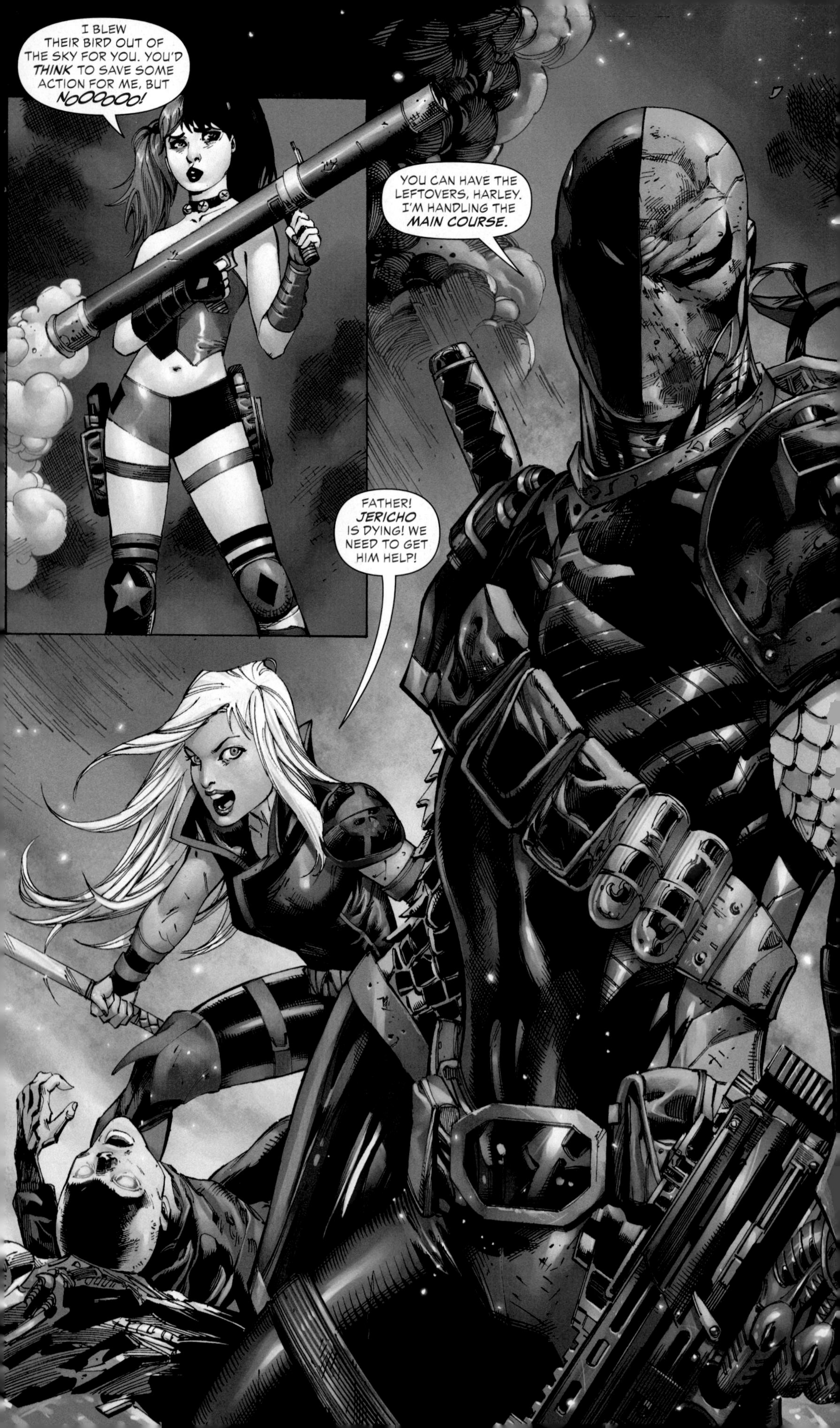
I BLEW THEIR BIRD OUT OF THE SKY FOR YOU. YOU'D *THINK* TO SAVE SOME ACTION FOR ME, BUT *NOOOOOO!*
YOU CAN HAVE THE LEFTOVERS, HARLEY. I'M HANDLING THE *MAIN COURSE.*
FATHER! *JERICHO* IS DYING! WE NEED TO GET HIM HELP!

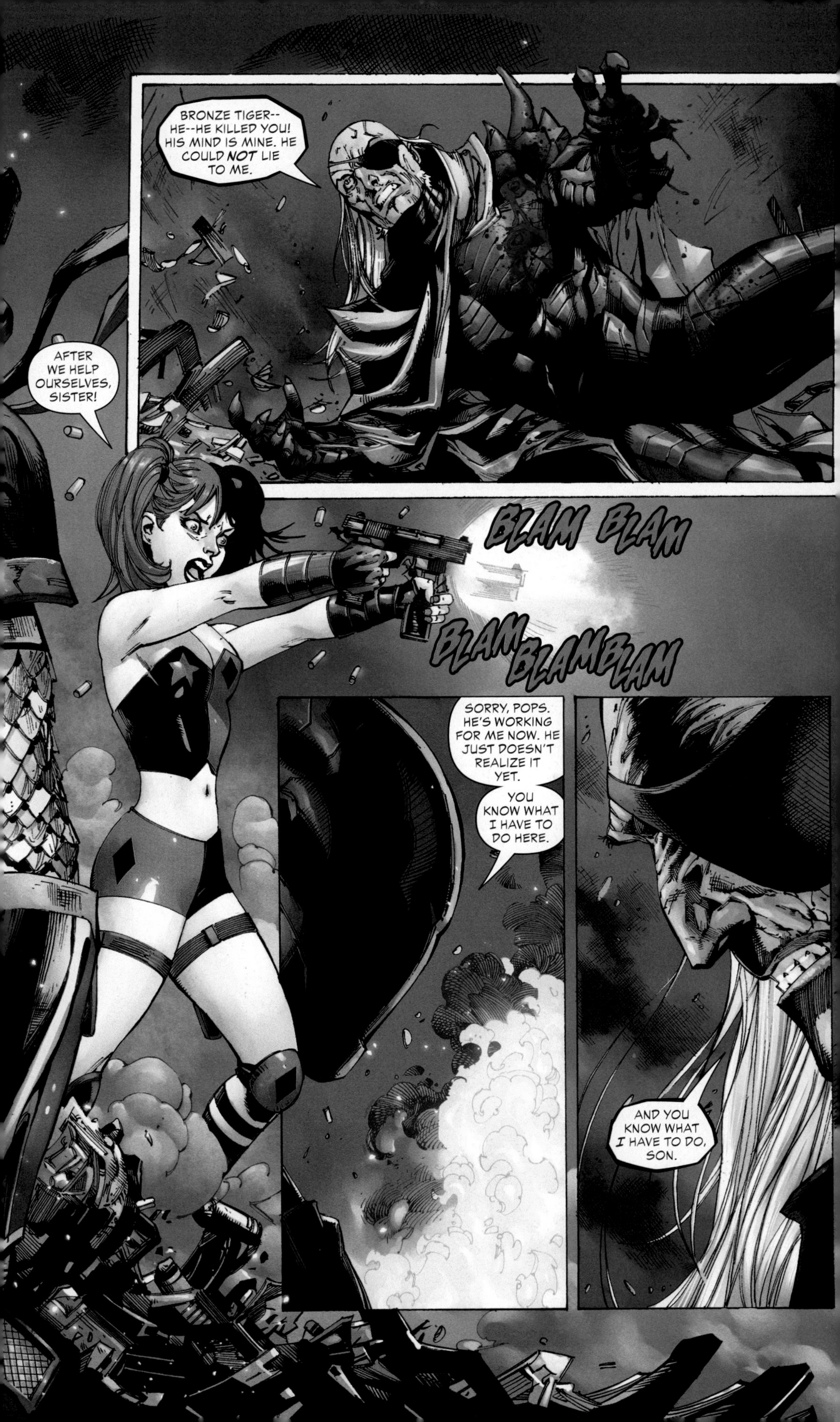
BRONZE TIGER-- HE--HE KILLED YOU! HIS MIND IS MINE. HE COULD NOT LIE TO ME.
AFTER WE HELP OURSELVES, SISTER!
BLAM BLAM
BLAM BLAMBLAM
SORRY, POPS. HE'S WORKING FOR ME NOW. HE JUST DOESN'T REALIZE IT YET.
YOU KNOW WHAT I HAVE TO DO HERE.
AND YOU KNOW WHAT I HAVE TO DO, SON.

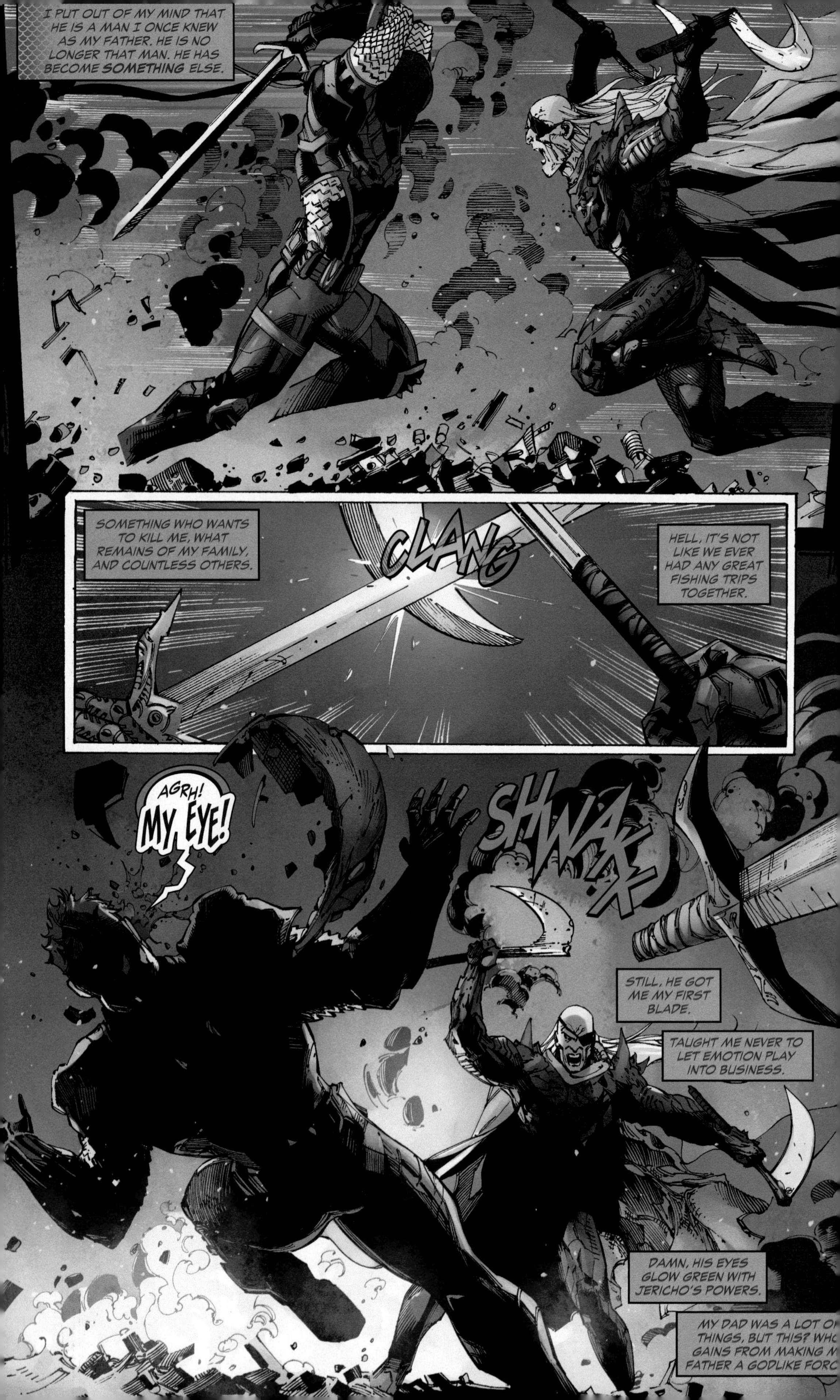
I PUT OUT OF MY MIND THAT HE IS A MAN I ONCE KNEW AS MY FATHER. HE IS NO LONGER THAT MAN. HE HAS BECOME SOMETHING ELSE.
SOMETHING WHO WANTS TO KILL ME, WHAT REMAINS OF MY FAMILY, AND COUNTLESS OTHERS.
CLANG
HELL, IT'S NOT LIKE WE EVER HAD ANY GREAT FISHING TRIPS TOGETHER.
AGRH! MY EYE!
SHWAKK
STILL, HE GOT ME MY FIRST BLADE.
TAUGHT ME NEVER TO LET EMOTION PLAY INTO BUSINESS.
DAMN, HIS EYES GLOW GREEN WITH JERICHO'S POWERS.
MY DAD WAS A LOT OF THINGS, BUT THIS? WHO GAINS FROM MAKING MY FATHER A GODLIKE FORCE

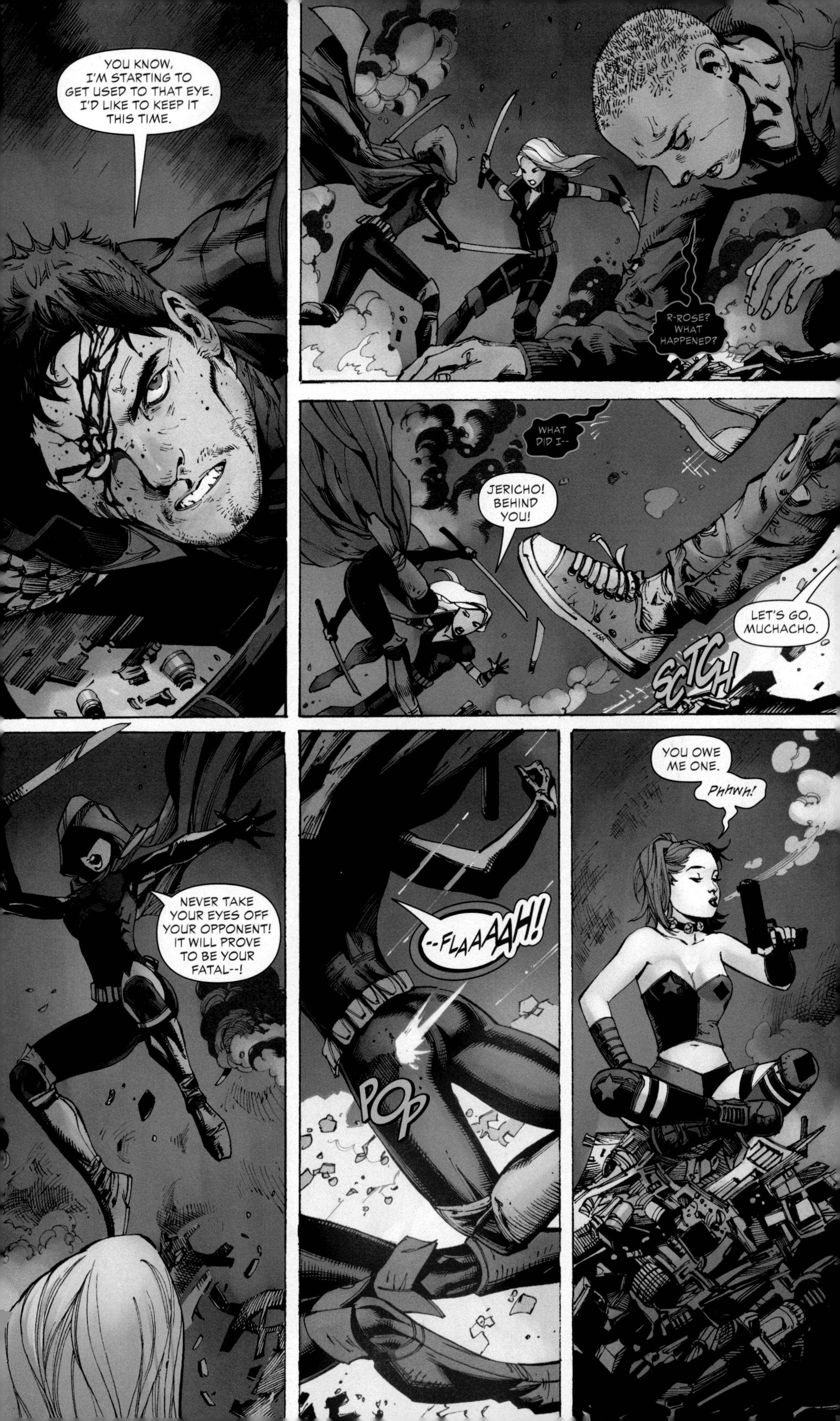
YOU KNOW, I'M STARTING TO GET USED TO THAT EYE. I'D LIKE TO KEEP IT THIS TIME.
R-ROSE? WHAT HAPPENED?
WHAT DID I--
JERICHO! BEHIND YOU!
LET'S GO, MUCHACHO.
SCTCH
NEVER TAKE YOUR EYES OFF YOUR OPPONENT! IT WILL PROVE TO BE YOUR FATAL--!
--FLAAAAH!
POP
YOU OWE ME ONE.
Phhwh!

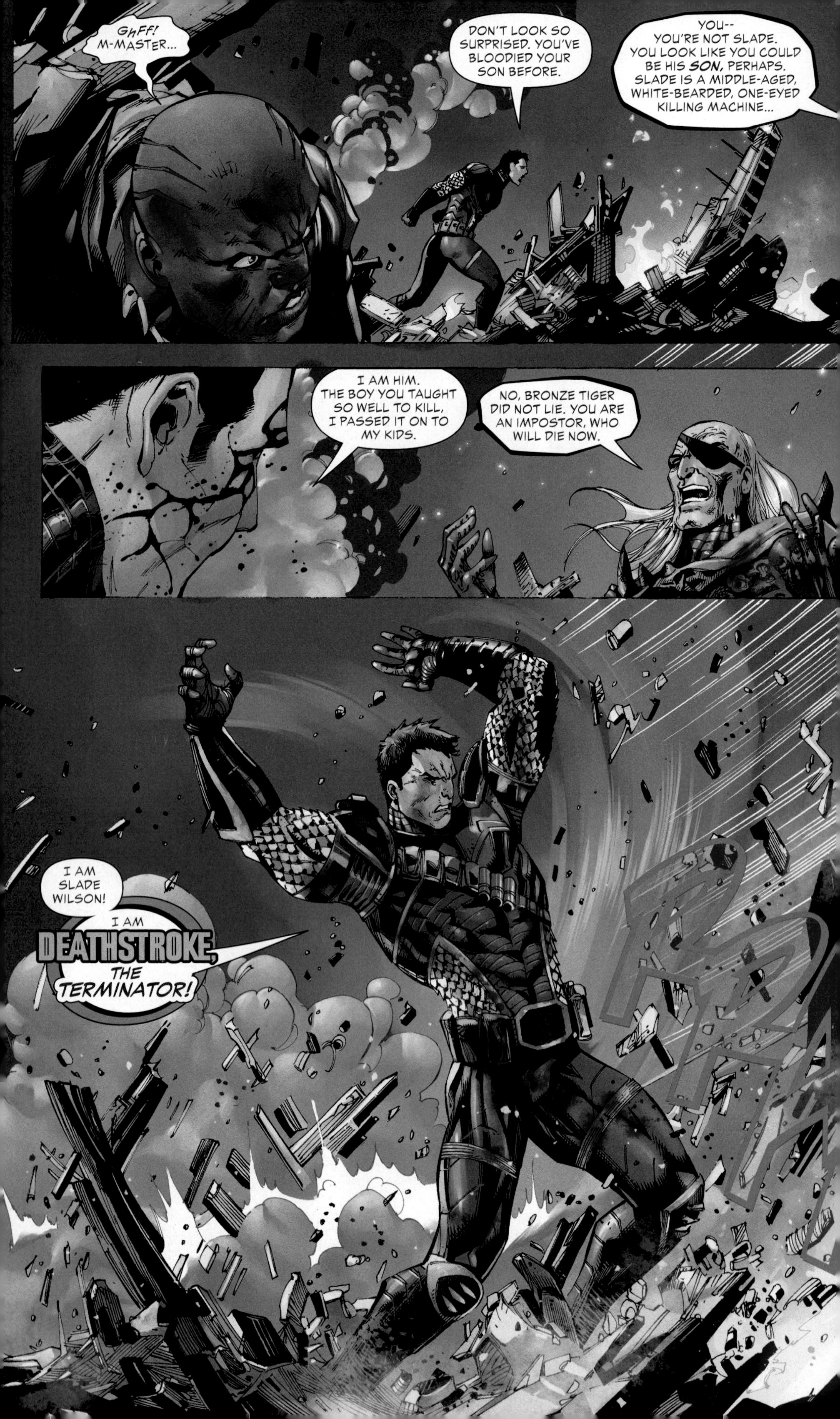
GHFF! M-MASTER...
DON'T LOOK SO SURPRISED. YOU'VE BLOODIED YOUR SON BEFORE.
YOU-- YOU'RE NOT SLADE. YOU LOOK LIKE YOU COULD BE HIS SON, PERHAPS. SLADE IS A MIDDLE-AGED, WHITE-BEARDED, ONE-EYED KILLING MACHINE...
I AM HIM. THE BOY YOU TAUGHT SO WELL TO KILL, I PASSED IT ON TO MY KIDS.
NO, BRONZE TIGER DID NOT LIE. YOU ARE AN IMPOSTOR, WHO WILL DIE NOW.
I AM SLADE WILSON!
I AM DEATHSTROKE, THE TERMINATOR!

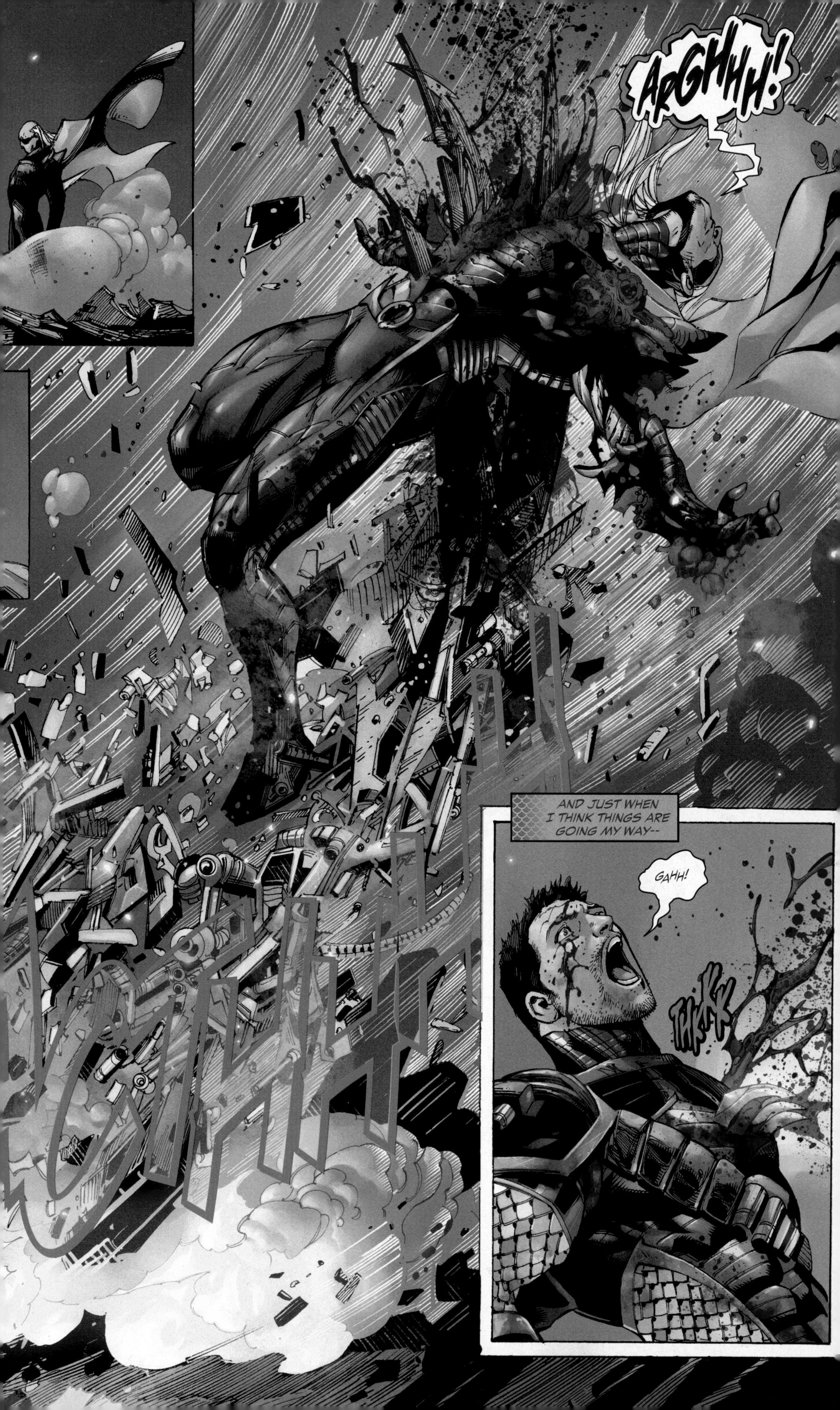
ARGHHH!
AND JUST WHEN I THINK THINGS ARE GOING MY WAY--
GAHH!
THKK

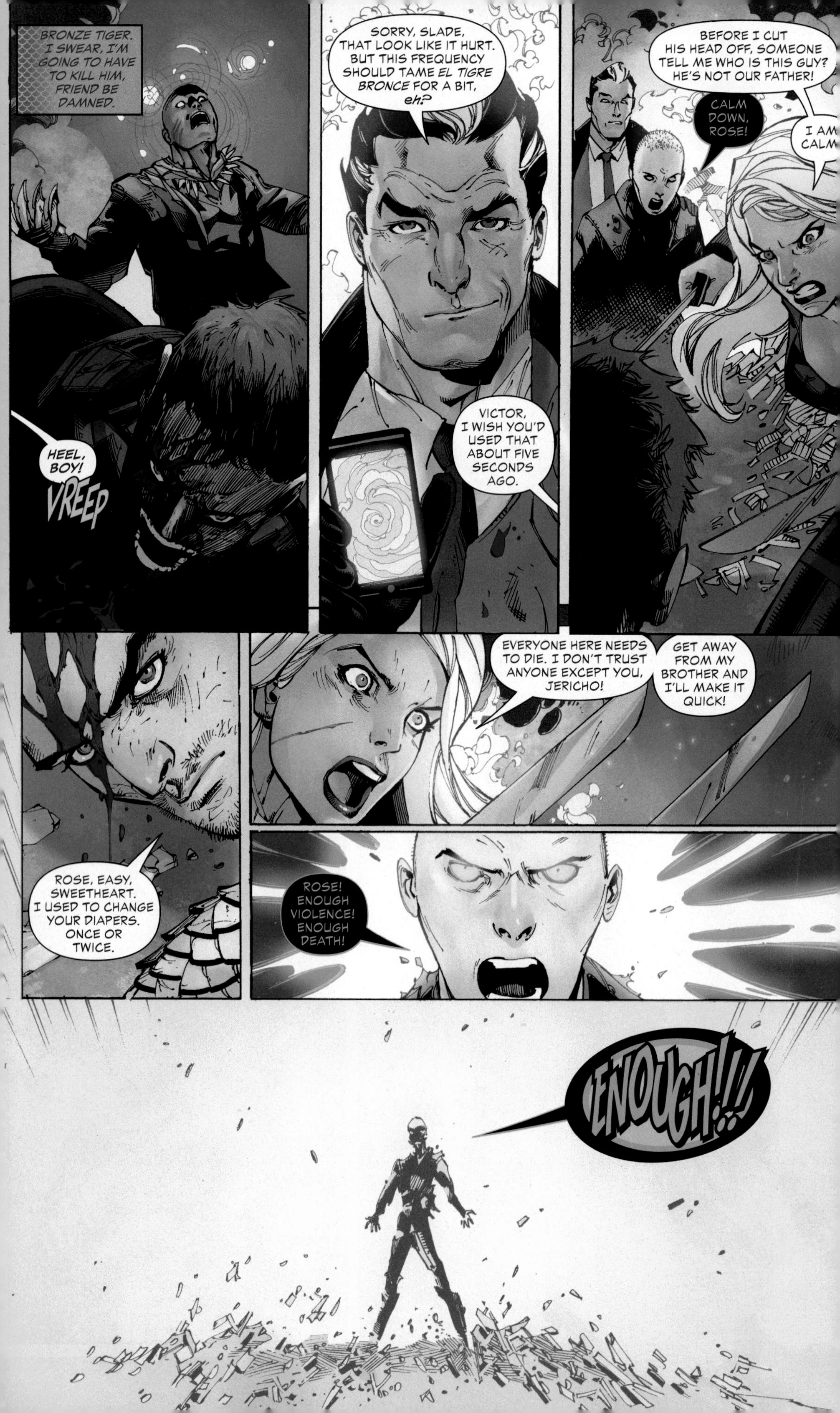
BRONZE TIGER. I SWEAR, I'M GOING TO HAVE TO KILL HIM, FRIEND BE DAMNED.
HEEL, BOY!
VREEP
SORRY, SLADE, THAT LOOK LIKE IT HURT. BUT THIS FREQUENCY SHOULD TAME EL TIGRE BRONCE FOR A BIT, eh?
VICTOR, I WISH YOU'D USED THAT ABOUT FIVE SECONDS AGO.
BEFORE I CUT HIS HEAD OFF, SOMEONE TELL ME WHO IS THIS GUY? HE'S NOT OUR FATHER!
CALM DOWN, ROSE!
I AM CALM
EVERYONE HERE NEEDS TO DIE. I DON'T TRUST ANYONE EXCEPT YOU, JERICHO!
GET AWAY FROM MY BROTHER AND I'LL MAKE IT QUICK!
ROSE, EASY, SWEETHEART. I USED TO CHANGE YOUR DIAPERS. ONCE OR TWICE.
ROSE! ENOUGH VIOLENCE! ENOUGH DEATH!
ENOUGH!!!!

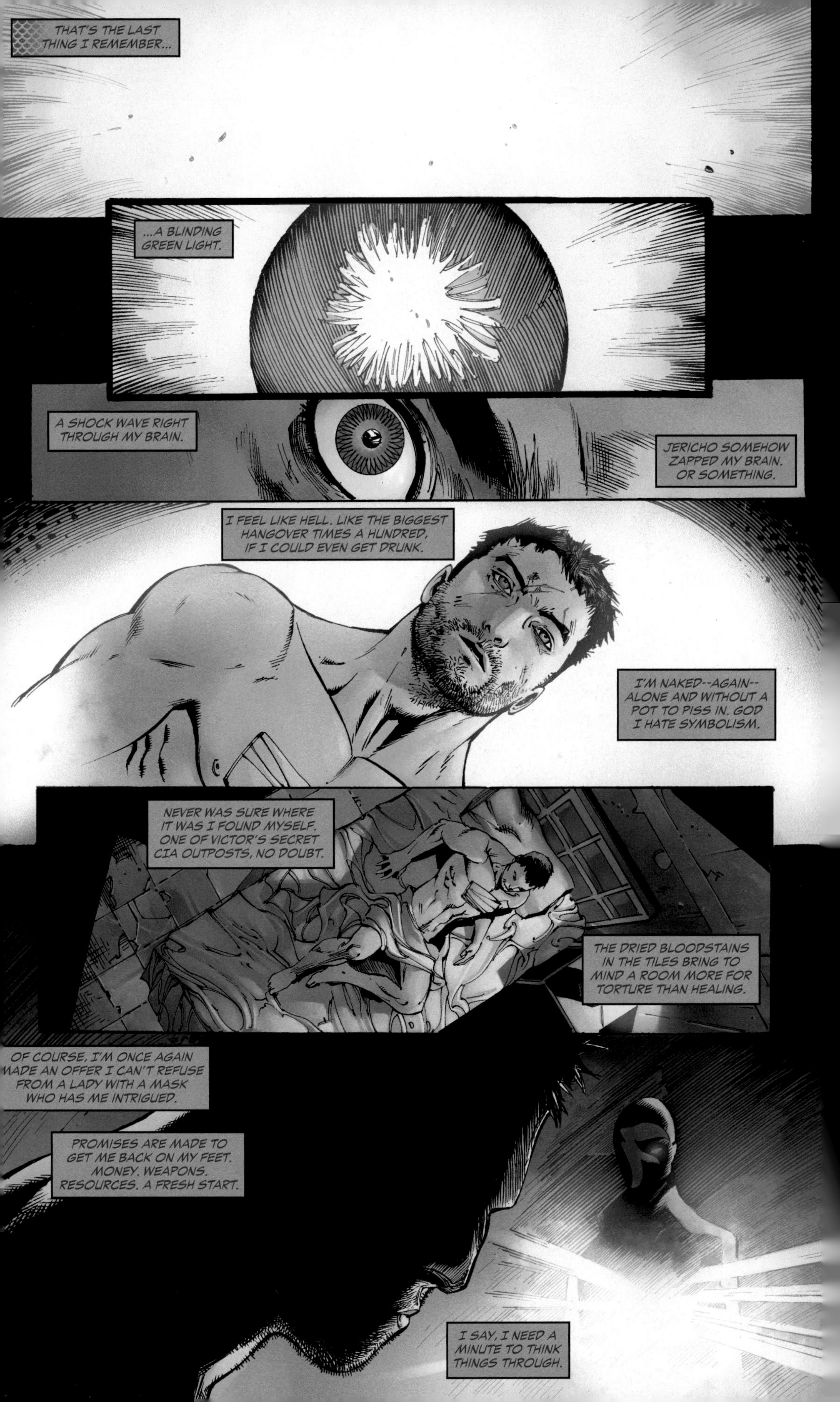

THAT'S THE LAST THING I REMEMBER...
...A BLINDING GREEN LIGHT.
A SHOCK WAVE RIGHT THROUGH MY BRAIN.
JERICHO SOMEHOW ZAPPED MY BRAIN. OR SOMETHING.
I FEEL LIKE HELL. LIKE THE BIGGEST HANGOVER TIMES A HUNDRED, IF I COULD EVEN GET DRUNK.
I'M NAKED--AGAIN--ALONE AND WITHOUT A POT TO PISS IN. GOD I HATE SYMBOLISM.
NEVER WAS SURE WHERE IT WAS I FOUND MYSELF. ONE OF VICTOR'S SECRET CIA OUTPOSTS, NO DOUBT.
THE DRIED BLOODSTAINS IN THE TILES BRING TO MIND A ROOM MORE FOR TORTURE THAN HEALING.
OF COURSE, I'M ONCE AGAIN MADE AN OFFER I CAN'T REFUSE FROM A LADY WITH A MASK WHO HAS ME INTRIGUED.
PROMISES ARE MADE TO GET ME BACK ON MY FEET. MONEY. WEAPONS. RESOURCES. A FRESH START.
I SAY, I NEED A MINUTE TO THINK THINGS THROUGH.

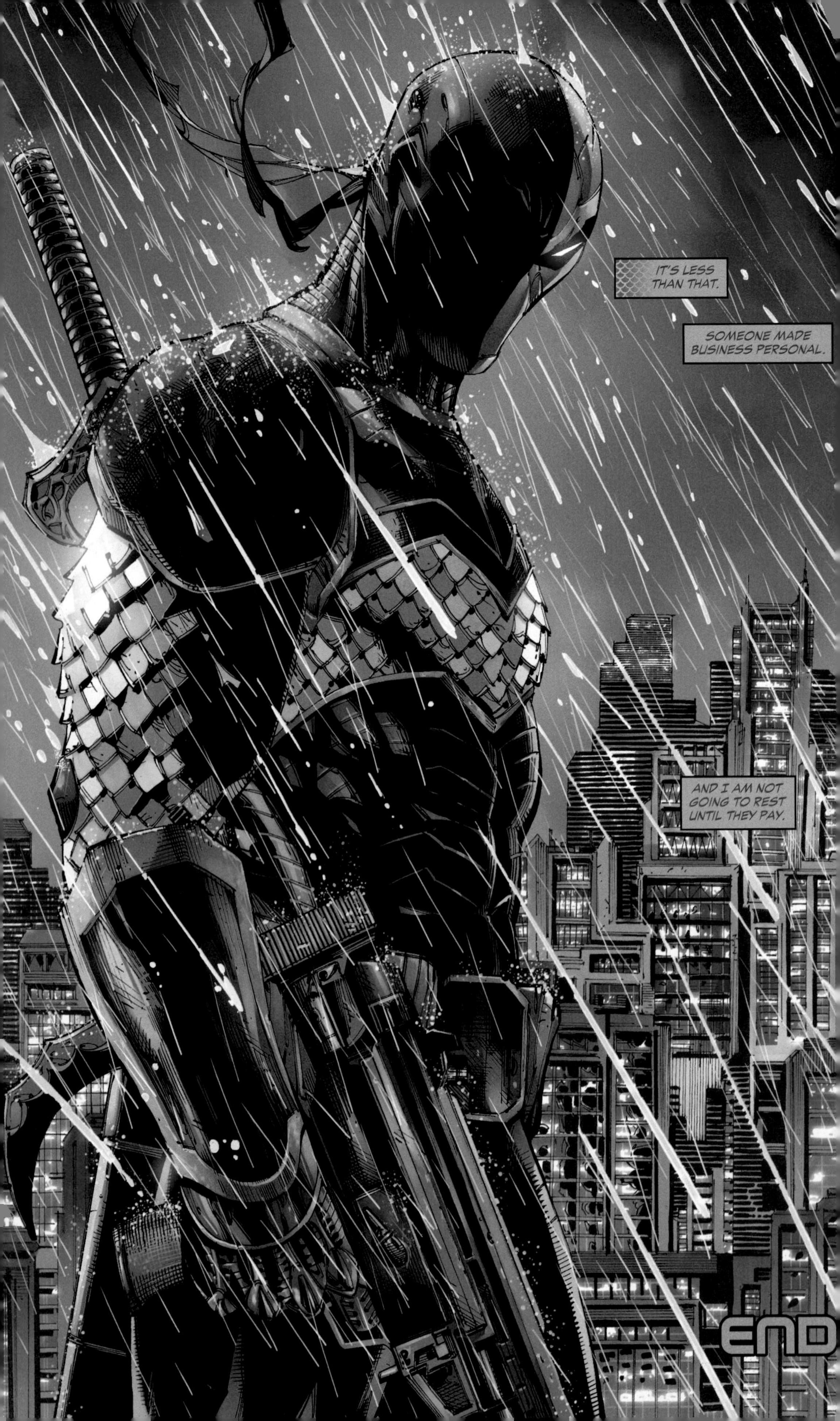
IT'S LESS THAN THAT.
SOMEONE MADE BUSINESS PERSONAL.
AND I AM NOT GOING TO REST UNTIL THEY PAY.
END

DEATHSTROKE #1
cover by TONY S. DANIEL and SANDU FLOREA

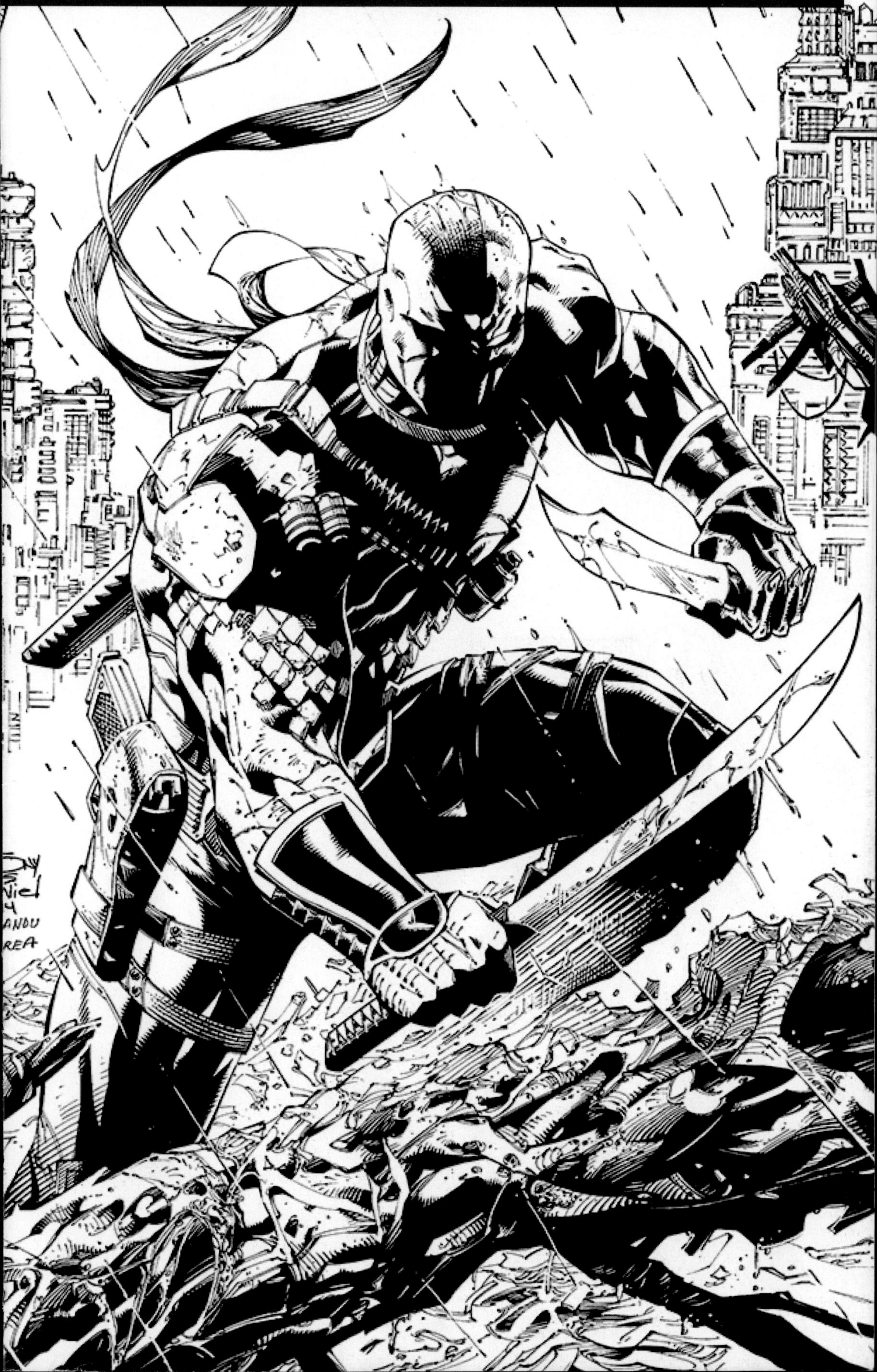

DEATHSTROKE #1
cover pencils by **TONY S. DANIEL**

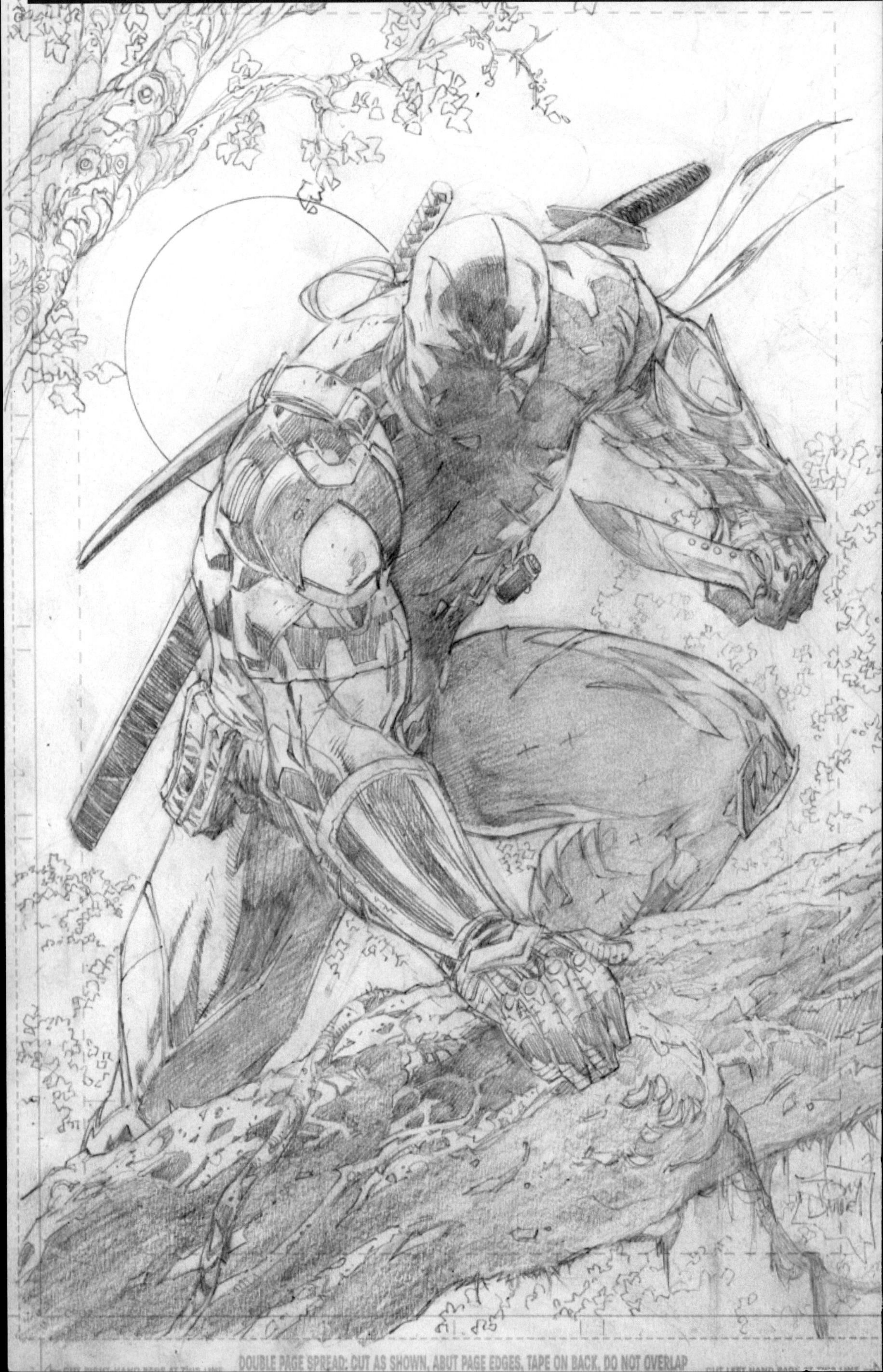
DOUBLE PAGE SPREAD: CUT AS SHOWN, ABUT PAGE EDGES, TAPE ON BACK, DO NOT OVERLAP

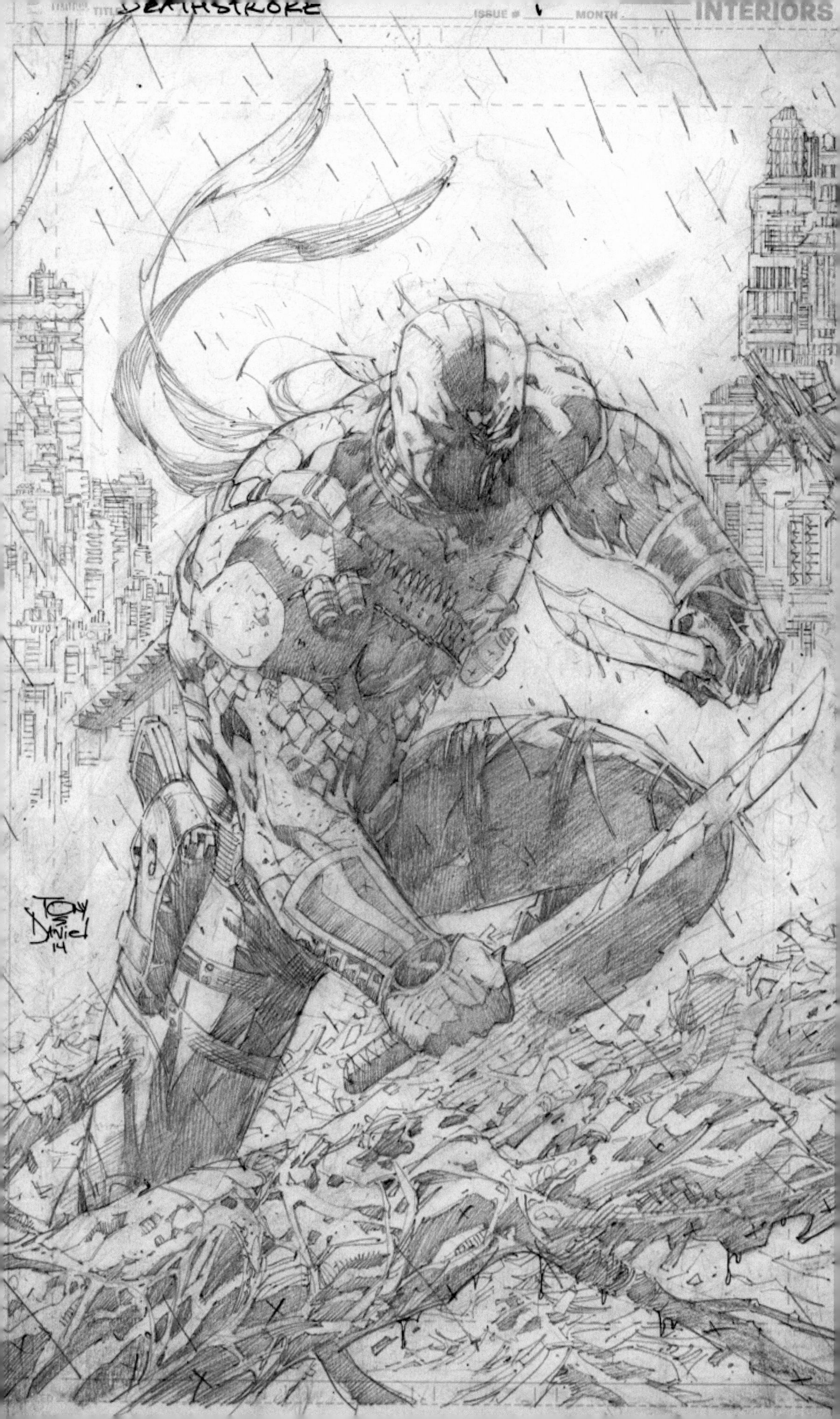
TITLE
ISSUE # 1
MONTH
INTERIORS

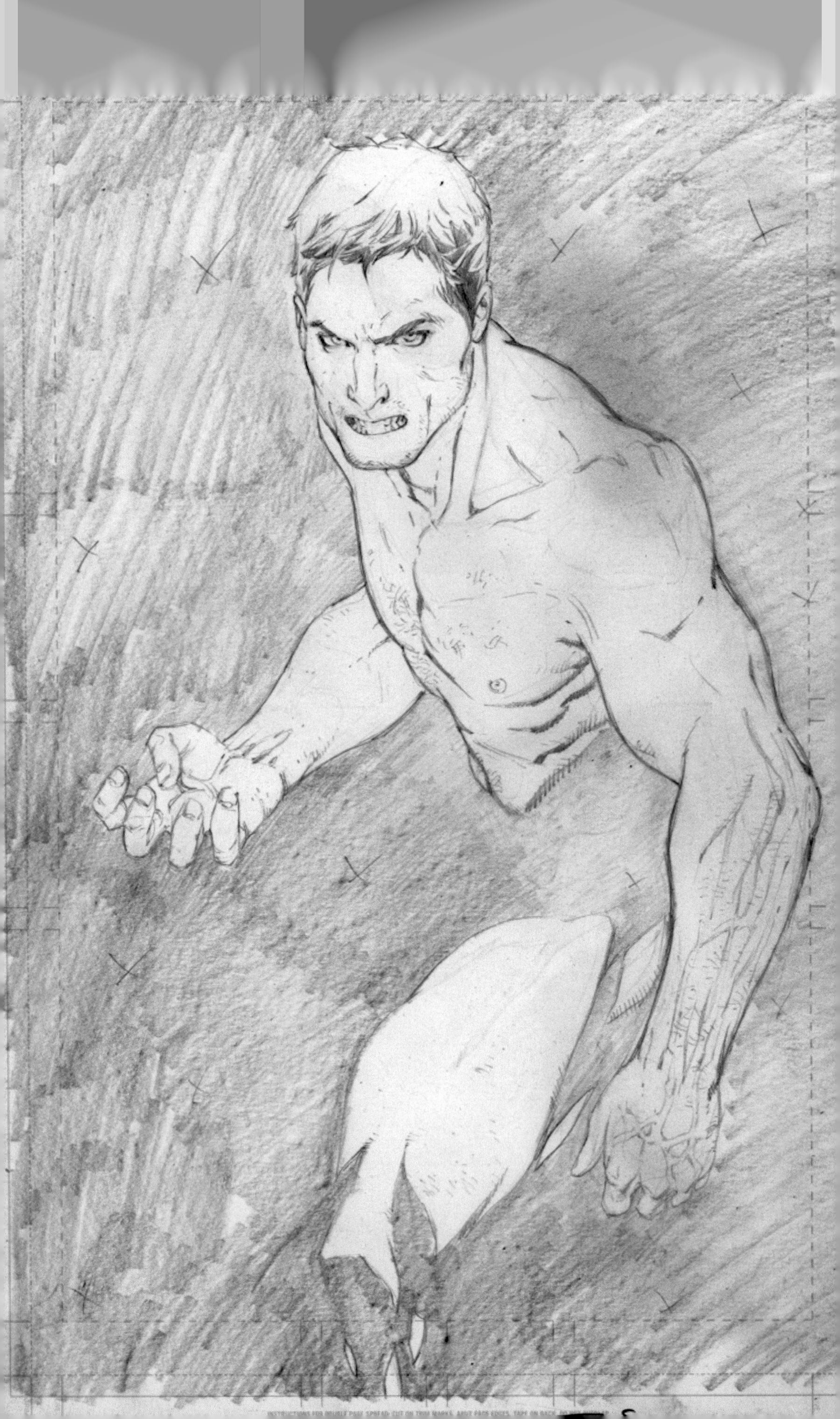

DEATHSTROKE #1 ALTERNATE PAGE 20
inks by SANDU FLOREA

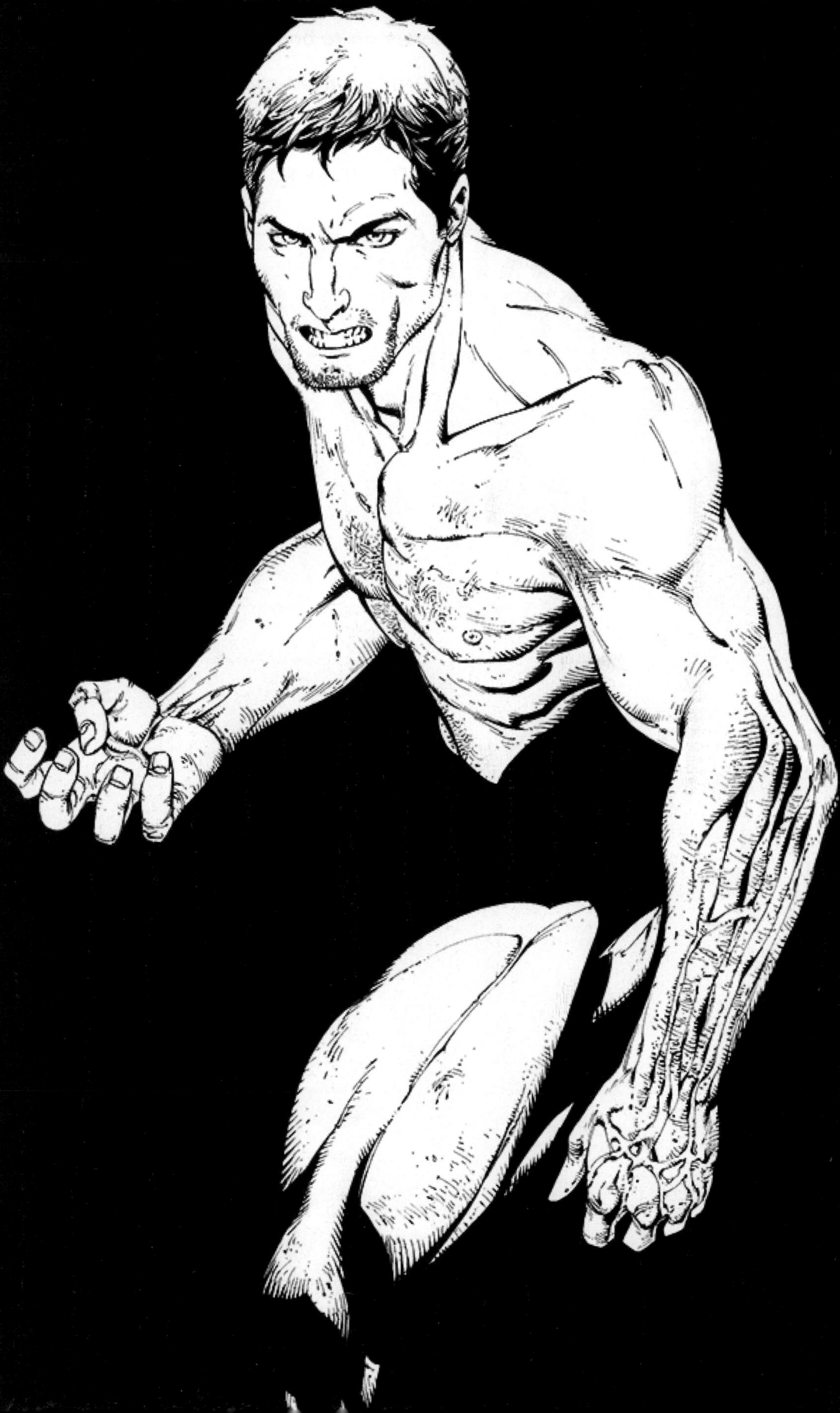

DC COMICS™

"This is your go-to book."—ENTERTAINMENT WEEKLY

"DETECTIVE COMICS is head-spinningly spectacular from top to bottom."—MTV GEEK

START AT THE BEGINNING!

BATMAN: DETECTIVE COMICS VOLUME 1: FACES OF DEATH

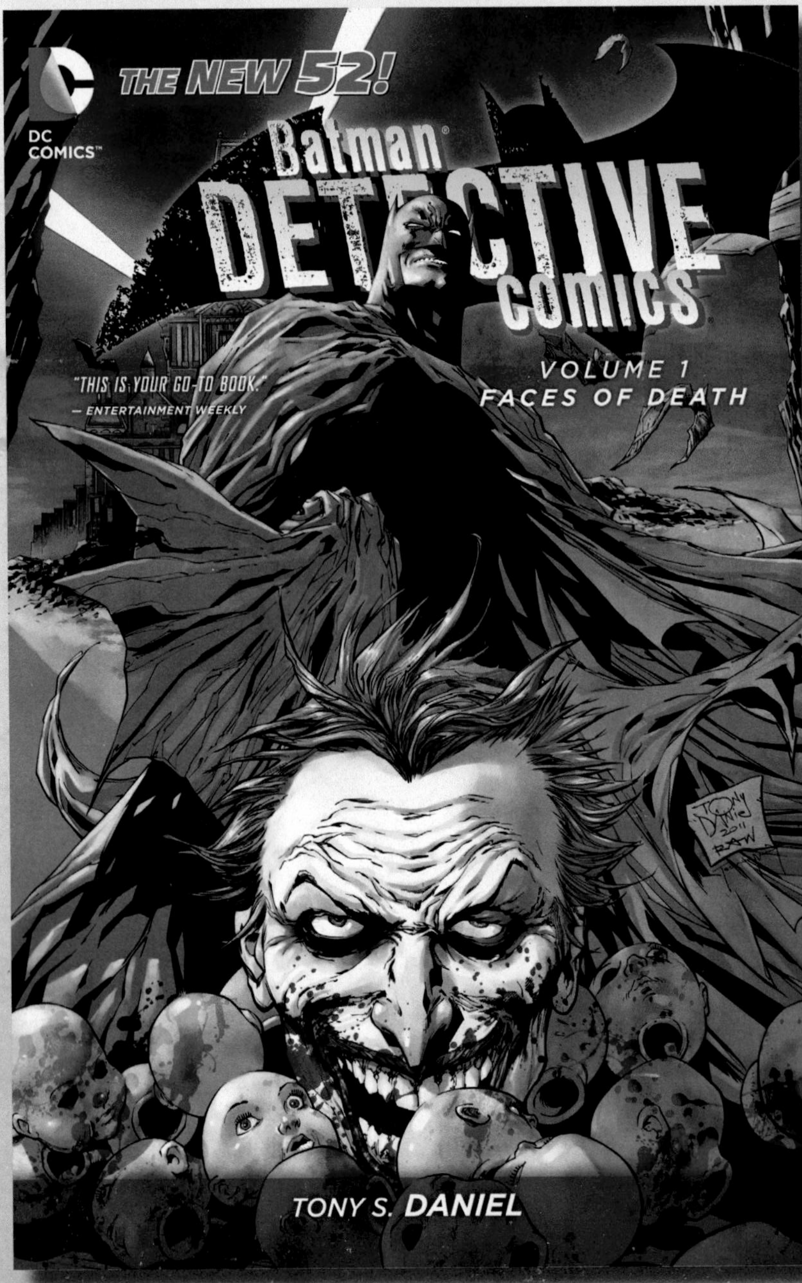
DC COMICS
THE NEW 52!
Batman
DETECTIVE COMICS
"THIS IS YOUR GO-TO BOOK."
– ENTERTAINMENT WEEKLY
VOLUME 1
FACES OF DEATH
TONY S. DANIEL

BATMAN: DETECTIVE COMICS VOL. 2: SCARE TACTICS

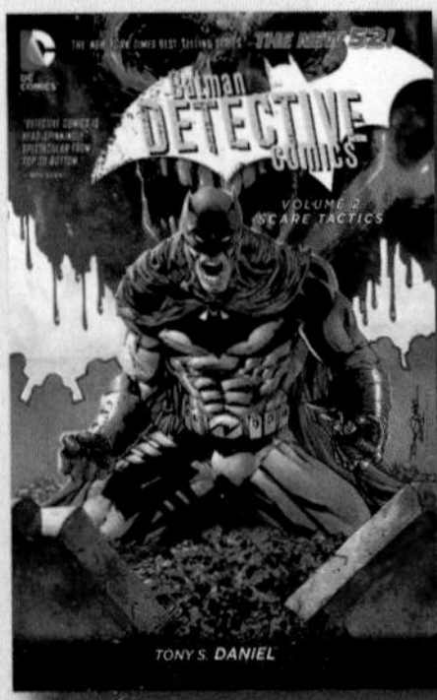
Batman
DETECTIVE COMICS
VOLUME 2
SCARE TACTICS
TONY S. DANIEL

BATMAN: DETECTIVE COMICS VOL. 3: EMPEROR PENGUIN

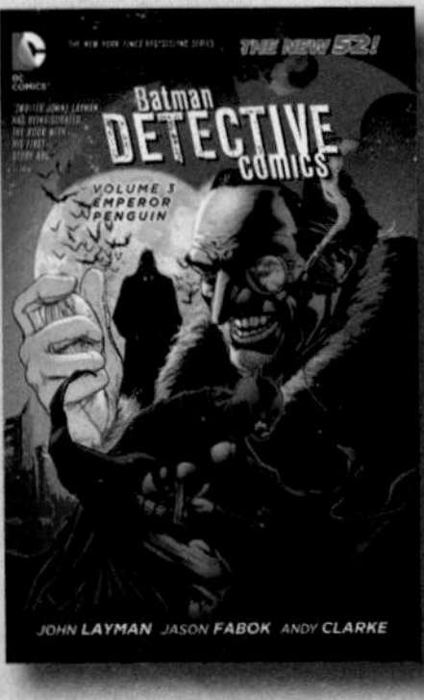
THE NEW 52!
Batman
DETECTIVE COMICS
VOLUME 3
EMPEROR PENGUIN
JOHN LAYMAN JASON FABOK ANDY CLARKE

THE JOKER: DEATH OF THE FAMILY

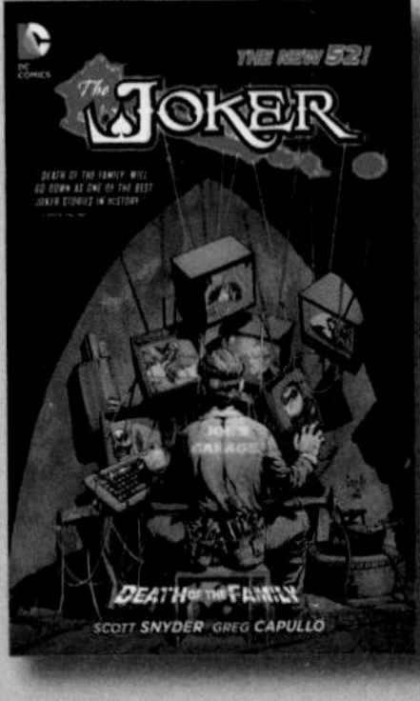
THE NEW 52!
The JOKER
DEATH of the FAMILY
SCOTT SNYDER GREG CAPULLO